High Adventure

High Adventure

Edmund Hillary

WITH MAPS BY
A. SPARK

AND SKETCHES BY
GEORGE DJURKOVIC

BLOOMSBURY

First published by Hodder and Stoughton Ltd, 1955
This paperback edition published 2003

Copyright © by Edmund Hillary 1955

Published by arrangement with Book Creation, LLC, New York

Photographs are copyright and reproduced under licence by The Royal
Geographical Society, London. All rights reserved.

The moral right of the author has been asserted

Bloomsbury Publishing Plc, 38 Soho Square, London W1D 3HB

A CIP catalogue record for this book is available
from the British Library

ISBN 0 7475 6696 8

10 9 8 7 6 5 4 3 2 1

Printed in Great Britain by Clays Ltd, St lves plc

Preface to the Anniversary Edition

Ever since I reached the summit of Mount Everest fifty years ago the media have classified me as a hero, but I have always recognized myself as being a person of modest abilities. My achievements have resulted from a goodly share of imagination and plenty of energy.

Modern developments in technology and equipment have produced major changes in the techniques of exploration. Aircraft and vehicles are in many cases replacing the human legs; oxygen bottles are giving new strength to air-starved lungs in the thin air that clothes the highest peaks; and satellite communication has removed the loneliness from even the most desolate spaces. But despite all this I firmly believe that in the end it is the man himself that counts. When the going gets tough and things go wrong the same qualities are needed to win through as they were in the past – qualities of courage, resourcefulness, the ability to put up with discomfort and hardship, and the enthusiasm to hold tight to an ideal and to see it through with doggedness and determination.

The explorers of the past were great men and we should honour them. But let us not forget that their spirit still lives on. Today, it is still not hard to find a man who will adventure for the sake of a dream or one who will search, for the pleasure of searching, and not for what he may find.

Sir Edmund Hillary

AUCKLAND
January 2003

Author's Preface

This book makes no attempt to be an official account of any of the expeditions in which I have taken part. It is simply a personal record of my own part in them. Inevitably many of my companions are hardly mentioned, merely because they didn't happen to be doing the same job as myself.

I have gained much from the mountains, and not least has been the companionship and friendship of many fine mountaineers.

IT IS TO FOUR OF THESE MEN
THAT I WOULD DEDICATE THIS BOOK

TO
HARRY AYRES
for his superb mastery of snow and ice

TO
ERIC SHIPTON
for his inspiration and unquenchable spirit

TO
JOHN HUNT
for his courage and singleness of purpose

AND

TO MY OLD FRIEND
GEORGE LOWE
for so many years of cheerful comradeship

Edmund Hillary

AUCKLAND,
March 1955.

Contents

CHAPTER ONE

First Footsteps

I WAS SIXTEEN BEFORE I ever saw a mountain. My father's rapidly expanding bee business had occupied all my holidays, and I'd learned to do a full-size job before I entered my teens. But in the winter of 1935 I'd saved a little money and I was allowed to join a School Ski-ing Party to Ruapehu – one of our large New Zealand volcanoes. I was in the Lower Sixth Form at the time – a tall, bony, clumsy-looking youth, far from being the brightest lad in the class; and I don't think I'd been more than fifty miles outside of Auckland. I'd heard glowing tales from the other boys about ski-ing holidays, but it didn't mean a great deal to me – all I wanted was a chance to see the world.

I saw my first snow at midnight when we stepped off our train at the National Park station. There wasn't much of it but it was a tremendous thrill, and before long snowballs, as hard as iron, were flying through the air. And as our bus carried us steadily up towards the Château, perched high on the mountain-side, its powerful lights sparked into life a fairy-land of glistening snow and stunted pines and frozen streams. When I crawled into my bunk at two in the morning, I felt I was in a strange and exciting new world.

For ten glorious days we skied and played on the lower slopes of the mountain, and I don't think I ever looked towards the summit. We had been told the upper parts of the mountain were dangerous, and I viewed them with respect and fear. I never dared to venture on them. I returned home in a glow of fiery enthusiasm for the sun and the cold and the snow – especially the snow!

But I didn't see a great deal of the snow in the next few years. It took two years of University life to convince my parents that I was unsuited to an academic career. I don't think I was particularly dull, but I was certainly lazy and couldn't work up much interest in a lecture on solid geometry. So I joined my father's business and became a full-time beekeeper.

It was a good life – a life of open air and sun and hard physical work. And in its way it was a life of uncertainty and adventure; a constant fight against the vagaries of the weather and a mad rush when all our 1,600 hives decided to swarm at once. We never knew what our crop would be until the last pound of honey had been taken off the hives. But all through the exciting months of the honey-flow, the dream of a bumper crop would drive us on through long hard hours of labour. I think we were incurable optimists. And during the winter I often tramped around our lovely bush-clad hills, and learned a little about self-reliance and felt the first faint stirrings of interest in the unknown.

When I was twenty years old I had my first long trip. With an older friend I visited the South Island of New Zealand. One of our plans was to spend two days at a famous tourist resort, The Hermitage, right in the heart of the giant peaks of the Southern Alps.

We had a magnificent drive through the mountains, and arrived at The Hermitage in the early afternoon. It was a perfect day and the great peaks around seemed to tower over our heads. I looked on them with a growing feeling of excitement – the great rock walls, the hanging glaciers, and the avalanche-strewn slopes. And then, strangely stirred by it all, I felt restless for action, and decided to go for a walk. The nearest snow I could see was high up in a gully in the Sealy Range behind the hotel. I set off towards it. For a long time I climbed upwards, stumbling over the loose rocks in my light shoes. I soon realised it was much farther than I had judged, but for some reason I kept on going. And at last I reached it – a tattered remnant of old avalanche snow spanning a mountain torrent. In an excess of enthusiasm I kicked steps up and down it, and then, with an astonishing sense of achievement, I climbed back down the long slopes to The Hermitage.

As I sat in the lounge that evening, I felt restless and excited. And then the hum of voices suddenly hushed, and I looked up to see two young men coming into the room. They were fit and tanned; they had an unmistakable air of competence about them. I could hear a whisper going around the room: 'They've just climbed Mount Cook.' And soon they were the centre of an admiring group. As I hovered a little forlornly on the outside, I heard one of them say: 'I was pretty tired when we got to the icecap, but Harry was like a tiger and almost dragged me to the top.' It wasn't until some years later that I found out that they were Stevenson and Dick, a famous climbing partnership, and they'd just completed the first Grand Traverse of Mount Cook from north to south.

I retreated to a corner of the lounge filled with a sense of futility at the dull, mundane nature of my existence. Those chaps, now, were really getting a bit of excitement out of life. I decided there and then to take up mountaineering. Tomorrow I'd climb something!

I approached my companion and he agreed to give it a try. But as we had neither experience nor equipment, he suggested we take a guide. All the necessary arrangements were made, and I went to bed in a fever of anticipation.

Fate was kind and next morning it was fine. After

breakfast, Brian and I met our guide. I couldn't help feeling a slight sense of disappointment. He certainly looked the part with his weather-beaten face and Tyrolean hat, but his mature years and excess weight didn't give the impression of dash and endurance. In rather dampening tones he informed us that we'd tackle 'Olivier', a small peak on the Sealy Range above The Hermitage. 'Of course, if it's too far we can spend the afternoon boiling the billy at the Sealy lakes!'

He led off at a slow and steady pace – too slow and steady for my liking, and before long I'd dashed on ahead. I climbed up the steep narrow track, and the cool crisp air and the wonderful sense of freedom as I rose above the valley spurred me on. I'd been at the lakes half an hour before our guide hove into view. Brian and I swam in the clear cold water while he lit a fire and boiled a billy. Then, with ravenous appetites, we attacked our lunch.

A thousand feet of snow stretched between us and the crest of the range. At my impatient movements our guide sighed deeply and reluctantly stirred himself. He led off up the slope. This was real mountaineering! The snow was pleasantly firm, and an easy kick produced a comfortable step. But the long slope underneath gave an impression of exposure, and I followed enthusiastically but docilely up behind. We reached the crest of the ridge and looked over into a magnificent valley of great glaciers and fine peaks. A few yards along the ridge was a rocky outcrop. I couldn't restrain myself any longer and scrambled quickly upwards. Next moment I was on the summit of my first mountain.

I returned to The Hermitage after the happiest day I had ever spent. And next day I returned home. But my new enthusiasm for the mountains went home with me and gave me little rest in the years that followed.

Two books became my climbing inspiration. One was *Camp Six* by Frank Smythe, and the other *Nanda Devi* by Eric

Shipton. With Smythe I climbed every weary foot of the way up the North side of Everest. I don't think I have ever lived a book more vividly. I suffered with Smythe the driving wind and the bitter cold and the dreadful fight for breath in the thin air. And when he was finally turned back at 28,000 feet, I didn't regard it as a defeat but a triumph. Shipton's story struck a different chord – one that I could more readily understand. For Shipton in his Himalayan explorations and climbs epitomised for the New Zealander the ideal in mountaineering. His problems, although on a larger scale, were the same as ours: the problems of limited finance, of the difficulty in moving quickly through tough, inaccessible country, of the need to carry all your own supplies, and of the constant battle against rain and weather and sheer misery.

By 1946 I'd had a good deal of experience in running my own trips. I'd carried a lot of heavy loads through plenty of rough country. I'd climbed a lot of small peaks and a few of the big ones. But I still didn't really know much about the technical side of mountaineering. And then I met Guide Harry Ayres. Harry was New Zealand's outstanding climber, with a tremendous reputation for brilliant ice-craft. He took me under his wing, and for three marvellous seasons we climbed the big peaks together. I learned a lot from Harry. I learned how to cut a step and when to cut it; and I learned a little of that subtle science of snow- and ice-craft that only experience can really teach.

And then in 1950 George Lowe set off the spark that finally got us both to the Himalayas. I had never climbed with George, but we were old friends and he had a fine record of difficult climbs. We were walking down the Tasman glacier together when George suddenly said, 'Have you ever thought about going to the Himalayas, Ed?' Actually I'd thought about it often, and told George so. But it was most exciting to find someone with the same views. We decided we'd plan together,

and organise a party and raise enough money to go. I was
leaving on a trip to England in a few months' time, and I
agreed to get all the information I could about equipment
and food.

I didn't really get much information in England, for it was
summer when I arrived there and most of the Alpine Club
seemed to be away in the Alps. So I went off to the Alps
myself. There were three of us, all New Zealanders, and we
enjoyed ourselves immensely. We went first of all to Austria,
and luxuriated in its large and comfortable huts and climbed
a lot of easy mountains. It was so different from the hardy
mountaineering we'd been accustomed to that it was a little
like a rest cure, and we made the most of it. And then we
went to Switzerland, and visited some of the places that had
become so familiar to us through the classic books on mountaineering. We climbed a number of fine peaks and found
them pretty easy on the whole, but that was probably because
we nearly always used the routes that the guide-books called
'la plus facile'. Our best period was when we climbed five
4,000-metre peaks in the Bernese Oberland in five successive
days. We were so unaccustomed to fine days in the New
Zealand alps that we felt we had to use every one.

One day we called in at the post office at the Jungfraujoch
to get our mail, and I received a letter from George Lowe.
It had exciting news. Apparently another group of chaps in
New Zealand had been making plans about the Himalayas,
and they'd invited George to join them. At his suggestion
they'd invited me too. They were a first-class group of
climbers, and their plans sounded really worth while. I wrote
back immediately accepting the offer.

When I returned to New Zealand, I found that organisation was already well under way. At first our plans were very
ambitious – a ten-man party to attempt Kanchenjunga. But
permission failed to come through, the bugbear of finance

reared its ugly head, and our party started dwindling. Finally there were only four of us left – Riddiford, Lowe, Cotter, and myself. At times it seemed as if we'd never get away, but Riddiford never lost heart. He was a man of tremendous enthusiasm and considerable organising ability. And finally we raised the necessary finance. Our main objective now was the peak Mukut Parbat, 23,760 feet, in the Garhwal Himalaya.

We were deep inside the Himalayas when we first heard about the new reconnaissance of Everest. Someone had sent us a newspaper cutting, which came up with our mail-runner. It was exciting and disturbing news . . . What we'd do to get on a trip like that! We avidly read all the paper had to say. It explained how all the early expeditions to Everest had approached the mountain through Tibet and had tried to climb it up its northern slopes. There had been seven expeditions since the first one in 1921 and, though they'd performed unbelievable feats of courage and endurance, they hadn't got higher than a thousand feet from the top. It almost seemed as though there was some invisible barrier at 28,000 feet through which no man could go. And then, for a period of over ten years, the mountain was left completely alone.

'After the war, changes in politics made Tibet a closed country to the European and it appeared that no further expeditions would be possible in the foreseeable future. But Everest lies on the border between Tibet and Nepal, although the Nepalese side of the mountain was generally regarded as impossibly steep to climb. The Nepalese had always carefully excluded Europeans from their country, but they now adopted a more liberal policy. In 1950, two famous mountaineers, the American Houston and the Englishman Tilman, were given permission to travel through Western Nepal towards the foot of the mountain. For some reason they approached no closer than a few miles, and then returned to report that in their opinion there was no practical route from this side.'

We already knew most of this, but the article carried things a step further: 'Despite this discouraging news, another small reconnaissance expedition is going out to examine the southern approaches to the mountain in the autumn of 1951 – that is, in only a few months' time. And the expedition is to be led by no less a person than Shipton himself!'

With envy in our voices, the four of us talked of the thrill it must be to go on an Everest Expedition. And then we returned to our own problems, although I think we all had our dreams.

By this time we had learned many lessons about Himalayan travel – lessons in handling temperamental coolies and in dealing with the local peoples. And we'd felt the strength drain out of our limbs and the will out of our minds in the thin breathless air at great heights. And we were learning fast. Lowe and I had formed an energetic and happy partnership. We reconnoitred the great glaciers at the foot of Mukut Parbat, and found a way through its formidable defences. We established Camp 3 at 21,000 feet. From this camp, on July 11th, Riddiford, Cotter, and Pasang reached the summit after a great struggle.

We returned to Ranikhet thin and wasted and without a penny in our pockets, but with a glow of modest pride at our seven new peaks. As we entered our hotel, unshaven and dirty, we were handed a cablegram. It was an invitation to two of us to join Eric Shipton's party.

We were on our way to Everest!

CHAPTER TWO

To Everest, 1951

RIDDIFORD AND I, WITH two of our Sherpas, Pasang and Nyima, arrived in Lucknow on August 28th. We had been instructed to meet Shipton and his party at the railhead of Jogbani on the Indian-Nepalese border, but first we had to purchase stocks of food and fuel. Finding suitable food for Himalayan travel in the bazaars of Lucknow was an almost impossible task, and we ended up with a large amount of bulky and exceedingly expensive tinned food. We loaded all of this and our equipment on to several horse-drawn carts and transported it to the station. Our train wasn't leaving for an hour, so we started in a rather leisurely way to complete the necessary official formalities entailed in getting all our luggage on the train. We emerged from a fog of utter confusion to realise that the train was leaving in a few minutes and that our luggage was far from being on board. With growing panic we summoned twenty coolies, hoisted the loads on them, and started at a jog-trot for the platform. We swept through the gates just as the guard appeared to blow his whistle. His firm cry of 'Too Late!' sounded the death-knell of our plans. But Riddiford was not the man to give in too lightly. His forceful persuasion (and judicious baksheesh) won the day. We leapt into a second-class carriage containing two Indian passengers, and then, to their utter horror, we

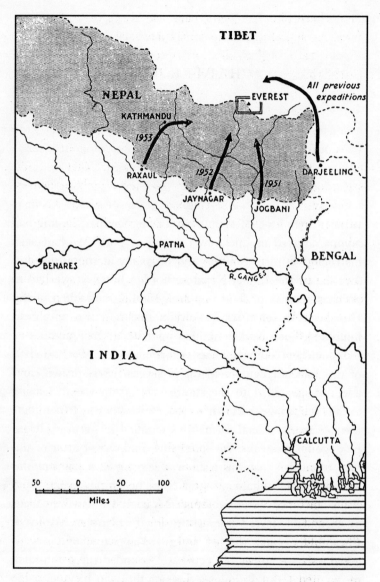

The Approaches to Everest.

commenced piling in tents, bags and boxes of food, tins of kerosene, and all the various paraphernalia of an expedition. A wild scattering of coins to our coolies, a sudden jerk that nearly threw us on the floor and another expedition had started.

It was midnight, two days later, when we arrived at Jogbani. And for the last twelve hours there'd been torrential rain. We unloaded ourselves on to the dim, dripping little platform, and looked miserably out into the night. What we could see of Jogbani wasn't very inspiring – a few crumbling houses, a muddy road, and large stagnant pools of water. All of it outlined by a few flickering lights and veiled by the pouring rain.

Pasang came to our rescue. He made some inquiries and then led us through the mud and rain to a more substantial building with a large verandah. With the unconcern of the East, he woke some bundles of bone and rags and sent them shuffling off out into the night. We inflated our air-mattresses and put them down on the verandah. It was too hot and muggy to need any bedclothes. We took off some of our damp clothing, and went to sleep to a mixed chorus of the high-pitched whine of the mosquito and the deep croak of the innumerable frogs.

The morning was fresh and fine, without a cloud in the sky. At an early hour we left our uncomfortable quarters and walked about a mile to a large jute mill. Nearby was the home of the chief engineer, a Scotsman. Mr and Mrs Law welcomed us in, and soon we were sitting down to a large breakfast. They told us that Shipton and his three companions were five days ahead of us, so we were going to have to hurry if we wanted to catch up. Mr Law was invaluable to us. He helped to get our luggage from the railways and through the Customs, and smoothed out the official difficulties of crossing into Nepal. Finally, he arranged for a large truck to carry us and our gear over the thirty miles of road between Jogbani and Dharan – a town in Nepal at the foot of the hills. As we were walking back to the house, Mr Law suddenly pointed and said 'Everest!' I looked at him in disbelief, and then glanced in the direction he was indicating. To my astonishment, in the clear morning air I could see a white fang thrusting up into the sky above the distant hills. What a long way off it was! So far that it still seemed like a dream. I felt a surge of excitement and was impatient to be off.

We loaded all our gear on to the large truck, and then the four of us climbed on board. With its great tractor-tread tyres and both front- and back-wheel drive, it looked capable of getting through anything. We waved to the Laws and then were on our way. We had been warned that in the monsoon this road was often impassable; we soon understood why. We began by bumping over rough cobbles and grinding through deep mud-wallows. Then we emerged into the more open country, and saw nothing but a sea of mud ahead of us. It seemed fantastic that we could get through it at all. But slithering and sliding and bucking and jerking, we chewed our way along. Sometimes we slid dangerously near the great ditches on either side of the road; sometimes we stuck in a great pool of slush and had to back out and have another go. I had achieved the firm belief that nothing could stop us when we shuddered to a halt in two feet of mud.

For half an hour our driver tried his best to move us, while fifty feet away a dozen hideous vultures fed noisily on the carcass of a dead cow. But it was all to no avail. There was only one chance, our driver said. If we unloaded all our luggage and carried it two hundred yards through the worst stretch ahead, he thought the lorry might get through. I looked with some distaste at the morass in front of us and then at my understandably reluctant companions. 'We'll have to do it, Earle. You unload the gear, and Pasang and Nyima and I will carry it along.' Riddiford readily agreed. At least it meant he didn't need to get his feet dirty.

I took off my shoes and socks and rolled my shorts up as far as they'd go. Then I lowered myself gingerly into the ooze. The two Sherpas shrugged and then followed me. Riddiford handed each of us a load, and we started wallowing our way along the road. Half-way to the next patch of dry ground was a small bridge, and this favoured viewpoint was quickly occupied by sons of the local landowners. Our misfortune caused them no small merriment, and a particularly hearty gale of laughter swept through them every time I went past, up to my knees in the mud. I tried to persuade some of them to help us with the loads and flashed a roll of rupee notes under their noses, but they had no intention of spoiling the fun or of getting dirty. Their leader was a very smartly dressed young man, and his witticisms, although I couldn't understand them, brought roars of laughter from his companions.

I am, I think, fairly long-suffering, but I have my limits. After I'd carried seven or eight loads through the mud, my temper was starting to fray a little. I was returning to the truck, covered in mud from head to foot, when the well-dressed young man produced another smashing witticism. It was too much! Behind him was a large ditch full of water. I took one step forward and pushed with all the energy of my pent-up feelings. His shriek of horror as he hurtled towards the water is still one of my treasured memories. I am pleased to say that from then on I crossed the bridge in a deep and respectful silence.

Relieved of its load, our truck took on new life. The driver succeeded in backing it out of the hole, and then drove it forward again with every bit of power. In a sheet of muddy spray it clawed its way through to the other side. And there we loaded it up again. We continued as before. A dozen times we bogged down to the axles and a dozen times we pushed the truck out again. Just as the sun went down, we bogged down for good and all. This couldn't have been more frustrating. It was the last stretch of muddy road before we climbed up from the plains towards the hills. But help was at hand. We saw the lights of a vehicle coming towards us from Dharan, and soon it stopped on the far side of the bog. There was a shouted conversation between drivers, and then we were informed that if we liked to tranship all our baggage we could go on in the other truck. In pitch darkness we started carrying once again through the deep, soft mud. We were too tired now to care how dirty we got, and splashed our way along in dull resignation. It was a great relief when we'd moved the last load.

We arrived at Dharan at 11.30 p.m. It had taken us eleven hours to do the thirty miles – a memorable experience.

At Dharan the road stopped and there were only tracks leading into the hills. All our loads from now on would have to be carried by coolies. We spent the next day recruiting seventeen of them. On September 3rd we left Dharan at 6.45 in the morning in perfect weather. For two days we travelled through a picturesque and hilly countryside. It was extremely hot at times, but we enjoyed some refreshing swims in the forest streams. At the end of the second day, we climbed up a long, steep hill to the town of Dhaunkuta, magnificently situated on an airy ridge at 4,000 feet.

The Governor of Dhaunkuta was very generous to us. He gave us the use of a small building in the pleasantly cool pine forests surrounding his home, and sent us some fruit, including a delicious pineapple. In the evening he visited us, and for two hours we discussed world affairs and the problems of our respective countries. We asked his advice on the next stage of the journey. We wanted to go to the town of Dingla, and go there as quickly as possible in order to try to catch Shipton. There were two routes we could take – one on the west bank of the Arun river and the other on the east bank. The Governor consulted with his advisers. Apparently Shipton had followed the west bank, as there were fewer big tributary rivers to ford. But if we were prepared to cross several very large rivers, the route up the east bank could save us several days. This was good news. Both Riddiford and I had had a good deal of experience of crossing flooded rivers in New Zealand, and we were quite prepared to have a go at getting the coolies over. As a last favour, the Governor gave us a military escort in the person of a rather bedraggled and weaponless soldier.

We had hoped to get away early in the morning, but were delayed for several hours; four of our coolies had failed to put in an appearance. We finally left at about 8 a.m., and climbed steadily up above the town on a long and pleasant ridge. On both sides of us the hills were thickly terraced and were green with the flush of their monsoon growth. To the north, long bush-clad ridges swept down from the Himalayas, and to the south we could see the distant plains of India. It was an exhilarating outlook. We crossed a small pass and descended a little to the small village of Pakaribus. Heavy storm clouds were approaching and our coolies seemed to be a long way behind, so we decided we'd better camp here. We obtained permission to use part of one of the larger houses, and then we quickly moved in under the roof. It was none too soon. Down came the rain in bucketsful, and with the rain, heavy thunder and sheet lighting. Our coolies straggled in half-drowned.

In the evening the weather cleared for a moment, and I went for a short walk up on to the hill behind the village. Below me I could see the great valley of the Arun river, and towering up in the far distance were the great walls of Chamlang and Makalu, glistening white in their mantle of monsoon snow. I looked at them almost with a feeling of awe.

It seemed hard to believe that I was really seeing the mountains that I had so often read about. Even as I watched them, they glowed a fiery red in the setting rays of the sun before being enveloped once again in the dark storm clouds.

It was a wild night, and we were very thankful for a roof over our heads. The thunder rumbled and rolled around the hills, the lightning split the clouds in jagged streaks of fire, and the rain lashed at us continously. Early in the morning the weather began to ease a little, and when we started off at 7.45 a.m. only light rain was falling. We had to descend to the Arun river, and we found the path was a very poor one. The hard clay had been polished by the rain, and the surface was slippery and treacherous. We were only wearing rubber-soled tennis shoes, so we had to watch every step. And along this path we found our first leeches. These blood-sucking monstrosities infest the Himalayas during the monsoon and reach out blindly with their suckers at every warm-blooded creature.

Half-way through the afternoon, we slithered down the last slopes to the floor of the Arun valley. The coolies seemed to be going very slowly and were a long way behind. Barring our way was a side-stream. In normal times it was probably nothing more than a thin trickle, but now it was a respectable torrent. Using my ice-axe as a third leg, I inched out into it. The water, although barely knee-deep, plucked at my legs with the strength of a giant. I was glad to reach the other side. I thought of the much larger rivers ahead and my heart sank.

The track continued on up beside the Arun river. And what a river it was! A great turgid mass of water tearing its way with relentless fury down into the plains of India. Huge tree trunks were sailing by faster than you could run, and the whole valley was filled with the moan of rushing waters. I'd gone only another mile before I came to another side-stream.

And this was a raging torrent. I waited until Riddiford arrived, and we viewed it together. We knew we'd have trouble getting the coolies over this, and decided to use a well-tried method for getting over ourselves. Standing close together, we both held firmly on to a horizontal ice-axe. Then shoulder to shoulder we entered the stream. Riddiford was upstream, and the force of the water wrenched at him and almost carried his feet away. But I was protected from the main force of the current, and could support him and drive us both to the other side. It was quite a struggle, and we knew the coolies could never cross without assistance.

Another two hundred yards farther on were the few huts of Legua Ghat. We had a cup of tea there, and then returned to the stream. The coolies had arrived on the other side, and by their wild gesticulations were obviously quite determined not to cross. But we were even more determined that they should. Off a nearby tree I cut a stick about seven feet long. Then, using this to support ourselves, Riddiford and I started to cross the stream again. When we were half-way over, a sudden surge of water almost engulfed Riddiford, and I only just managed to support him. We reached the bank even wetter if that were possible.

We appealed for a couple of volunteers to make the first crossing. For a while we had no response, but finally two men agreed to give it a go. We put them between us on the stick and moved down into the water. I could feel the coolie next to me shivering with fear and admired him for his courage. As the water plucked fiercely at us I could hear his frightened gasps. But the combined strength of four of us enabled us to cross much more easily. The other coolies gained a little courage from seeing their companions safely on the other side, and we finally managed to persuade them all to follow suit. By the time we'd completed the ferry, Riddiford and I had crossed the river about a dozen times, and we were only too thankful to walk the few yards to Legua Ghat and camp there for the night.

Judging from the map, we were likely to strike one of the biggest rivers on the next day's march. Heavy rain could easily make it impassable. We were having our breakfast when Pasang brought us a message from the coolies. They wanted to cross the Arun river by canoe and follow up the west bank – the same route as Shipton had used. They didn't like the look of the weather, and they were afraid of getting drowned in one of the fords. We didn't like the weather either – the clouds were heavy and dark – but we wanted to make good time and persuaded them to go and have a look at the first river.

We continued on up the valley as fast as we could. Even the sombre, threatening sky couldn't spoil our appreciation of the beautiful scenery as our narrow track climbed up and down the steep cliffs above the Arun. In places there was a sheer drop of several hundred feet to the river. Riddiford and I pushed on ahead. We wanted to get to the large side-stream before the rain started. But it was a vain hope. Before long it was raining heavily. We rushed across a long tongue of sand, turned a big corner, and there was the river. We stopped aghast! To our worried eyes it looked as big as the Arun. A great stream of water, fifty yards wide, was surging down in a series of big waves. On either bank little groups of coolies crouched miserably over their fires. Some of them had obviously been there for some days.

We decided we'd try to cross. Holding on to the ice-axe as before, Riddiford and I descended into the river. It got deeper and deeper. Before long it was up to our hips and the water was breaking around Riddiford like the bow-wave of a destroyer. It was impossible for him to keep his feet all the time, but he was protecting me from the full force of the current, and I managed to keep my feet on the bottom. We were certainly holding our own, and we took a fierce joy in it. It gave us new strength, and we battled our way across in fine style.

We realised that our coolies weren't going to regard this crossing as a sport. They'd probably want to join all these other coolies and sit around for a week until the river went down. I went up into the bush with my ice-axe and cut out a heavy pole about twenty feet long. Two of us could just carry it with comfort. This would give us weight and stability in the river. We stood uncomfortably around in the rain until all our coolies had arrived and gathered in a frightened, chattering bunch on the other side. Then we started to cross. The weight of our great pole forced us down on to the river-bed, and we churned our way over in a sheet of spray. It must have been an impressive sight, and we hoped it would fill our coolies with confidence and courage.

But far from it! We landed to a chorus of impassioned pleas ranging from a desire to sit and wait, to an outright request to be paid off. For half an hour we argued with them. And then the same two brave souls came to our rescue and offered to cross. Pasang came, too, and the five of us spread along the pole and then dashed into the torrent. It must have been an exciting trip for our passengers – the water always seemed to be up to their necks – but to us the familiarity and the extra weight made it appear a lot easier. We left them on the far side, and then battled our way back for the next group. With monotonous regularity we crossed back and forth. Our coolies seemed unending. It wasn't until we'd brought the last group over that I realised there were no longer *any* coolies crouching around their fires. For some time we'd been acting as public transport.

We pressed on for another two hours. The rain had stopped and the sun was shining weakly through the clouds. The humidity was most oppressive, and our perspiration washed the mud and dust from our faces. We were passing now through a very dry stretch of country with few habitations, so that when we came to a small village with a spring of fresh water we decided to camp for the night. Nyima scouted around and found a suitable dwelling. It was a frail bamboo structure, with a large roof but no walls at all. It had two floors – the animals lived on the ground-floor and the humans on the floor above. This had certain disadvantages if one had a delicate sense of smell, but, on the other hand, the soft breeze had an unhindered passage through the building and it kept remarkably cool. Pasang was a very competent cook, and he produced a fine meal of roast chicken, roast potatoes and pumpkin, and a green vegetable rather similar to spinach. Our air-mattresses were spread out on piles of fragrant corn, and I sank into a deep and dreamless sleep.

We had an early breakfast and left before seven o'clock. I was feeling rather energetic and raced on ahead. There was another big river marked on the map, and I wanted to see what it was like. I came over the top of the hill and saw it beneath me. It was colossal. None of our river-crossing technique was going to serve us here. I wandered aimlessly up and down the bank, wondering what on earth to do; it seemed ridiculous to have to turn back after coming this far. Riddiford had just appeared in sight and was coming down towards me. I was turning to go up to meet him and tell him the bad news when I suddenly noticed two men walking down to the far bank. They went towards what appeared to be a stranded tree trunk. And then, with rising hopes, I realised it was a dugout canoe. They dragged it into the water and with a casual air stepped aboard. Next moment they were in the grip of the fierce current, but a few great sweeps of their paddles brought them across and they landed a hundred yards down-stream. Then they dragged the canoe up the bank to where we were standing.

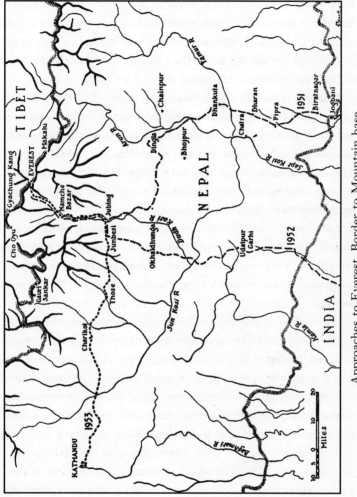

Approaches to Everest. Border to Mountain base.

Riddiford, Nyima, and I crossed first. We squatted down inside the canoe, and Nyima's snort of fear only echoed my own thoughts as the canoe rolled alarmingly. And then we were out in the current and being swept rapidly down-stream. But the great paddles were guiding us cunningly to the other side, and almost before we'd had time to worry we were grating on the far bank. We left Pasang to conduct the rest of the coolies across and went on.

Our aim was to reach Dingla that night. We were rather afraid that if we didn't do so, Shipton would have moved on again. It didn't look as though the coolies would get there, but they could follow on the next morning. We started climbing down towards the Arun river. Dingla was high up on the other bank and we had to find the ferry. It was extremely hot. We asked everyone we met the way to the ferry, but our rough Hindustani produced only a blank stare. Finally, one of the men pointed and we went down to the river bank. Out on the sand was a small shelter, and resting in this were three men. A large dugout canoe was tied to the bank.

We looked at the river. Above and below were enormous rapids. A man couldn't live for a minute in them before being battered to death. But here the water poured down in enormous, oily surges, travelling at great speed. It looked impossible to get across the river before being swept into the rapids below. I noticed that the river here was split by a shallow shingle bar – but it still looked impossible.

Feeling decidedly scared, I crawled after the others into the canoe and sat down on the bottom in an inch of water. The steersman took his place in the stern, and the other two of the crew untied the canoe and started dragging it farther up the river. When the bar in the middle of the river was a couple of hundred yards below us, they gave a great shove and leapt aboard. They grabbed their paddles and started working furiously. The current caught us and we started hurtling downwards at unbelievable speed. I could see the broken water of the rapids getting steadily closer. Suddenly, to my astonishment, the man in the bow calmly dropped his paddle and leapt overboard. And then I realised he was on the bar. Straining against the tug of the current, he brought the canoe to a stop. Then, in ankle-deep water, he started slowly dragging the boat up the river again. I couldn't keep my eyes off the next stretch of water. This was the main stream, and the great swells were sometimes four feet high. But I didn't feel quite so bad about it. These men seemed to know what they were doing, even if their safety limits were a bit fine. We reached the end of the bar and the bow man leapt on board. Once again their paddles flashed furiously. We were rolling and tossing in the grip of the current and the bank was flashing past. I couldn't see how we'd get ashore without being dashed to pieces. A great rock was looming up, thrusting out from the bank. The crew bent to the task, and we shot round it to the calm waters of an eddy on the other side and gently grated on the sandy shore. I paid my eight annas (eightpence) and thought, 'What a way to make a living!'

It was getting late and Dingla was still 2,500 feet above us. Riddiford and I started off at a fast pace and soon left Nyima behind. As we climbed rapidly upwards, I couldn't help wondering what the four men we were meeting would be like. Of course we knew all about Shipton, his tough trips, his ability to go to great heights, and his policy of having cheap and mobile expeditions by living largely off the land. He was certainly the most famous living Himalayan mountaineer. But what did he look like? And what about his three companions? I'd never heard of them. I looked at Riddiford. Thin and bony, with a scraggy beard and scruffy, dirty clothes, he didn't look a particularly prepossessing type. I knew from experience that I probably looked a lot rougher. But these Englishmen – for all I knew they might shave every day; they might be sticklers for the right thing. We'd have to smarten up a bit and watch our language.

Dingla was a good deal farther than I had anticipated, and our enthusiasm was wearing a little thin by the time we reached its outskirts. As we entered the village we were met by a cheerful-looking Sherpa who informed us that the 'Burra Sahib' was waiting to meet us. Feeling not a little like a couple of errant schoolboys going to visit the headmaster, we followed the Sherpa into a dark doorway and up some stairs into the upper room of a large building. As we came into the room, four figures rose to meet us. My first feeling was one of relief. I have rarely seen a more disreputable bunch, and my visions of changing for dinner faded away for ever.

Shipton welcomed us and quickly put us at ease. He introduced his three companions: Bill Murray, a dour Scotsman who had led the first all-Scottish expedition to the Himalayas the previous year; Dr Michael Ward, a well-built young chap with an easy, impetuous manner; and, last but by no means least, Tom Bourdillon. Bourdillon was an enormous chap and was obviously as strong as a horse. I knew he had a fine record of formidable climbs in the Swiss Alps.

Shipton explained that they'd already spent three days at Dingla as they were experiencing great difficulty in getting enough porters. The local inhabitants didn't like travelling in the monsoon; they feared the flooded rivers and, in any case, were busy on their own crops. They were, however, slowly signing coolies up. In this work Angtarkay, Shipton's famous sirdar, was proving invaluable. Angtarkay was small and compactly built, with great vitality. It was impossible not to like his patient and kindly face.

Sunday, September 9th, we all spent at Dingla. Shipton and Angtarkay conferred at length with the village headman, and finally achieved some success. They agreed on a rate of pay of forty-five rupees for the trip to Namche Bazar. But the headman had stipulated that the coolies must carry loads of 90 lb. each. He was afraid he might get into trouble if we were delayed in his district any longer, and this was the only way he could get his small number of coolies to move us. We knew that a load of 90 lb. on the wet and slippery tracks would make for extremely slow progress, but at least it was better than none at all.

Monday morning was very wet. The coolies arrived late, and we left a good deal later. We tramped uphill over muddy tracks with frequent rests to dislodge leeches from our legs and feet. There was little sign of the coolies, and when we reached the village of Phaldobata at 5 p.m. we decided to stop. The coolies dragged in very slowy, and not all of them had arrived by nightfall. Now that they were out of range of their headman, they started complaining about the weight of their loads. We had obtained a few extra men, so we decided to reduce all the loads to 80 lb. – still a formidable weight for these steep, slippery tracks. It took us a day to do it, in miserable weather with continual mist and rain.

On September 12th we started off again. We began climbing steadily upwards along narrow tracks, deep in mud. The dense, wet mist gave an eerie air to the whole country-side, but it was obvious we were getting very high and into an area of few habitations. The leeches lined every path and reached out blindly towards us. I was walking a little ahead, hunched miserably under my umbrella, when I saw a move-ment at the side of the track. Next moment a slender snake about two feet long wriggled across my path. My sole weapon was my umbrella. I lowered it quickly and leapt to the attack. Just as the snake was about to disappear inoffensively into the brush, it received a couple of fearful thuds over the head and expired. I picked it up by its tail and carried it triumphantly down towards a group of Sherpas. Their violent and terror-stricken scattering made me realise for the first time that the snake was probably poisonous.

We were now making our way along the crest of a ridge at over 10,000 feet. Visibility was practically nil and our progress extremely slow. In the afternoon, torrential rain started falling and life became very miserable. We searched anxiously for some sort of shelter for the night, as our tents would be poor protection. After a long hunt through the fog and rain, we discovered a little deserted hovel in a sea of mud. It was a shepherd's hut made of plaited bamboo mats. Wet, dirty, and rather cold, we crawled in underneath it and the Sherpas started a crackling fire of bamboo splinters. Life became a little brighter.

For a change, it wasn't raining when we started in the morning. We were anxious to locate ourselves and rushed up on to a hill. Row after row of high bush-clad ridges stretched in front of us, and in the distance we could see a wonderful view of Makalu and Chamlang. We really seemed to be getting closer now. But, even as we looked, the fog closed in again. We trudged up and down along the ridge, continual mist blotting out the view and the rain coming down. Late in the afternoon, we started searching for another shelter. And then a Sherpa brought us a message from Pasang, who was bringing up the rear. Apparently the coolies had decided to stop for the night under some primitive huts about a mile back. We'd hardly done more than five miles all day, so Shipton wrathfully set off back to stir them into further action. I rushed on ahead to try to find some form of habitation.

I'd only gone a mile when I came on some rude dwellings – squalid and dirty, they were primarily a bamboo protection for the hardy high-country cattle. But at least we'd have a roof over our heads. I hastened back to tell Shipton. As I approached the place where the coolies had stopped, I met hurrying groups of startled Nepalese with their loads on their backs and pots of half-cooked rice in their hands. I arrived in the clearing to find a fiery Shipton stirring the few remaining coolies into rapid flight. Pasang explained his inability to stop the men camping here by a lugubrious, 'Me only one Sherpa; they sixty coolies!' But apparently one Shipton had been sufficient. It must have been an impressive sight.

Life was pretty grim when we settled down for the night. All our clothes were wet and so were our sleeping-bags. And the smell was hard to put up with. The rain was pounding down on our flimsy roof and it was leaking in a dozen places. But nothing seemed able to disturb Shipton. Sitting in his sleeping-bag, with his umbrella over his head to divert the drips, he puffed at his pipe and read a novel in the flickering light of a candle. He couldn't have looked more contented in an easy chair at home in front of a cosy fire.

It rained hard for the next seven days, and we were never comfortable or dry. The leeches had a veritable feast off us. We climbed up and down muddy tracks, crossed flooded rivers, slid and slipped on steep hillsides, and camped wherever we could get a rough roof over our heads. Although the constant fog and rain limited our views, it was quite apparent that we were passing through a very beautiful country. There were great gorges with streaming waterfalls, wild and turbulent rivers, and magnificent forests. In a few brief gaps in the weather we caught glimpses of the great white walls of Chamlang, Makalu, and Lhotse.

On September 21st we woke to our first fine morning. It seemed a propitious sign, for we were fast approaching the mountain country. We left early, and had a delightful walk up a pleasant track through the bush and up to a tiny pass. From here we had a magnificent view up the great valley of the Dudh Kosi river. On each side towered great rock peaks,

and at the head was the shapely spire of Khumbila. Our
Sherpas enthusiastically pointed out places of interest. This
was their homeland, and from our lofty viewpoint we could
see many of their villages and pastures. As we travelled up
the Dudh Kosi valley, we received a warm and enthusiastic
reception wherever we went. We were dragged into their
homes and plied with their alcoholic beverages, *chang* and
rakshi. Sherpas who had carried loads on Everest and other
mountains came from all directions, proud to renew their
acquaintanceship with Shipton. And Mike Ward laboured
enthusiastically on their numerous ailments and diseases.

We camped at night in the small village of Phakding.
Although we were at a height of nearly 10,000 feet, fresh
vegetables were plentiful. We dined on a remarkable meal of
soup, corn, lamb chops, potatoes, pumpkin, and green peas.
For dessert we had rice pudding. And we slept out under the
stars.

We climbed up next day through a great gorge towards
the capital of the district, Namche Bazar. As we got steadily
higher, our excitement increased, for more and more great
peaks were coming into view. We turned a corner to see the
vast rock and ice-wall between Nuptse and Lhotse filling the
head of the valley. And over it all towered the summit pyramid
of Everest – only twenty miles away but still 20,000 feet
above us. We were met outside the village of Namche Bazar
by the headman and welcomed to his domain. The size of the
place astonished us. In terraces on the side of the hill were at
least sixty dwellings and a large, brightly coloured Buddhist
monastery. After the traditional welcoming ceremony of
drinking Tibetan tea and *chang*, we had a large house put at
our disposal. There we paid off our coolies and sorted out
our equipment.

It took us several days to recruit some Sherpas and issue
them with warm clothing. We accumulated some stocks of

local food, and we aired all tents and sleeping-bags to dry out the musty monsoon smell. We took possession of our own equipment – string singlets, woollen underclothes, wind-proof trousers, nylon-pile jackets, down jackets, double-layered windproof parkas, balaclavas, and silk, woollen, and leather gloves. Enough, we felt, to keep us warm in the most rigorous conditions.

We had decided to establish our Base Camp on the Khumbu glacier, and make from it a thorough investigation of the southern approach to Everest. Actually, we weren't particularly optimistic about our chances of finding a route. The only photograph we possessed of the slopes leading to the South Col was a rather unsatisfactory aerial one. It made the upper slopes look impossibly steep. We called it out 'horror photograph', and it was produced whenever one of the party became too optimistic. After perusing it for a while, even the most enthusiastic Everester tended to develop the attitude of: 'Let's go and find we can't climb it! Then we can go away and get down to some really enjoyable exploration!' It was something of this attitude that influenced us to take only seventeen days' supplies with us. If we needed any more, we could send down for them.

CHAPTER THREE

Discovery of the Southern Route

FROM NAMCHE BAZAR IT took only three days to get to the foot of Everest, but in many ways they were the most exciting and dramatic days I had ever spent. The rivers foamed through great gorges; the hillsides were clothed in dense forest, broken only here and there by a sheer rock face or a sharp crag. And then, high above the early autumn tints, towered the unbelievable peaks of the Khumba region – mighty ice-fluted faces, terrific rock buttresses, and razor-sharp jagged ice ridges soaring up to impossible summits. These peaks were rarely more than 22,000 feet high, but I found it hard to believe that they would ever be climbed.

Perched amongst them all on a wooded spur is the Monastery of Thyangboche, one of the spiritual homes of the Sherpas. No temple could have a more glorious setting. Ageless, it is wrapped in an aura of peace and meditation. The Lamas proved to be kindly, gentle folk and entertained us regally. We had great difficulty in dragging ourselves away from their hospitality.

As we went on, the weather became rather unsettled, and we had frequent snow showers as we climbed up beside the Khumbu glacier. Altitude was having its inevitable effect, and although Riddiford and I, who had been high recently, and Shipton, who seemed to acclimatise automatically, were

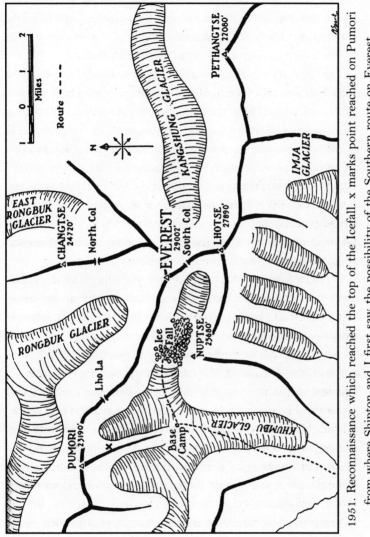

1951. Reconnaissance which reached the top of the Icefall. x marks point reached on Pumori from where Shipton and I first saw the possibility of the Southern route on Everest.

all reasonably happy, the other members of the party were finding the going very hard indeed. It took us several days of reconnaissance to find a suitable Base Camp, but we finally pitched our tents in the lateral trough of the glacier beside an excellent spring at a height of 17,500 feet.

On the afternoon of our arrival at Base Camp, Shipton and I took a pair of binoculars and went for a scramble on the pile of moraine behind the camp. From here we had a thrilling view of Everest, immense and remote with its long, graceful plume of wind-driven snow. It still looked as far off as ever. We examined with interest the southern side of the mountain. We knew there was no direct access to it, for the way was barred by a great ice-filled valley called the Western Cwm. Nobody had even looked into the Cwm, and we were far from confident that there was a way up its obviously precipitous sides on to the mountain.

Getting into the Western Cwm was going to be a formidable task. On every side it was surrounded by an immense mountain wall over 25,000 feet in height. There was only one break – where the glacier filling the valley drained through a narrow gap between the tremendous precipices of the west ridge of Everest and of Nuptse. In one great leap this glacier, crushed in the narrow gap, falls in a shattered chaos of iceblocks and crevasses to the Khumbu glacier 2,500 feet below. Through the glasses the lower icefall seemed quite possible, but we returned to the camp in a far from optimistic mood.

On the morning of September 30th it was fine and clear. Four men left to examine the icefall – Riddiford, Bourdillon, Ward, and Pasang, who had proved himself a forceful climber in Garhwal. Shipton wanted to climb to a position where he could get a look into the Western Cwm, and invited me to accompany him. We left camp and scrambled on to the bottom of a ridge which came down off Pumori (23,190 feet). We were both fairly fit and climbed steadily upwards. But the

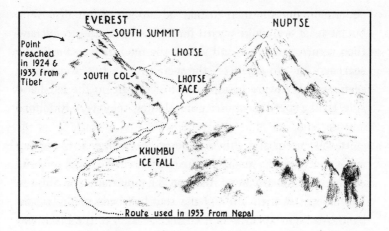

height started taking its toll. In the rarefied air our lungs were working overtime and rapid movement was impossible. At 19,000 feet we stopped for a short rest and admired the wonderful views that were opening up around us. Then we pushed on up the last pitches. We scrambled up a steep rock bluff, chipped a few steps over some firm snow, and collapsed with relief on a little ledge at 20,000 feet.

Almost casually I looked towards the Western Cwm, although I didn't expect to see much of it from here. To my astonishment the whole valley lay revealed to our eyes. A long, narrow, snowy trough swept from the top of the icefall and climbed steeply up the face of Lhotse at the head of the Cwm. And even as the same thought was simmering in my own mind, Shipton said, 'There's a route there!' And I could hear the note of disbelief in his voice. For from the floor of the Western Cwm it looked possible to climb the Lhotse glacier – steep and crevassed though it appeared – and from there a long and steep traverse led over to a saddle at 26,000 feet on the south side of the mountain – the South Col. Certainly it looked a difficult route, but a route it was. In excited voices we discussed our find. We had neither the equipment nor the men to take advantage of our discovery, but at least we could try to find a route up the icefall and then return next year and attack the mountain in force. We searched for the party on the icefall. Only two were to be seen, and they were gaining a lot of height on the left-hand side. By the speed they were going I knew they were Riddiford and Pasang.

It was warm and comfortable on our ledge, and with an air of contentment we slowly ate our lunch. We had a remarkable view of the northern route on the mountain, and Shipton pointed out to me all the places that had been made famous by the earlier expeditions – Camp 5, Camp 6, the black and the yellow bands, and the great couloir. And certainly 28,000 feet, the point reached by so many brave men, including Shipton himself, seemed only a step from the summit. I returned down the ridge in a daze of excitement – I'd been one of the first men to look into the Western Cwm, I'd seen a new route up the mountain, and I'd had the old classic route explained to me in detail by one of its most famous characters. What more could I ask!

The icefall reconnaissance party came back to Base Camp after a long day. Bourdillon and Ward had examined the right-hand slopes until increasing difficulties and lack of acclimatisation had forced them to give up. Riddiford and Pasang had been a good deal more successful. As I had suspected, they were the two who'd gone to the left, and they'd reached over a thousand feet up the icefall without too much difficulty before stopping in a rather broken area. This was encouraging news.

Next day, while the others recovered from their efforts, Shipton and I crossed the Khumbu glacier and climbed a long ridge to the north of the icefall. From a height of nearly 20,000 feet we had an excellent view of it, and could readily trace out the route followed by Riddiford. There was still a long way to go to the top and the climbing higher up was much harder, but we thought we could see a reasonable way and determined to try it.

On October 2nd, Shipton, Bourdillon, Riddiford and I moved a camp over to the foot of the icefall. Murray and Ward were not acclimatising too well and stayed back at Base. It was a miserable snowy day, and we hurriedly pitched our tents and crawled inside them. Three of our Sherpas stayed with us. For the next day and a half it snowed steadily, and we didn't move from the tents. But on October 4th the morning was fine and cold. We left for the icefall at 8 a.m. The snow was deep and loose, and it was hard work making a trail. We all took turns at it. The going was surprisingly easy. We wandered in and out amongst blocks of ice well buried in the snow, and crossed large numbers of well-bridged crevasses. The snow was bitterly cold, and Riddiford and I in particular were suffering agonies from frozen feet. When we reached a sunny spot, we had to take our inadequate boots off and chafe our feet back to life.

It didn't take us long to reach Riddiford's highest point. We estimated it was about 19,000 feet. Bourdillon was finding the altitude a little too much for him, so he decided to stop and wait here for us. From now on the climbing became much more difficult. We fought our way upwards in deep and doubtful snow. Only a short distance ahead of us was a great shelf which stretched across the middle of the icefall. But barring our way from it was a tangled mass of unstable-looking crevasses and ice-blocks. The heavy monsoon snow turned out to be a blessing. It bridged the crevasses and filled in between the ice-blocks. We ploughed our way through it with determination, and scrambled up on to the middle shelf.

The way ahead didn't look too easy. Great blocks of ice were embedded in the deep snow, and many of them looked as though they could tumble down with ease. And we were very conscious of another danger. High above us on the cliffs of Everest and Nuptse were hanging glaciers. Periodically great masses of ice detached themselves and swept out on to the icefall, spreading ruin and destruction in their paths. To dodge these we were going to have to keep well into the middle. Still, taking turns with the leading in order to spread the effort, we struggled upwards around crevasses and under towering pinacles of ice. By one o'clock we had just about had enough so stopped and ate our lunch, sitting on top of an ice-bulge in the sun. The food and rest gave us new strength, but we continued on in some trepidation. Great ice séracs lined the route, and we stumbled over the debris that had split from their sides. We were climbing now up some very steep slopes and the snow condition was giving us some concern. It was loose and very deep, but it was tied together by a crust packed by the wind. We were afraid it might avalanche. But we could now see the crest of the icefall and felt the urge to continue. Our progress was pitifully slow. The lack of oxygen strained our lungs to the utmost as we plunged upwards in snow that was often hip deep. We needed frequent changes, and the higher we got the more often we changed. We dragged ourselves up a steep gully and on to a snow shelf, and saw in front of us the last great crevasse before the crest of the Western Cwm.

It was a very wide crevasse, partly filled in with snow, and the upper wall, instead of being vertical, was a long and very steep snow slope. It looked a nasty problem. Two of our Sherpas asked to remain behind, but Pasang continued. It was my turn to lead, and I started off down into it. Floundering around in waist-deep, feathery powder snow, I made a track across the lumps of ice, up a vertical ice-wall, and then, very cautiously, across the fragile bridge that spanned the icy depths. I stopped, exhausted, on a little snow ledge at the foot of the steep slope. I was far from happy about the condition of the snow. It seemed decidedly dangerous, and my only ambition was to get away from it as quickly as possible.

The others climbed up to join me, and as nobody mentioned the snow condition I shrugged and kept silent. 'Perhaps I'm being unduly cautious' was my thought. The obvious route on the face was to go vertically upwards for sixty feet and then to traverse out to the right. It was Pasang's turn to do some of the work, and the fact that we let him lead in such a place as this was an indication of the indecision in all our minds. He plunged upwards in the deep snow, and Riddiford and Shipton followed him. I belayed the party with my ice-axe sunk deeply into the slope. When they reached the top of the vertical section, I moved up to them and belayed again. It was a most impressive place, for we could look straight downwards into the green depths of a crevasse.

With a tightening of my stomach muscles, I watched Pasang struggling across the snow in a steadily rising traverse. I didn't like the place at all and felt we shouldn't be there. Almost instinctively I thrust my ice-axe a little deeper. But Pasang was making considerable progress, and Riddiford soon followed him out on to the face. Before long Pasang, Riddiford, and Shipton, about twenty feet apart, were spread out on the face and inching their way across. I had almost persuaded myself that my fears were groundless when, with a sudden crack, the whole slope broke up into large blocks and started sliding with horrifying rapidity towards the gaping maw of the crevasse. The snow under my feet quivered, slid an inch, and stopped. I threw all my weight on my ice-axe and watched the other three being swept downwards. They were fighting for their lives.

Pasang was near the edge of the avalanche. With a leap in the air like a cat, he shot off the moving blocks and thrust his ice-axe deep into the stable snow above. Shipton was

1951. The Avalanche in the Icefall.

dashing towards me. With remarkable balance he leapt from lump to lump and threw himself on to the relative safety of my belay. But for Riddiford there was no such escape. He was rapidly carried down to the edge of the crevasse where the snow blocks were disappearing with a dull roar. And then our ropes came tight, cutting into Riddiford's waist as the weight of the avalanche came against him, but he rolled on to his back and wriggled free. He lay there suspended on the slope, exhausted.

It took us quite a while to calm our pounding hearts and gasping lungs. And then Riddiford started slowly moving. We tugged on the ropes and slowly he dragged himself across towards us. He didn't seem to be injured – he was more winded than anything else – but he'd had a narrow escape. With extreme caution, we climbed back down over the crevasse to safe ground on the far side.

It was now after four o'clock and we'd been going for eight hours. We were very tired. Depressed and discouraged by the dangerous snow condition, we started off down. We didn't want to be caught out in the dark, so we drove ourselves as hard as we could. We reached Bourdillon, and found him stamping around trying to warm himself. By ten past six we were back at camp. Too tired to eat anything solid, we supped on tea and soup, then lay in our sleeping-bags and discussed the day's activities. There didn't seem much point in persisting with the icefall while the snow was in such bad condition. It would be much better to return to it in a couple of weeks, when it had had a chance to consolidate. And later, too, the other members of the party would be better acclimatised and could do a useful job. Shipton decided that we'd break the party up into two groups and go off on exploratory trips for a few weeks, then come back to the icefall and examine it thoroughly.

The next fortnight was one of the most exciting I have

ever spent. Shipton had invited me to accompany him on an exploratory trip to the south-east of Everest. This in itself was exciting enough, for I was to have as my companion the most admired and respected of Himalayan explorers. But combining this with the fact that the area we were visiting was completely unexplored and unmapped, it looked to me like a perfect expedition. The other four members of the party were to explore some equally unknown ground to the west.

Shipton and I descended into a paradise of blazing colour. In our short ten days up the Khumbu, every leaf and branch and twig had assumed its autumn coat. To my eye, accustomed to the evergreen forests of New Zealand, it was almost unbelievable. It was like being in a new world. A world of crimson and gold, and above it the slender white purity of soaring ice and the deep dark blue of the sky. For ten days we climbed and explored in country that men had never seen. We crossed difficult passes and visited great glaciers. And at the end of it, it wasn't so much our achievements I remembered, exciting as they had been, but more the character of Eric Shipton: his ability to be calm and comfortable in any circumstances; his insatiable curiosity to know what lay over the next hill or around the next corner; and, above all, his remarkable power to transform the discomfort and pain and misery of high-altitude life into a great adventure.

On October 19th we arrived back at Base Camp on the Khumbu glacier. The other party hadn't yet arrived, so we decided to spend some time improving the route through the icefall. Our first task was to establish a more comfortable camp at the foot of it. We had with us a large dome-shaped tent, and we carried this across and pitched it on the flattest place we could find. It was very comfortable indeed, and as it was built to withstand the gales of the Arctic, we felt we could now laugh at the weather. Then we tackled the lower part of the icefall. We found that in our absence there had been many changes for the worse. Crevasses had opened up and séracs had fallen over our path. But the snow itself was unquestionably a good deal safer. We varied the route to dodge the more dangerous of the séracs, and we cut stairways up two ice-walls to escape difficult crevasses. And then, on October 23rd, we decided to try once again to get to the top of the icefall and into the Western Cwm.

It was bitterly cold at 7.45 a.m. when we left the dome tent, and the sun was still far away. But in the crisp, invigorating air we made fast time up our established track. We reached Riddiford's point at nine o'clock, just as the sun bathed the icefall in its warm light. We started along the old route and immediately struck trouble. A series of new crevasses had opened up across our path. Investigating every step with care, we crawled over some dubious, bottomless snow and scrambled around the side of a slippery ice-block. This led us to a fragile snow bridge, and another crevasse was behind us. We cleared the last one with a long jump and climbed up towards the crest of a snow bump. We knew that the only thing dividing us now from the shelf in the middle of the glacier was a tangled area of crevasses and ice-blocks. As we came over the crest we looked for signs of our old track – and then we blinked our eyes and looked again. The whole area had completely changed. It was as though some vast subterranean vault under the glacier had collapsed and the ice had fallen into it. Below us was a great depression filled with an unimaginable chaos of shattered ice-blocks. Our old route had disappeared into the heart of the glacier.

It shook us up a bit to see the complete destruction of ground on which we'd been confidently walking only two weeks before. And we didn't really know whether to go on. But finally we decided that we'd have to examine this new stretch and see if it was possible to cross it. We tied our two ropes together. I was in the front, Shipton a hundred feet behind, and then Angtarkay and Utsering. Held on a tight rope by Shipton, I descended on to the fresh ice-blocks. They rang with a hollow sound when I cut at them with my ice-axe, but they didn't rock under my weight, so I went on. It was hard going. I cut a trail over and around hundreds of the blocks, and was slowly moving over to the far side. And Shipton and the Sherpas were moving out after me on to the 'Atom Bomb' area, as we were already calling it.

On the far side was a line of ice-cliffs – freshly cracked and unstable looking. I worked my way towards a large sérac which I thought might give me access on to them. It was very steep and a large bulge of ice was barring my way. I set to work to cut the bulge off with my ice-axe. A few hard blows and a lump as big as my head fell off and rolled into a gaping crevasse. For a moment nothing happened. And then an astonishing crashing and rumbling noise came up from the depths. Decidedly puzzled and not a little frightened, I chopped off another piece and watched it fall into the depths. There was another long pause and then again the eerie sub-terranean rumbles. I was about to chop off a third lump when I heard a shout from Shipton. I turned around, and to my amazement saw our two Sherpas lying flat on the ice. I moved across to them and Shipton explained what had occurred. As each of the lumps of ice fell into the crevasse, the area on which he and the Sherpas had been standing had shaken like an earthquake. The Sherpas in fear and dread had followed their instincts and thrown themselves to the ground. And, as Shipton wryly put it, 'I'd have done the same myself if I didn't have to be a pukkha sahib!'

We decided to try to get up somewhere else. After a good deal of careful work, I managed to get on top of the cliffs, to find that they were criss-crossed with recently made cracks – the whole area was completely shattered. Rather daunted by all this, we retreated with some speed to safer ground.

Then we tried to find a way around this bad patch. To the left was impossible; great ice-cliffs barred the way. We examined the right side. After a long spell of route-finding amongst the séracs we emerged well over to the right, only to find an area of much greater devastation. This was all very worrying. Whereas it might be justifiable for climbers to take the risk of crossing such an area, Shipton wasn't at all sure that it would be fair to take laden Sherpas over it. We returned to camp, worried and depressed over what we had found.

On October 25th, Murray, Bourdillon, Ward, and Riddiford returned from their explorations to the west. They were all looking much fitter and their trip had helped their acclimatisation a good deal. A day or so later, we all climbed up on to the ridge under Pumori and examined the Western Cwm and icefall in detail. The others agreed that the route out of the Western Cwm on to the South Col looked decidedly promising, but also agreed that the icefall seemed to have deteriorated in our absence. We decided to make one last attempt to reach the Western Cwm.

On October 28th, the six British members of the party, together with Angtarkay, Pasang, and Nyima, set off from the large dome tent at the foot of the icefall. It was 7.15 and a cold, dark autumn morning. We climbed rapidly up our well-established track, and by 9 a.m. we were at the edge of the 'Atom Bomb' area. As far as we could tell, it didn't seem to have changed in our absence. We started across it. Not without some trepidation we climbed over the tumbled ice-blocks, scaled the shattered cliffs above, and moved as quickly as possible over several hundred feet of cracked area to unbroken ground. It still wasn't a nice place, but we had to admit it was a lot more stable than it had been the time before. We continued on upwards, making rapid time until we reached the steep slope on the crest of the icefall where the avalanche had stopped us on our reconnaissance three weeks before. We split up into three parties and examined different approaches. Two of our parties were turned back, but Bourdillon by vast exertions shovelled all the loose surface snow off the lower corniced lip of a crevasse running steeply up the right-hand side of the slope, and forced a somewhat dubious route to the top. Certainly the hearty creaks the cornice emitted as I climbed up Bourdillon's route did little to endear it to me. With some excitement we climbed up on to a long snowy shelf and looked ahead. We could see a deep and narrow valley sweeping away from us. And at the head of it was Lhotse. We were on the threshold of the Western Cwm!

There was only one problem in our way. A vast crevasse split the glacier from side to side. We could see no ice bridge across it and no way into it or out the other side. Without any suitable equipment, this was as far as we could go. We debated as to whether we'd bring a camp up here and try to push farther into the Cwm, but finally decided that the route was too dangerous for laden porters. Angtarkay and Pasang heartily endorsed our view.

We returned to Base with the strong feeling that the icefall was the key to any attempt on Everest from the south. Our experience had shown that it was dangerous but that it could be climbed. We made ambitious plans for our return the following year equipped with rope and tackle and ladders. But Shipton was far from happy about subjecting Sherpas to such a route – it hardly worked in with the deep-seated British tradition of responsibility and fair play. But, in my heart, I knew the only way to attempt this mountain was to modify the old standards of safety and justifiable risk and to meet the dangers as they came; to drive through regardless. Care and caution would never make a route through the icefall. If we didn't attack it that May, someone else would. The competitive standards of alpine mountaineering were coming to the Himalayas, and we might as well compete or pull out.

We descended to Namche Bazar amid the early signs of winter. There was fresh snow on all the mountains, and Everest's long plume told of strong and bitter winds. At Namche we parted. The four English members went north to the Nangpa La and the Menlung valley. Riddiford and I had been away from home for a long time and had to rush back to catch an early boat, so we decided to return to Kathmandu over a pass known as the Tesi Lapcha. This pass was regarded by the Sherpas as a very difficult one, and was only used by them on infrequent occasions during the months of July and August. We could expect a certain amount of trouble in attempting to cross it so late in the season.

Riddiford and I said our farewells to our other companions, and left Namche on November 4th, with a dozen porters carrying our luggage. Two days later we camped under the pass. It was a wonderful place, and on every side we were surrounded by great ice-fluted peaks. We left next day at 8 a.m. It was fine but a strong wind was blowing. We climbed steadily upwards for several thousand feet on moraine-covered glacier, and then moved out on to the clear ice. We found our way through an easy icefall and then up the slopes above it. We were making very rapid height, and I was pleased to find the route so much easier than I had expected. But then we came to a very steep and broken icefall. We were forced to get on to the rocks on the right, and we climbed up these until we were stopped by a thirty-foot high rock bluff. This was a bit of a problem, but by using a crack in the middle of it I managed to reach the top. I hauled Pasang up on the rope, and we belayed ourselves and dragged the rest of the party and the gear up, hand over hand.

I cut a line of steps over a steep ice-slope and we emerged into a large snow basin. Ahead of us now we could see the pass – a V-shaped notch in the great wall which still towered thousands of feet above us. The wind was blowing furiously, but we dragged ourselves up the last slope and looked over the pass into a magnificent sweep of unexplored country. Below us was a very large glacier, and we quickly dropped down about a thousand feet of easy snow, then chipped a track for the porters in the hard snow of the final hundred feet. It was now 4.30 p.m., and as the men were obviously tired, we decided to camp, although still at nearly 19,000 feet. It proved to be the coldest night we had experienced in the Himalayas, and although Riddiford and I were warm enough in our double bags, the porters had a miserable time. Next morning they were only too happy to leave.

Several of them had crossed this pass before at the normal time of the year, so following their advice we set off down the left-hand side of the glacier towards the icefall. After chipping for two hours down an icy trough, we reached an unclimbable drop of several hundred feet, and the Sherpas admitted that the easy snow slope usually running up here seemed to have completely disappeared. Next we tried the right-hand side of the glacier, and climbed down steep rock beside the ice until we were finally stopped by a sixty-foot overhanging bluff. It was easy to see how this could be negotiated when spring avalanche snow was present, but it was now the autumn and the route had gone. It was 4 p.m. and everyone was feeling rather tired. We decided to camp for the night and lower everyone down the bluff in the morning. But three of the Sherpas (two of them old Everest men) had no desire to camp in such an unhealthy place, and did some further investigation of the icefall. They found an amazing route running diagonally down across an almost vertical icewall. Riddiford quickly organised all the porters while Pasang and I hacked a staircase down this fault. Soon we had them all down. Darkness fell, and we had an unpleasant time scrambling down through the lower icefall and finding a difficult way through the bluffs below. It was a great relief to reach the moraine and crawl into our sleeping-bags.

On November 8th we put in a long day. First of all we spent hours descending the moraine of the glacier. We hadn't had any breakfast and we couldn't find any fuel. We were feeling quite weak by the time we came down into the scrub at the terminal face of the glacier, and stopped for a long rest and a large meal. Below us was a lovely valley – sweeping down between enormous mountain walls and disappearing into the ill-famed Rolwaling gorge. The whole valley was a blaze of autumn colouring. We walked down the track in a dream world of crimson and gold. And when the sun disappeared behind the mountains, the colours faded slowly as the darkness of night came creeping up the valley.

We were pretty tired by the time we reached the village of Beding. We found this was mainly inhabited by Buddhist Lamas, and Pasang received a royal welcome, for he is a Lama himself. We were given clean and pleasant quarters in the monastery, and went to sleep in an atmosphere of grinning gods and delicate incense. We rested here for a day, and in the evening we attended a Buddhist ceremony of thanksgiving for our safe crossing of the Tesi Lapcha. It was a long ceremony and, to our uneducated eyes and ears, a singularly monotonous one, so we crept out half-way through. But we made our peace with a gift of money, and the Lamas drank and celebrated deep into the night.

For the next eight days we travelled quickly through the beautiful Nepalese countryside; walking over narrow bush tracks, camping by swift-flowing rivers, and crossing the high ridges. In the villages harvesting was in full swing, and every night we heard singing and dancing until the early hours. It had been a good harvest, and their houses were stacked high with grain and their trees bowed low under their crops of oranges. I have never seen such a happy and contented people.

On November 17th we arrived at Kathmandu, and sank

into that haven of rest for tired mountaineers – the British Embassy. Mr and Mrs Summerhayes welcomed us with kind and generous hospitality, and before long a hot bath and clean clothes had made us almost human again. And then we heard the latest news – the Swiss had been granted permission for an attempt on Everest in 1952. Our dream castles tumbled merrily down around our ears!

CHAPTER FOUR

Preparation on Cho Oyu

THIS NEWS WAS A serious and unexpected blow to our hopes and plans, but the Joint Himalayan Committee of the Royal Geographical Society and the Alpine Club acted with admirable courage. They decided to go ahead irrespective of the Swiss attempt. Permission had been granted by the Nepalese Government for a British Expedition to Everest in 1953. The Himalayan Committee decided to spare no effort to prepare for this, and at very short notice agreed to send a training expedition to the Himalayas in 1952. This would have the very useful purpose of providing a pool of climbers who had shown that they could function effectively at great altitudes. It would also give an opportunity to carry out experiments with the existing oxygen apparatus with a view to developing something suitable for use on Everest.

It was a great moment when I received a cable from Shipton. He had been asked to lead the Expedition to Cho Oyu, 26,867 feet, the seventh highest peak in the world. And he wanted me to go along too. But I think the biggest thrill was that George Lowe had been invited as well. Cho Oyu is only about twenty miles to the west of Everest, and the glimpses I'd had of it made it look extremely difficult. But at the conclusion of the 1951 Everest Reconnaissance, Shipton and his three companions had examined Cho Oyu from several directions, and considered there was a good chance of climbing the mountain. Riddiford was coming again and so was Bourdillon. Two more of the party had Himalayan experience – Dr R. C. Evans and Campbell Secord. A. Gregory and R. L. B. Colledge had fine alpine records, and Dr L. G. C. Pugh was attached to the party to carry out physiological research.

We all met on March 29th at Jaynagar, a railhead station on the Nepalese border about a hundred miles to the west of Jogbani. George and I had flown over together from New Zealand, and all the others had come from England. It wasn't long before the veneer of civilisation had vanished and in old ragged clothes and sprouting beards we were struggling with the problems of organisation and transport. There were twenty-five miles of hot, sandy plains between us and the village of Chisapani at the foot of the hills. We decided to carry our loads over this by ox-cart and then recruit all our coolies for the onward carry at Chisapani.

We made good progress with our packing, and on March 31st we were ready to go. In the atmosphere of noise and confusion that always seems to characterise Indian activities, we loaded all our gear on to eight ponderous ox-carts and watched them draw slowly away from our bungalow. It is always a good moment in an expedition when the last details are finished and you really start moving towards the mountains. And this was no exception. Perhaps the temperature of well over a hundred degrees made us all the more anxious to get up into the snow. We had a quick check to see that nothing had been left behind and then started off after the carts.

We didn't have far to go. They were parked in the busiest part of the town, with the oxen quietly chewing their cud and no sign of the drivers. We searched indignantly for them, and finally ran one man to earth. He explained that they were busily buying food with their advance pay, but we judged from the powerful odour wafted to us from our informant that it was mostly liquid in form. Shipton urged them to hurry, and then the ten of us walked out into the desert.

A clear but slow-moving river wound its leisurely way across the plain, and on the left side of it was an easy track. It was fiendishly hot, and we travelled erratically from the shade of one tree to the next. Most of us were wearing shorts and shirts, and some didn't even have shirts. By midday we'd consumed all our water and were racked with thirst. We sat under the meagre shade of a straggly tree and waited for the carts to appear. But nothing emerged through the dazzling heat haze. Late in the afternoon we started to get worried. Passing travellers had assured us that this was the way to Chisapani, so what could have happened to the carts and all our equipment?

We decided to push on and find a village. The sun was low in the heavens and it became pleasantly cool, but we were tired and thirsty and not a little angry. It was quite dark before we stumbled on to a little group of thatched huts. At our calls, startled faces appeared at the doors, and we were soon led to the headman's hut. Shipton explained our need for food, water, and shelter, and the headman agreed that we should stay with him. He also gave us the information that there was another track on the other side of the river, which was more commonly used by travellers going to Chisapani. All was now clear. The ox-carts, with our Sherpas watching over them, were probably camped a few miles away from us on the far side of the river. It would be hopeless to try to find them in the dark.

Our host prepared us a meal of curry and rice. I took a mouthful and then frantically gasped for breath. The curry was as hot as fire. Disregarding all our health rules, I asked

for a drink of local water and quenched the flame in my throat.
Then with alternate mouthfuls of curry and water, I was able
to finish my meal. We examined our quarters for the night.
There was a hard wooden bench which might take four of
us; the others would have to sleep on the floor. I was one of
the lucky ones on the bench – or perhaps lucky isn't a suitable word. Crowded together for warmth, we shivered our
way through the night, wriggling desperately to ease our soft
hips on the hard boards. Before daylight we'd had more than
enough. We paid the headman and, gathering our few belong-
ings, plunged off across the river.

We found the other track without difficulty, and followed
along it. It was soon daylight, and without any warning the
sun rose and we were bathed in sweat again. We came to a
large village and sat down under some cool trees. Shipton
persuaded one of the local inhabitants to cook some food for
us, and we ate a meagre breakfast of eggs and chupatties.
Then one of the ancients of the village spoke to us at length.
I could see by Shipton's surprised air that it was something
rather unusual. He translated for us. The old man was sug-
gesting we hire the village elephant as a taxi. This appealed
to us immensely, not so much for the labour it would save us
but more for the effect it would create if we caught up with
the ox-carts on an elephant. The old man was advised of our
interest, and some boys were sent off to get the elephant.
Great was our disappointment when they returned and told
us that the elephant was on its way to another village to do
a day's work.

We started off into the blinding heat of the day. We'd only
gone about three or four miles when we saw a group of carts
beside a dry stream bed. The oxen were grazing on the sparse
pasture. As we approached there was no sign of life until a
hearty yell brought our Sherpas and the drivers out from
their midday rest in the shade of the carts. It was a relief to

see Angtarkay and the other Sherpas again, and they were kind enough not to laugh at us – at least not when we were looking. We arrived at Chisapani late in the afternoon, and immediately sent out a call for coolies.

All next day men gathered from the villages around, and Shipton and Angtarkay debated with their leaders the question of pay. The men were keen to work and wanted to carry large loads for high pay. It was never to our advantage to have men carrying more than 60 lb. each; they became too slow and too many of them dropped by the wayside. But these men refused to consider carrying 60 lb. They wanted to carry 120 lb. and get double the pay. We were forced to agree. Sixty-eight coolies signed on and were issued with a load, and on April 3rd we set off with them into the foothills.

The next five days were extremely pleasant. We took advantage of the coolness of the mornings for easy travelling. We'd leave before 5.30 a.m. after a quick cup of tea, and then walk briskly through the crisp air for two or three hours. Then as the sun rose and the heat of the day returned, we'd find a shady spot beside a river and have a large and leisurely breakfast. The remainder of the march would be done in the heat of the midday sun, but we crossed many rivers and cooled ourselves with frequent swims. We were making gradual height the farther we got in amongst the hills, and on April 7th we climbed up several thousand feet to the village of Okhaldunga – the capital of No. 3 District of West Nepal. In its magnificent location at 6,000 feet on a hilltop, it catches every cooling breeze. Here we had to change our coolies. The men with 120 lb. each had carried magnificently, but in the rougher country ahead we limited the loads to a maximum of 80 lb.

Our route now lay in the high country, and we spent much time in the delightfully cool temperatures of 10,000 feet and over. In the early morning we often caught glimpses of the

Everest massif, and I can remember feeling a slight touch of envy that I wasn't going back there myself. But later on, the great ice-topped bulk of Cho Oyu came into view and our interest and enthusiasm flared into life. On April 16th we climbed up out of the Dudh Kosi valley to the village of Namche Bazar, and were enthusiastically welcomed by many old friends. The Swiss Everest party had left for the Khumbu glacier the previous day.

The next few days at Namche were spent in re-sorting loads and engaging Sherpas to carry them. We signed on ten Sherpas to act as high-altitude porters, and we fully equipped them. We received our own equipment at the same time, and were like a bunch of children at Christmas time as we excitedly unpacked things and tried them on. Included in all this high-altitude gear were rubber-soled boots, down jackets, down trousers, down hoods, and down gloves; there were double-thickness windproof trousers and parkas, air-mattresses, reindeer skins as sleeping-mats, and large and efficient sleeping-bags. Apart from the windproof suit, which was too heavy and badly designed, the equipment proved satisfactory, and the down clothing was extremely good. Amongst the clothing were long woollen underpants and long-sleeved woollen singlets. George and I examined these with pleasure – they seemed particularly soft and warm, so we decided to put them on immediately. We managed with great difficulty to get into them, but found to our consternation that they were so tight we were unable to bend our legs or arms. They'd obviously been designed for midgets and couldn't cope with our six foot two. George produced a sharp knife and we went to work. Before long we had a nice and comfortable, though rather ragged, set of short underclothes.

On April 19th we left Namche with three weeks' supplies, and set off up the Bhote Kosi river to examine the approaches to Cho Oyu. Cho Oyu lies on the main Tibetan-Nepalese watershed some seventeen miles to the north-west of Everest, and it is easily approached from the south by either the Bhote Kosi or the Dudh Kosi valleys. In 1951 Shipton and Ward saw the southern side of Cho Oyu from a small peak up the Pangbuk valley and, although they were a long way off, they thought they could see a feasible route. At the same time Murray and Bourdillon had crossed the first saddle to the west of Cho Oyu, the 19,050-foot Nangpa La, and examined the north-west face of the mountain from there. They also thought a route existed from that side. So we had two possible lines of attack.

After two days' travelling up the Bhote Kosi, we came to the small, deserted grazing village of Chule at over 15,000 feet. The sturdy stone huts were still half-covered with winter snow, but we dug away the snow from the doors and made ourselves comfortable inside. From this village most of the party climbed a peak of 18,900 feet, and from it they examined closely the southern route on to Cho Oyu. I had a touch of fever, and was down in the huts when they returned, decidedly disappointed. Contrary to our expectations, it appeared that access to the mountains from the south was going to be difficult, if not impossible. Our only hope was that the route might improve on closer examination.

We tramped for another day in deep, soft snow up beside the Nangpa glacier, and then established our Base Camp at the grazing ground of Lunak, which was well covered with winter snow. It was at an altitude of about 17,000 feet, and a more cold, uninviting, and desolate spot it would be difficult to imagine. But it was the only place we could find to suit our purpose. The Sherpas, however, thought it was quite satisfactory. They had uncovered a large rock-and-sod hut, and Thondup, our cook, had appropriated it for his cook-house. In the dark and smoky atmosphere they crouched around the fire, telling jokes and rocking with deep-chested laughter.

The weather was very unsettled next morning, but we all set off to examine more closely the southern approaches to Cho Oyu. We climbed up about 2,000 feet on steep snow slopes, but clouds enveloped the mountain and restricted our view. However, there didn't seem to be much doubt that an unclimbable 2,000 feet of bluffs separated us from the commencement of the south ridge. In order to confirm this, Evans and Gregory were to take a camp and a few days' food over to the foot of the ridge and examine it more closely. Meanwhile, Shipton asked George Lowe and myself to take six days' food and cross the Nangpa La to reconnoitre the north-west approach to the mountain.

On April 24th we had a very early breakfast, and then George and I left Base Camp at 5.20 a.m. We had with us three excellent Sherpas – Angputa, Tashi Phuta, and Sen Tensing, who was an old, experienced man and had been nicknamed the 'Foreign Sportsman' seventeen years before on the 1935 Everest Reconnaissance Expedition. We all had fairly heavy loads, but the cold, crisp air and the excitement of a new task kept us going at a steady pace up beside the Nangpa glacier. On every side of us unclimbed peaks shot fantastically upwards in ice-clad buttresses and towers. Search as we would, we were unable to see the faintest chink in their defences.

The snow was soft, and it was hard work plugging a trail. When the sun came out we were overcome with lethargy. We were still quite unaccustomed to the altitude, and our weakness was aggravated by the heat and glare. After five miserable hours we'd had enough, and decided to camp on the moraine-covered ice beside the glacier, which our Sherpas said was called Jasamba. We pitched our tent on a pile of rock and rubble, and the five of us crawled inside as snow started falling. Behind us avalanches were grumbling down the great ice-cliffs.

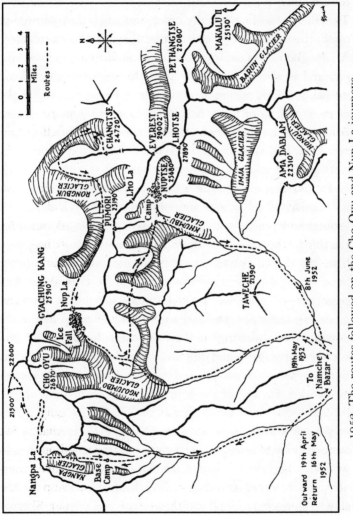

1952. The routes followed on the Cho Oyu and Nup La journeys.

I had a splitting headache and, judging from George's sour countenance, he had one too. I offered him a codeine, and he took it, then lay down with his face to the wall of the tent. The Sherpas were unusually quiet, and when they pointed at my bottle of codeine I realised that they also had headaches. All the glamour of exploration had gone. Nothing but discomfort and weakness remained. Even the slightest effort made me pant, so I lay miserably down beside George, and thought of the comforts of home and the pleasure of good, thick air. Before long the codeine quietened the hammering in my brain and I went to sleep.

It snowed all the evening and most of the night. In the early morning everything looked incredibly desolate, with its blanket of snow and the whirling mist. We were still feeling very poorly and had resigned ourselves to spending the day in the tent. And then from somewhere I dragged a little bit of will-power. 'We'll never get acclimatised lying here, George! Let's get going and work it off.' George was reluctant to agree, but I stirred some life out of the even more reluctant Sherpas and we started to pack. I crawled outside and, shivering in the cold wind, looked at all our snow-covered gear and the snow on the tent. My resolution started to weaken. And then a bleary-eyed George pushed his way out of the door, so I went on making up the loads.

We were away at 9 a.m. The Nangpa La is used quite frequently by Sherpas, even though it is 19,050 feet high; but we were the first to cross since the winter, and there were no signs of other travellers. With leaden feet we climbed slowly up an easy icefall which was covered in six inches of fresh snow. We had to wind in and out amongst the crevasses, and in one place some snow gave way and Sen Tensing slipped in up to his waist. I couldn't help wondering how the Sherpas and their animals managed to cross this area repeatedly without disaster. Perhaps they waited until some of the snow had melted and revealed all the cracks in the ice. Our lungs were straining to get enough air as we made a deep trail up gently rising snowfields. It was a long way and the flat monotony made it seem a lot longer. But soon after midday we reached an indeterminate crest, and saw a long, broad glacier sweeping down in front of us. Far in the distance were the brown hills and fleecy clouds of Tibet. We sat down wearily in the snow beside a clump of Tibetan prayer-flags. Bad weather was already approaching again and clouds were blotting out the peaks. We scrambled to our feet and walked quickly down the easy slopes to the Kyetrak glacier. We pitched our tent on the snow at about 18,900 feet, and before long we couldn't see a hundred yards in the snow and fog. Once again the whole party had bad headaches, and we dosed ourselves liberally with codeine and tried to forget our discomfort in sleep.

It was bitterly cold when we woke our Sherpas at 3 a.m., and everything seemed to take a long time. It was 6 a.m. before we had our breakfast – a large mug of tea liberally strengthened with *tsampa*. We crawled out of the tent and everything was clear and sharp. Above us towered the north-west face of Cho Oyu and our hearts sank as we looked at it. Bourdillon had told us that he thought he'd seen an easy route the year before, but it looked decidedly impressive to us. Rising from the glacier were almost 1,500 feet of steep, loose rock bluffs topped by a glacial cap. From this icecap, a narrow, twisting ridge ran up to a series of great ice-cliffs which cut right across the face and obviously could not be turned at either end. Above the ice-cliffs were several large snow basins which led up to a great, banded rock face, now heavily plastered with fresh snow. The summit itself was out of sight, probably a thousand feet higher and some distance back from the banded rock. It looked pretty formidable to us, but we thought that if we could find a way on to the icecap above the bluffs, it might be possible to tackle the ridge and the ice-cliffs from there. It was quite obvious, however, that the upper rocks stretching from 24,000 to 26,000 feet could easily be impossible under their heavy burden of snow.

George and I and Angputa set off on a reconnaissance. In the deep, fresh snow we crossed the Kyetrak glacier and followed up its northern side. The air was completely still and the sun glared down. Before long we were feeling weak and lethargic, but drove ourselves on to well over 19,000 feet. It became obvious that there wasn't an approach to the icecap from this side. We hadn't the strength left to try anywhere else, so we dragged ourselves slowly back to camp. The heat was unbearable. For four hours we lay gasping in our tent, with practically nothing on and perspiration streaming down our bodies. The glare, the heat, and the altitude had given us all frightful headaches which no amount of pills could alleviate. And then, at three o'clock, the sun went behind a storm cloud and our tent changed to an ice-chamber. We hastily dressed and crawled into our sleeping-bags. A few moments later we were being peppered by torrential hail, which drummed on the canvas in a continuous roar. Some of the hailstones were half an inch in diameter, and we were afraid they might cut the material. We were relieved when the hail changed to softly falling snow. By evening it was almost clear, and only a gusty wind was shaking the tent.

On April 27th we left the tents much earlier, and made our way well up the Kyetrak glacier. Here we found a subsidiary rock spur which appeared to give a good approach to the icecap. We could also see something of the route above the icecap, and although it looked rather difficult, it was by no means impossible. We returned to our camp with the conviction that we had seen sufficient to warrant an attempt

on the mountain. Once again it was very hot in the afternoon, but we seemed to be getting hardened to it and didn't
suffer as much. George rummaged around in his pack and
produced a pack of cards and we passed an hour quite pleasantly playing crib. The Sherpas watched us with some
interest, so when we had finished George went to some
trouble to explain to them all about cards. He showed them
the different cards and the different suits, and strained his
Hindustani to the limits to describe how a game was played.
The Sherpas listened politely and intelligently to this simple
discourse. Exhausted by his efforts, George placed the pack
in Sen Tensing's gnarled hand. With a skill that would have
shamed a professional card-sharper, Sen Tensing shuffled the
cards and then dealt them in a fluid stream to his companions. Next moment they were deep in the intricacies of Sherpa
poker. It takes a lot to make George blush, but this time his
face rivalled the setting sun in its crimson hue.

We decided to return to Base Camp at Lunak with our
information. But we were feeling fairly fit now, and we determined to try to climb a peak on the way back. To the west
of the Nangpa La were several fine snow peaks more than
21,000 feet in height, and we resolved to tackle one of these.
We were away at 5 a.m., and left the Sherpas to pack up camp
and cross the Nangpa La by themselves.

We crossed the pass and climbed rapidly up some steep
snow slopes, which were broken only by a few long crevasses.
Ahead of us was a long snow basin rising up to a little saddle
at about 20,500 feet. We were going particularly well. Our
initial acclimatisation lethargy had disappeared, and in the
crisp conditions we kicked steps with enthusiasm. The slope
steepened considerably, but we drove on and with a last few
hefty kicks moved up on to the saddle.

From here a steep and exposed ridge ran up to the summit
at 21,100 feet. We investigated this ridge and found it was

composed of a layer of loose powder snow over hard ice – a difficult and often dangerous combination. But what did it matter! In our new fitness this was only a whetting of our appetites. With some wild New Zealand yells we cut our way upwards. We moved one at a time, taking turns with the work, and we made height rapidly. We soon reached the horizontal ridge, slightly corniced on the west, which twisted gracefully up to the sharp summit. Some cautious shuffling, an exhilarating sense of exposure, and we were on top of our peak.

Our pleasure in success, our satisfaction in our improving physical condition, and the stimulation of the wonderful peaks in every direction, proved too much for us, and once again we split the Himalayan silence with exuberant shouts. A reaction, as we found later, rather more noisy but no more enthusiastic than the rather reserved 'Jolly good climb, chaps!' of our English companions. George and I were unquestionably a noisy pair.

Our view of the face of Cho Oyu was most impressive. It was obvious that the ice-cliffs were going to be a difficult proposition, and from here the upper rocks looked extremely steep. We examined it in detail and then descended carefully to the saddle. We raced down over the Nangpa La after our Sherpas, and arrived at Jasamba to find them preparing a brew of tea. We were impatient to be off, but a mug of 'char' was worth waiting for at any time. Then on again down the glacier and a mad rush into Base Camp – hot, panting, and excited. All the party were there, and we quickly gabbled out our story. It was received with mixed feelings. Evans and Gregory had found that the approach from the south was quite impossible, so our route appeared to be the only feasible one.

Griff Pugh invited us into his tent. He was carrying out a physiological experiment – counting the number of red corpuscles in the blood. Apparently the theory was that the number of red blood corpuscles governed the degree of acclimatisation. I felt pretty confident; there was no question but that George and I were the fittest pair in the party. Pugh took hold of my ear, and with the unnerving impersonality of the scientist he jabbed it violently with a sharp instrument. The resulting blood was passed through a battery of instruments and emerged as a reading on a dial. Pugh couldn't understand it. And neither could I when he explained. My blood count was just about the lowest of the lot. This meant that, theoretically, at 20,000 feet I shouldn't be able to put one foot in front of the other! There and then my faith in science and scientists disappeared for ever.

I returned to the large mess-tent to find a heated discussion in progress. A message had come in saying that the Chinese Communist troops, who had taken control of Tibet, were only a short distance away on the far side of the border. Shipton felt we might be taking a grave risk attempting Cho Oyu from the north-west. I felt this was a far too pessimistic view of the situation. We knew that in the Nangpa La area the border was ill-defined, but as we had no intention of going below 18,800 feet I failed to see that we could possibly attract undesirable attention. 'Let's give it a go' was my attitude. But, as the day passed, the argument waxed and waned, and I could feel my confidence evaporating and the cold breath of Siberia freezing my blood. By evening, Shipton had decided that we'd examine the mountain from the north-west, but that only a light mobile party would be used and that our base would be Jasamba, far down on the Nepalese side of the frontier. The length of our communications and the limits of mobility would make a powerful attempt impossible, and I think that already we were doomed to failure. Certainly I went to bed that night with shattered morale and dreamt uneasily of Communist bayonets.

The next week was spent in bringing up stores to Jasamba and in preparing for an attack on Cho Oyu. Most of us by now were getting fairly fit, and in this period we all climbed a number of peaks over 19,000 feet in height. On May 5th we crossed the Nangpa La and camped in the middle of the Kyetrak glacier. We were all slightly nervous and couldn't resist frequent glances down the glacier into Tibet. At the slightest sign of a Chinese we would have bolted back to Jasamba. On the following day six climbers and eighteen laden Sherpas went up the glacier for three hours, and established a camp at about 19,000 feet by the foot of the spur giving access to the ice plateau. I was in an exploratory mood and continued on up the spur. It was fairly steep in places, but the rock was broken and loose and it was easy enough to make a way up it. I climbed up on to a snowy shoulder and plugged steps slowly up to the foot of a very steep slope. This was a different proposition! It was hard ice covered with a foot of unstable powder snow. I must have been a thousand feet above the camp, and decided it was too risky to go on without a companion to protect me with the rope. I raced down again with the good news that some progress was possible.

The whole party started upwards next morning. I was a little worried by the loose nature of the first rocky section, and afraid that something might be dislodged on the heads of the slower members of the party. So I went on to a steep snow gully that split the face and cut up it a long line of steps. It was invigorating work. The hard, frozen snow sparkled in the morning sun as I mastered it with smooth, easy sweeps of the ice-axe. There was soon a stream of icy chips tinkling merrily downwards, and I zig-zagged my way to the top. In a little more than two hours I was at the foot of the ice-slope.

George Lowe and I roped up, and while he protected me

I tackled the slope. It was hard work. First I had to scrape away the deep powder snow, and then I attacked the gleaming ice beneath. I hacked out great bucket steps, safe enough for even the clumsiest Sherpa. It took me nearly an hour to make a stairway up a hundred feet of ice, and then I climbed up on to a rock outcrop and had a much needed rest. Above, it looked a little easier – a broad, steep ridge with a mixture of deep snow, ice, and rock.

I was joined by George, and he went on plugging upwards, beating a trail from rock island to rock island. It was very exposed and a slip might have produced an uncontrollable slide. Some stretches were treacherously loose and we couldn't rely on the Sherpas not to fall off. They were expecting us to make a safe way for them. Some of the others brought up some rope, and we attached 350 feet to jutting rocks and strung it as a handrail across the steps. Even so, some of the Sherpas had difficulty in getting up, and sprawled helplessly on the slope, hanging on to the rope for dear life. I ploughed up and down recutting damaged steps and placing flaying feet into them. And where necessary I put a very firm shoulder under reluctant Sherpa seats.

In this fashion we escorted the whole band up on to the ice plateau, and then dropped down on to a little hollow at the beginning of the snow ridge which twisted its way up towards the higher reaches of the mountain. We were at 21,000 feet and a hard and bitter wind was blowing. We decided to pitch camp immediately, hacking out platforms in the solid ice. We kept only six of our best Sherpas with us. Bourdillon and I escorted the remaining ones down over the difficult section, and saw them start off on their way towards the Nangpa La and Jasamba.

A boisterous wind flapped the tents noisily all night and it was very cold. I felt a tremendous sense of isolation. We had only five days' food with us and our base seemed a long way away over a high pass. If the Chinese came up the glacier we'd be cut off like rats in a trap. The improbability of such a thing didn't seem so great in the dark hours of the night, and I tossed and turned miserably. Evans had developed laryngitis and was having a trying time. I could hear his heavy cough and laboured breathing from the other tent even above the shriek of the wind. In the morning all of us were weak and spiritless.

At 9.45, five of us, shod in crampons, examined the ridge ahead. It was of mixed snow and rock and appeared to be of a high alpine standard. But as we climbed upwards we found the snow was not in good condition. In places deep powder lay uncomfortably on hard ice and slid off under a careless step. Elsewhere it had been packed by the wind into a crust and we feared the dreaded windslab avalanche. It was quite a relief to reach a series of rock towers, and as we climbed over them we rejoiced in the feeling of firm rock under our hands. By midday we had gained only 500 feet, but the visibility was nil and it was snowing steadily. We returned carefully down to camp.

We were hoping next day to push up the ridge a good deal farther, but even though the morning was sunny, a howling wind whipped the snow off the mountains and buffeted the tents. It would have been impossible to work higher up. Evans was still very ill and was obviously incapable at the moment of going any higher. In fact, remaining at this height could be dangerous for him. Later on in the day he started off down the mountain with Secord and a Sherpa assisting him, and slowly made his way back to healthier levels. We were all still far from being well acclimatised. We were very conscious of our poor selection of food and were eating very little. Pemmican, dried soups, half-brewed cups of tea, hard biscuits – all seemed revolting to us as our minds lovingly dwelt on tinned fruit and juicy steak. We passed the time with innumerable games of crib. At 4.30 p.m. the weather cleared a little, and we could see a lot of fresh snow farther up the ridge.

I don't think I slept much that night. In the morning I felt thick and heady and a sharp cough rasped my sore throat. I felt I was getting a cold. But the weather was fine and I knew we had to make the most of it. Gregory, Bourdillon, George Lowe, and I left our tents at 7.30 a.m. in an attempt to get up to the ice-cliffs. George and I were roped together and we went on ahead. Most of our tracks had been wiped out, but we steadily chipped and cramponed our way up the ridge. My feet were agonisingly cold and so were George's. We soon reached our highest previous point and continued on. It was very steep and the surface here was most unpleasant – a thick windcrust over deep unstable snow. I didn't like it at all and felt it could avalanche at any moment. We crawled on to a rock island which protruded through the slope and sat on a narrow ledge. It was a bit warmer here, and we took off our boots and beat our frozen toes back into life. Gregory and Bourdillon laboured slowly up towards us. Bourdillon wasn't going well, and he admitted quite frankly that he was greatly afraid of the snow conditions. They started unlacing their boots and George and I went on. We took every opportunity to keep on the crest of the ridge, and when forced in places to traverse on the south face, we did so one at a time, on a tight rope. We were making gradual height, and we climbed carefully over a long snow bridge over a great crevasse. Then we came to the end of the ridge, and sat down gratefully in a warm little hollow out of the wind. Once again we rubbed our numbed feet.

Our view was superb. Already we were above many of the nearby peaks, and far away to the west we could see the towering 26,000 feet of Gosainthan. The ice-cliffs above us

looked grim and forbidding. They were hundreds of feet high
and quite unclimbable. But there was a breach in this great
rampart. Out to the left, across a very steep ice gully, a bare,
hard slope of solid ice swept up between the cliffs. It looked
fiendishly steep and I estimated that it was 300 feet long. We
decided to look at the route more closely.

Between us and the ice-cliffs was a long and steep snow
slope. Fortunately this snow was firm and safe. We cut a
zigzag of steps up it, and I felt sharply conscious of the
tremendous drops beneath as we approached the great wall.
The ice-cliffs seemed to loom over our heads as we inched
our way over to the edge of the ice gully. It was a real death-
trap. Hanging above it were some great fractured fingers of
ice which periodically avalanched and swept remorselessly
down to the glacier 3,000 feet below. To cut steps underneath
this active ice would demand a high degree of courage or
rashness. And even if we took the risk and got on to the great
ice-slope, we were far from confident that we could get laden
men up a route of such length and steepness even if we
attached fixed ropes, and we had neither ropes nor pitons for
this purpose.

We were nearly 22,500 feet up and it seemed hard to turn
back now, but we didn't hesitate. We just weren't prepared
to take the risk and, anyway, we had neither the equipment
nor resources to take advantage of it if we succeeded. We
climbed slowly down to our warm hollow. Cho Oyu had been
a series of worries and frustrations. We seemed so cut off
from the main body of the expedition and our resources
seemed so slender. And there was always the nagging fear
that a squad of soldiers might be waiting for us at the bottom
of the ridge. I was glad that we'd at least been stopped by a
tough problem, but under the circumstances I wasn't sorry
to be leaving the mountain.

Someday Cho Oyu will undoubtedly be climbed, but it will

be by a party that is prepared to accept the risk of over-hanging ice and is determined to push on despite it.

We were back at our tents by 1.30 p.m. Despite my sore throat and threatening cold, I felt very fit and decided to go on down to the foot of the mountain. I made a load of my sleeping-bag and air-mattress and started off. I raced down the fixed ropes and plunged down the snow slopes below. With every step I could feel my spirits lightening. I glissaded down the bottom slopes in a cloud of dust and boulders, and had to stop for a moment to get my breath. A few hundred feet below me was our first camp. With a start I saw a line of black figures climbing up towards it. *'Who are they?* My mouth went dry and I mentally cursed the noise of my un-controlled descent. And then, with an enormous sense of relief, I recognised Shipton. With a shout of greeting I con-tinued down to meet him and Riddiford and a group of laden Sherpas.

I told Shipton of our retreat from the ice-cliffs above. Now that I was safely off the mountain, its difficulties and dangers were beginning to fade, and I felt almost a sense of shame that we'd allowed ourselves to admit defeat so readily. I suggested that Shipton go up and have a look for himself. But Shipton's responsibilities as leader of the party made him more conscious than any of us of the proximity of the Communist troops, and he had no hesitation in accepting our judgment. He decided that the whole party should retreat back over the Nangpa La to Jasamba.

In the morning we sent some Sherpas up the ridge, and the whole of our high camp was evacuated. We had decided to move the same afternoon to Jasamba, so we made all the gear into suitable loads. George Lowe and I had a word with Shipton. From high on Cho Oyu, we'd examined closely the group of peaks to the north of the Kyetrak glacier, and we thought that several of them were climbable. We wanted to attempt them. Shipton agreed, and we quickly made up a small camp with about four days' food. Our own personal Sherpas, Angputa and Tashi Phuta, were to accompany us. We divided everything into four loads, and parted from the others with their cheerful 'good luck' in our ears. It was unusually hot. The sun was shining through a thin layer of hazy cloud and not a breath of wind stirred. There was something ominous and oppressive in the complete stillness. Under our heavy loads we laboured across the glacier, wet with perspiration and weak with lethargy. A sudden chilling of the air gave us a little much needed relief, but soon the air was full of silent drifting snowflakes. We couldn't see any suitable place for a camp, but hacked away the top of an ice bulge to make enough room for our tent. And then we all crawled inside.

All night it snowed spasmodically, and in the morning the glacier was covered with a deep white blanket. The clouds were down around us and we couldn't see more than forty feet. We decided to remain where we were – we'd certainly get lost if we started out, and, anyway, this fresh snow could well avalanche on the steep slopes above. An increase in warmth after midday told us the mist was clearing, and we looked out of the tent to see a patch of blue sky above. Soon we were sweltering once again in the heat of the sun and praying for the night.

It was a bitterly cold night and the weather in the morning was still a little doubtful, with long streaks of high cirrus cloud glowing in the early morning sun. But we packed up quickly and started off at 7 a.m. Our objective was a little saddle between two of the peaks. The route to the saddle was still dark and shaded, but I thought I could see a practicable route up some snow gullies beside a tumbling glacier. I was feeling particularly fit, so went on ahead. I soon climbed up to the first gully and found the snow steep and hard. I started chipping a long line of steps. At first the cumbersome load on my back made me feel uncomfortable and off-balance, but I soon adjusted myself to it and achieved a smooth and easy swing. The air was freezingly cold – so cold, in fact, that it hurt my throat to breathe it. I pushed on as hard as my straining lungs would let me. Only activity could counteract the agony of the cold. I traversed out to the left to dodge a beetling ice-cliff, and then cut another line of steps back to the right to get on top of it.

George and the Sherpas were labouring steadily up behind, but I could tell from their grim expressions that they were suffering as much as I was. The slopes ahead seemed much easier, and I plugged a line of steps up them in soft snow, keeping close to the edge of the glacier to avoid hidden crevasses. I had now moved into the sun, but its feeble warmth was more than outweighed by the increasing wind. Just before nine o'clock I climbed up on to the saddle, and looked over it down across the bare hills of Tibet. I couldn't help a feeling of childlike awe as I looked again on that mysterious country. I'd always been rather interested in comparative religion, and down there was the home of ancient magic and holy Lamas. My soliloquy was cut short by a great surge of frigid air.

I searched for a camp site. A snowy hollow looked promising, but I quickly retreated when my questing ice-axe revealed a wide, hidden crevasse. I started clearing a ledge at a safer spot beside some rocks. George and the Sherpas joined me. George was suffering severely with cold feet and was afraid of frostbite. He removed his boots in a spot out of the wind, and then he and the Sherpas massaged back his feet into painful life. We pitched our tent, got into our sleeping-bags, and finished the thawing-out process with a mug of steaming soup.

We estimated our height as 20,600 feet. To the west of us was a fine peak of 21,500 feet. I was keen to climb it. George wasn't feeling too well, but was determined not to be left behind. By 11 a.m. we were warm and rested, so we dressed again in all our clothing and roped up. We emerged into the biting wind. I shouted a few instructions about having a hot drink ready for us to our Sherpas, who were comfortably resting in their sleeping-bags. '*Tikh hai* (O.K.), *Sahib!*' they replied, and snuggled a little farther down into their bags.

The ridge started up almost directly from our camp. There was only 900 feet to go, but there were some steep pitches. We clambered slowly upwards. We were protected from the worst of the wind, which was just as well, as George was climbing with difficulty. 'Will we chuck it in, George?' But George shook his head and struggled grimly on. We came to the foot of a vertical step in the ridge. We couldn't climb it direct, so we turned it on the left up a steep gully with loose, sliding snow. Then we carefully traversed over a steep rock face to the right. The approach to the summit was a formidable snow ridge. It was steep and exposed, but the snow was mostly in good condition and I made an airy but safe track up it. George drove himself on with courage and determination. We reached the corniced summit and shuddered to the full force of the wind. But we had a thrilling view of Tibet, and could also see, over the Nangpa La, the fantastic peaks and the cloud-filled valleys of Nepal. It was too cold and windy to linger, so we turned back down our tracks. We were welcomed to our tent by the cheerful congratulations of our Sherpas and a large mug of hot tea.

All night the wind rocked the tent. And it was very cold. In the early morning I poked my head out of the door to have a look at the weather. It wasn't too promising. There was a high layer of grey clouds and great cumulus were surging over the Nangpa La, and the wind was fresh and strong. We started to prepare our breakfast and forced down a mug of tea thickened with *tsampa*. At seven o'clock I had another look out – it hadn't improved at all; but it hadn't got worse, so we decided to leave. We planned to attack a peak to the east of us. It was 22,600 feet high and a tough-looking proposition; not the sort of place to get caught in in bad weather. We put on every bit of clothing we had and then crawled outside. Under the dull sky all the snowy peaks were a sombre, threatening grey. We put on our crampons and tied on the rope. Then, with a wave to the Sherpas, we started off.

First of all, we had to drop down on to the saddle and wind our way across between gaping crevasses. We were already starting to feel cold, and George complained that the straps of his crampons were constricting his feet. I knew we were unwise to go on, but felt we still had a chance to climb this fine peak. From the saddle we had to ascend a very broad ridge, practically a face, in order to reach the summit ridge at about 22,000 feet. This face was cut by a few crevasses, but they didn't look difficult to turn. The main problem seemed to be several very steep pitches of hard, clear ice, which would obviously require steps cut in them.

We cramponed steadily upwards, swinging well out to the right to dodge one of the crevasses. And then we came to one of the icy patches. George cut a line of steps across it. The sun was obscured by haze and the wind was very cold. I could feel my feet becoming blocks of ice, and knew that George's were probably worse. But we were making gradual height. All the valleys now and many of the peaks were shrouded in billowing clouds, and I could see powder snow whipping off the summit of our own peak. A tug on the rope told me George had stopped. 'I have to warm my feet!' He sat down in a hole he had dug in the slope and proceeded to take off his boots. Then he massaged his toes fiercely. I couldn't help a slight feeling of resentment. My toes were cold, but if we pushed on hard we could get back to camp and comfort all the sooner. Half an hour later, by the time George had his boots on again, my feet were frozen.

I pushed on at an angry pace, miserable and irritable. I cut steps up some ice slopes and gingerly crossed some unstable areas of wind-crusted snow. Poor George hadn't yet struck his best form and was finding the altitude a bit much for him. The rope between us was let out more and more, and soon I was a hundred feet ahead in my mad rush up the slope. A sharp tug brought me to my senses. George was sitting on the slope again fumbling with his crampons.

'I have to warm my feet again. Come down and give me a rub!'

'My feet are cold too – why not push on and then get back to the tent?'

'I'm doing them now!'

'Come up here and I'll give them a rub.'

'I'm doing them here!'

'Then do them yourself!'

In fuming silence we sat a hundred feet apart, perched on our little shelves. Before long my feet were so cold I had to take my boots off too, and then we were both sitting there massaging our feet.

I don't know why we didn't go back to our camp. But when we finally started off again most of our irritation had vanished. George was quite frank: 'I'm not going too well today, but if you can do the work and don't go too fast I'll get there.'

Feeling thoroughly ashamed of my tantrums, I plugged on. The slope steepened considerably towards the crest, and it was hard work making a trail up an almost vertical pitch on to the summit ridge. I belayed carefully and brought George up to me. Up here we were exposed to the full force of the wind, and it was painful to look into it. But we had a remarkable view of the north face of Cho Oyu. Conscientiously George produced his camera and took a number of shots. Next moment we were enveloped in cloud and pelted by hard-driven ice particles. We were thoroughly miserable but decided to keep on.

We knew that farther along the summit ridge it was corniced, so I kept well down on the right-hand side. Kicking and cutting steps, I forced out an exposed track. Sometimes the snow was loose and unstable, and I was very conscious of the bluffs beneath; and sometimes it had avalanched off to leave hard ice and a long spell of step cutting. The clouds were completely obscuring our view and it was hard to know where we were.

At 1.30 p.m. we staggered on top, having had quite enough. We saw nothing of the view, and my main memory of the summit is a shrieking inferno of wind-whipped rock and ice. We turned immediately back down the ridge directly into the face of the blizzard. With a feeling of panic, I searched for our upward tracks. Already most of them had been obscured. Our faces and beards completely froze, our glasses fogged up, and we literally felt our way down on a tight rope. In places we crouched desperately over our ice-axes as gust after gust of wind tore at us. With the strength that comes from desperation we battled against it, and climbed down more by

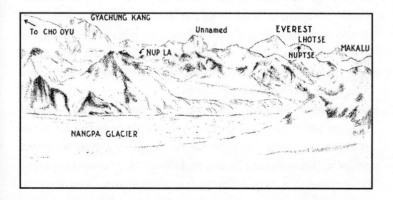

memory than anything else. To drop down off the ridge on to the face and out of the full force of the wind was like a blessing. We cramponed straight down the slope in a flurry of wind and snow. With the last shreds of our energy, we climbed slowly up the slope to our tent. Our two Sherpas scrambled out, helped us off with our crampons and pushed us into the warm interior. Soon we were inside our sleeping-bags and wearily sipping mugs of hot tea and soup. The tent rocked in the wind, but we could afford to ignore it in the comfort and security of our sleeping-bags.

Why did we persist with this climb – even at the risk of frost-bite or worse? I think it was mainly a reaction from Cho Oyu. We didn't want to be beaten a second time, so we pushed things a lot harder than we would normally have done. And also this peak had exerted the peculiar fascination of being higher than any peak we had yet climbed. Certainly, whatever the reason, I have never had to struggle harder for a peak before or since.

On May 15th we packed up our camp and descended down to the Kyetrak glacier. We crossed the glacier with our heavy loads, keeping a careful look-out down towards Tibet. We unconsciously hurried up the slopes to the top of the Nangpa La, spurred on by the sight of a little group of figures moving slowly up towards us from below. It was a great relief to cross the pass and descend rapidly down into Nepal. We arrived at Jasamba to find a group of Sherpas moving out the last loads. We raced on ahead of them down the glacier and round the corner to unload our packs from our aching shoulders at the camp at Lunak.

Now that our main objective had come to its unsuccessful conclusion, Shipton decided that the party should break up into smaller groups and explore and climb where they willed. Shipton himself, with Evans and Gregory, intended on doing an exploratory trip to the west. Riddiford had twisted his back and had decided to return home. Pugh had obtained three guinea-pigs in Bourdillon, Secord, and College, and they were all going to carry out oxygen tests at 20,000 feet in the Pangbuk valley. And finally Shipton suggested that George and I might like to have a go at crossing for the first time a pass to the east of Cho Oyu called the Nup La. We enthusiastically agreed. But first we wanted a few days to rest and reorganise.

On May 16th George and I walked the twenty tedious miles down to Namche Bazar. We arrived tired and footsore, and were met by Professor Lombard, the geologist of the Swiss Expedition. He told us that the Swiss had battled through the icefall and into the Western Cwm; that they had built up a good stock of supplies and food in the Cwm, and that now they were coming to grips with the next big problem – getting to the South Col. It made our own efforts somehow seem rather paltry and we went quietly off to bed.

CHAPTER FIVE

Across the Nup La

I HAD ALWAYS WANTED to attempt the Nup La. In 1951, Riddiford and the others had tried to get up its great icefalls, but had been forced back. Quite apart from the satisfaction of making the first ascent of this formidable pass, George and I had other, more secret, plans. The Nup La is the pass at the head of the Dudh Kosi river and the Ngojumba glacier. On its far side it leads into the West Rongbuk glacier and the northern slopes of Mount Everest. We thought that, if we managed to get over the pass, we'd do a quick trip around the north side of Everest, visiting many of the famous places of the early expeditions and perhaps attempt some climbs. Even to see the face of Everest, that had become so real to us through books and photographs, was an exciting prospect. But first we had to get over the Nup La.

On May 19th George and I left Namche Bazar and climbed up a thousand feet to the village of Khumjung. This was where our Sherpas Angputa and Tashi Phuta lived. We spent the night in Angputa's house, and were royally entertained by his charming young wife and his aged parents. The Sherpa home is a strongly built and commodious structure. A well-to-do home is of two stories with the walls made of rock plastered together with mud. The roof is usually overlapping slabs of pine with great rocks to hold it all down. The ground-floor is the storeroom and the shelter for their animals, while the family lives on the second floor. George and I crouched around the crackling fire and ate a great repast of omelet (specially produced in our honour) and boiled potatoes, followed by a dessert of curds and *tsampa*. A cup of tea completed our feeling of contentment. Our air-mattresses and sleeping-bags had been laid out for us in a corner, so we retired to rest after a judicious splashing around of flea-powder.

For the next two days our little caravan wound its way slowly up the deep valley of the Dudh Kosi. The scenery was superb, and as we were travelling at a leisurely pace we enjoyed every bit of it. We had three of our permanent Sherpas with us – Angputa, Tashi Phuta, and Angje – and half a dozen casuals, mostly fresh-faced and energetic youths. In the middle of the second day we came to a small village, with only one of its houses inhabited, as it was still fairly early in the year. Here we managed to purchase 80 lb. of potatoes and employed a very attractive young Sherpa girl to carry them. Immediately the whole atmosphere of the party lightened. All the young men were dashing about like a bunch of young colts, seeking to outdo each other with witticisms and laughter. The loads on their backs were quite forgotten and they fairly galloped up the valley. It was significant, however, that although all the young men did their best to impress our fair employee, not one of them offered to carry part of her considerably heavier load. Amongst the Sherpas a woman expects and receives no favoured treatment when it comes to carrying a load.

In the afternoon we climbed up the trough beside the Ngojumba glacier to a small grazing village beside a lovely lake called Dudh Pokari. Across the lake a range of fine glaciated peaks dominated the skyline, and I have rarely felt more at peace with the world than I did as I lay in the door of my tent and looked across the shimmering waters at their lofty summits. This village, too, had few inhabitants – only a handful of hardy souls tending the grazing yaks and milking them each evening. It started snowing late in the afternoon, and all our Sherpas moved into one of the rock-and-sod huts. George and I joined them there for our evening meal. We stumbled into the dark and smoky atmosphere of the hut, and were given places of honour beside the small yak-dung fire. A bowl of excellent stew was thrust into our hands and we attacked it enthusiastically. The Sherpas are rarely quiet, and before long their deep-chested laughter rang through the hut. The warmth, the soft hum of voices, and the air of complete contentment were too much for me and I gradually nodded off to sleep.

It was still snowing next morning and we felt very reluctant to start. But at last we summoned up the will to depart, and tramped up the valley in soft snow with a heavy mist obscuring everything. We'd only been going about an hour when the weather cleared remarkably quickly, and the snow started melting before our eyes in the sun's fierce heat. It was a typical Himalayan change – one moment it was miserably cold and the next unbearably hot. We pitched our tents on a little mossy terrace beside a crystal-clear glacial pond, and gathered armfuls of fuel from the stunted shrubs clothing the hillsides. I climbed up on to the edge of the glacier for a look at the way ahead. Towering over us on the left was the enormous face of Cho Oyu, and to the north of it, in one great sweep, stretched peak after peak, culminating in the summit pyramid of Everest itself. I wondered what the Swiss were doing there and how far they'd got. I strained my eyes hopelessly to pick them out on that great bulk twenty miles away, and then reluctantly turned to the immediate task. I couldn't really tell where the Nup La was, but it was quite obvious that next day we'd have to cross the glacier in order to approach it.

In the morning it was clear and frosty, and we started off very early. I felt a growing excitement as I realised that today we were going to see the approaches to the Nup La. We continued up beside the glacier for a short distance, and then dropped down a steep moraine wall on to the bare ice. It was surprisingly easy going. Stretches of bare ice were divided by moraine-covered humps, but we wound our way through from one long channel to the next. We were soon on the far side, and continued on up it to where the glacier turned sharply to the left. On the corner the ice was crushed and broken, and it took us a long time to find a way through it. We were forced to climb up another steep moraine wall into the trough behind it, and then, having followed up this trough for a short distance, came up on to a little crest. We stopped aghast at the view ahead.

It was far worse than I had expected. In front of us a great icefall tumbled down thousands of feet in an utter chaos of shattered ice. The icefall was split by a great rock buttress, and the ice surged around it like the bow-wave of a destroyer. It was a vast and spectacular sight, but I felt completely subdued at the thought of finding a way up it. The right-hand icefall, with its row after row of tottering ice pinnacles, looked decidedly dangerous, and the left-hand one crashed over an enormous rock bluff almost continuously. No wonder the other party in 1951 had brought back such lurid tales.

We pitched our tent on the ice at the foot of the right-hand icefall, and paid off all the Sherpas except our three permanent ones. They'd been a very happy party and extremely willing workers, and I was sorry to be losing their companionship. As they disappeared down the glacier, I stood with George and Angje looking up at the icefall. '*Bohut kharab* (very bad), *Sahib!*' said Angje. With the worthy intention of bolstering Sherpa morale, I assured him that it was perfectly safe and that we'd find a way up it without difficulty. Even as I spoke there was a sullen rumble and a hundred yards of ice-cliff leaned over and avalanched downwards with frightening force. When the grinding noises had stopped and the dust clouds had settled, I agreed whole-heartedly with Angje that it was indeed '*Bohut kharab!*'

In the afternoon I went off on a rather aimless solo reconnaissance. I had noticed a small gap between the right-hand icefall and the rock buttress, and wanted to see if it was possible to get far up it. I found it quite easy scrambling over loose boulders, although I had the unhappy feeling that I was liable to be showered with loose rocks from the left and chunks of ice from the right. Finally I couldn't get any farther – the ice-cliffs closed into the rock in an impassable wall. I tried climbing up the rocks, and reached about forty feet up a smooth watercourse before realising that it was effectively blocked by an overhanging waterfall. And then I had to get down again. The smooth, slippery surface was much harder to descend, and I arrived at the bottom with quivering muscles and shaken nerve. It was obvious that this gap promised only trouble for us, and I got out of it as quickly as I could.

I walked over to the foot of the main buttress and examined it closely. It looked a difficult problem, but I thought I could see a line of ascent at least up the first half. The greatest danger seemed to be falling rocks, which came down regularly every few minutes; but I felt we could pick a route to dodge them. I returned to camp in the evening and told George of my discoveries. We decided to attempt the rock buttress next day.

Our meal was cooked over the unusual luxury of a wood fire, as we'd brought a load of dry juniper wood up with us. As we crouched around it, warming ourselves in the chilly night air, Angje took a few glowing twigs and placed them on a small flat stone. He then added a tiny dab of butter, and watched it splutter and smoke while he murmured softly to himself. We asked him the meaning of this little ceremony. He explained that it was a little offering to propitiate the gods of the ice so that we might have a safe passage. The gift of butter, together with the Buddhist prayer '*Om Mane Padme Hum*', assured us of the kindly attentions of the gods. We went to sleep with Angje's prayers a soothing background to our worried minds.

George and I were at the foot of the bluffs by 7.30 next morning, before the sun had loosened the rocks from their frozen beds. We scrambled on to the bottom of a narrow ledge that climbed steeply up the face, and made our way up it as quickly as we could. It was loose shingle, which slid uncomfortably away from underneath our feet but was easy enough to climb. We reached the end of the ledge, and climbed a steep pitch of rock on to another shelf and raced up that. Then we relaxed and rested for a moment, for we felt we were out of danger of any rockfall.

Above us now was a steep rock couloir. I led off up it and found it quite easy going. But at the top was a great chockstone completely blocking the way. I couldn't see any way over it. The right-hand side of the couloir looked far too steep to climb, but I thought I might be able to get out of it on the left side. I cut a line of steps across the steep, hard snow below the chockstone, and while George climbed up to join me I looked gloomily at the move ahead. It was a smooth, holdless slab, and there was nothing but friction to get me up it. George assured me he had a reasonable belay in case I fell off, and with these comforting words as my staff I laid my hands on the slab. Three times I started to throw myself up it and three times I stopped myself, my stomach tight with fear. George waited patiently. I roundly abused myself for being faint-hearted and, summoning up a little courage from somewhere, I plunged upwards. With quivering muscles I balanced on the steep slab on my hands and knees, and then quickly threw a hand over the top and dragged myself to safety. I took in the rope and George unashamedly called for a tug and slithered up to join me. We agreed that any hope of getting laden Sherpas up here was pretty remote. But we decided to keep going.

An hour later we were a hundred feet farther up the cliff and fairly sure we couldn't get a foot higher. We were almost equally sure we couldn't get down again either. We lowered our packs on to a little ledge, and then slowly eased ourselves down. It took us a long time. It was a tremendous relief to get back to the chockstone. I lowered George down the steep slab, and then he climbed well up on the far side of the couloir so that he could more directly protect me with the rope. I eased myself on to the slab and, using all the friction I could get, inched my way down it. I wasn't sorry to feel a firm snow step under my foot again.

By now rocks were rattling down the lower bluffs with some regularity. We'd have to run for it! We raced down the couloir, dislodging a stream of boulders, and then ducked quickly aside to let them shoot past and go bounding down the cliffs with sickening thuds. We dived on to the first terrace, slid to the end of it, climbed down the rock pitch and then, with a tight feeling between our shoulders, we dashed down the last shelf and out to safety on the glacier.

We arrived back in camp a quiet and subdued pair. We were met by Angje with the familiar '*Bohut kharab*'. He told us that the Sherpas had watched our progress with great admiration, but that they had no intention of following our example and going up the bluffs. We assured him that the Sahibs had no further intention of going up there either. He didn't look completely convinced, and I knew that tonight the sacrificial fire would burn more brightly than ever. I felt strongly inclined to burn a little butter myself.

Later in the afternoon Angputa and I went for a stroll up

the left-hand valley to examine the other icefall. It was an impressive place. The main body of the icefall came to a sudden halt at the edge of a thousand-foot bluff and broke off in huge chunks and crashed to the glacier below. We kept well away from it on the other side of the glacier, but found that even here we were stumbling over avalanche debris from small hanging glaciers perched high on the great rock walls behind us. It looked a hopeless lead and a dangerous one, but I decided to go on a bit farther. I now climbed up on to a rounded ridge of moraine and ice that swept along in a great curve to the left-hand side of the icefall. It was quite easy going and certainly safe enough. The farther we got along the ridge, the more the route opened out before us. I stopped and had a long look. I felt stirrings of excitement. Although the icefall was well broken on this side, it wasn't as active, and it appeared that there might be a route up on to the ice-cliffs above the bluffs. I went on a little farther, and the closer I got to it the more convinced I became. It didn't look by any means an easy route, but it was the only place on the whole icefall that looked at all safe from overhanging ice. Darkness was approaching and we hadn't time to go any farther, so we hurried back to camp.

George and I set off at 6.30 a.m. next morning to try to follow this route. We were feeling very fit, and reached the limit of my previous day's explorations in a very short time. George, no doubt with memories of the rock buttress in his mind, was a little doubtful of my enthusiastic 'easy route', but as he looked ahead he started to thaw out a little and admitted that it had decided possibilities. We roped up, put on our crampons, and then started upwards, working together with the smoothness and confidence that came from months of hard climbing.

At the start we made quite good progress up some moraine between the icefall and the high rock bluffs on the left. But

slowly we found ourselves being forced into the icefall itself.
It was a criss-cross of deep crevasses – a problem that was
going to take a long time to solve. But this was the sort of
job we really liked. We hacked steps up ice-walls; cautiously
crossed slender snow-bridges; cut our way down into
crevasses and out the other side. In one place I chipped out
an airy highway on the thin crest of a blade of ice. It was
exhilarating work and we were making substantial height.
We had only one worry. The angle of the crevasses was slowly
but surely driving us towards the shattered edge where the
icefall took its last long jump. We could even feel the subterranean quiver as each fresh acre of ice broke off. We were
getting uncomfortably close when fate relented and we found
a snow-bridge which led us back to the centre again. At 10.30
a.m. we cramponed on to a snowy knoll, and saw in the far
distance, across the snowfields, the Nup La – a gentle 19,400-
foot dip between 24,000 feet precipices.

It was a great moment! For a few seconds we shouted and
waved in self-esteem and satisfaction. It was still a long way
to the saddle, but there didn't seem to be many difficulties in
between. All our troubles were over. We decided to return
immediately to camp and to start carrying up equipment the
next day. We followed our tracks easily downwards in a glow
of contentment.

The Sherpas greeted us as cheerfully as usual, but there
was a certain restraint in the atmosphere when we told them
of our plan to take them up the icefall with loads. And that
night the 'Om Mane Padme Hum's' reached a new crescendo
of feeling with all three Sherpas joining in.

I had a restless night due to the excitement and woke very
early. There was only need for one of us to take the Sherpas
up, so George was having a day off. I roused Angputa and
asked him to start preparing our breakfast. We left the camp
at 6 a.m., and it was cold and crisp. We all had substantial

loads, but the Sherpas were going very well. When we roped up and put our crampons on, the pace dropped off considerably, and I heard Angje's familiar '*Bohut kharab!*' as we came to each new and difficult pitch. But Angje, for all his dubious comments, was a strong and stout-hearted chap. It was Tashi Phuta who displayed the least confidence in his Sahib. Each snow-bridge was examined by Tashi Phuta with extreme care, and he poked so many holes in them with his ice-axe that he reduced their efficiency by at least half. Then he crawled across on his hands and knees. But, despite this, all of them were really climbing extremely well, and on the difficult stretches I helped them up with a hearty tug on the rope. We reached the crest of the icefall at 9.30 a.m.

I decided to continue a little farther. We dropped down off the snow mound and crossed an easy flat ahead. Confident that there were no difficulties in front of us, I walked dreamily on, feeling in imagination that we'd already dropped our loads on the Nup La. I stopped on the edge of an enormous crevasse. It was a vast chasm at least a hundred feet wide, and it split the icefall from side to side. All my dreams collapsed! This was the toughest problem we'd struck yet. I looked over the edge – sixty feet down, the crevasse was bridged with unstable-looking snow, itself split by minor crevasses. It looked a ghastly place, but I thought that if we could get down on to the bridge we might get across.

I searched along the crevasse until I found a place where the lower lip had broken in a little. The Sherpas seemed a little reluctant, but I made sure they had a good belay and then started to cut a staircase down the fractured ice-wall into the snow-filled bottom. It was difficult work and I had to make big steps, so it was over half an hour before I could step cautiously out on to the bottom. I thrust my ice axe firmly into the side of the crevasse as a belay, and then persuaded the Sherpas to follow me down.

We stood in a subdued little group in the depths of this great chasm, and I looked across at the other wall. It towered sixty feet above us – hard, clear ice. But there was a possible gap in its armour – in one place, banked up against the wall, was a cone of snow which almost reached the top. It was worth a try. I warned the Sherpas to keep the rope tight, and then I started picking my way cautiously across the snow, stepping over the numerous cracks in its surface until I reached the other wall. The snow cone shot up very steeply, but it seemed to be firm and stable. I didn't really like doing such technical climbing with only Sherpas on the rope, but I had to make a route somehow. I cut a steep flight of steps twenty feet upwards, and then dug out a platform large enough to stand on comfortably. Then, with a tight rope, I brought the three Sherpas up and anchored them safely on this platform. They didn't say anything, but their wide, frightened eyes showed they weren't enjoying it much.

I cut another line of steps to the top of the snow until only six feet of hard vertical ice separated me from the top of the crevasse. Feeling very exposed on my minute perch, I commenced hacking a route up the ice-wall. It wasn't easy work. In order to keep on the steps, I had to cut out handholds and take all my weight on these. It was a good moment when I reached over the top and thrust my ice-axe firmly into the hard snow. A wriggle and a grunt and I was out. I stood there for a moment regaining my breath. We were well over 19,000 feet, and an effort such as this was a great strain on the lungs.

I looked ahead. To my utter disgust another crevasse almost as big as the one I'd just crawled out of barred my way. Where was the nice easy route that George and I had seen? We must have been blind! The faint cry of 'Sahib! Sahib!' brought me back to my senses, and I hastened back to look down at the three Sherpas clinging to their airy ledge forty feet below. I knew I'd have to haul them up the last section. Getting a good, firm stance and placing the rope over my shoulder, I called to them to come on up. Then, like three sacks of coal, I dragged them firmly over the top. They were very glad to be there.

It was increasingly obvious to me now that there was still some very difficult country between us and the Nup La, and I sadly regretted that George wasn't up here to give me a hand. I decided to leave all our loads in this spot and to do a reconnaissance ahead without them. I moved up and had a look at the next crevasse. Well, at least it was a bit easier to get into it, although the snow in the bottom looked decidedly unstable. Once again on the other side there was a sharp ridge of snow climbing up the ice-wall and petering out about six feet from the top.

I cut a few steps, and then we all lowered ourselves cautiously into the depths. The snow in the bottom quivered at my footsteps, but it held as I carefully picked my way across to the other side. And then I commenced getting up this wall as before. I cut a long line of steps up the slender crest of the snow ridge, and then forced a route up the ice-wall at the top. Finally, after some more hearty tugs on the rope, the Sherpas joined me once again.

We continued on over some dangerously crevassed country. And the farther we went the more there seemed to be between us and the Nup La. We stopped, in the end, on the edge of a great drop which overhung the shattered morass of the right-hand icefall. This way was impassable. It might be possible to get around to the left, but I wanted George up here with me before I dared try it. We returned to the two great crevasses, and I lowered the Sherpas down their steep walls. And then, with a feeling of frustration, I led them back through the labyrinth of the icefall and down to camp.

At first I didn't feel very optimistic as I told George about

our day's efforts. We were lying in our sleeping-bags in the
tent, and the Sherpas were softly chanting their prayers. But
somehow, down here talking to George, the problems up top
seemed so much easier. In the end we decided to make an all-
out attempt to reach the Nup La on the following day.

We had packed up all our gear and had breakfast by 8 a.m.
It was unusually mild, and we didn't like the heavy clouds
down the valley. The season was quickly passing – it was
now May 27th – and we feared the onset of the monsoon.
We didn't waste any time as we went up the easier part of
the glacier, especially when we found part of our tracks had
been wiped out by an avalanche of ice falling from the hanging
glaciers clinging to the bluffs above us. We were soon roping
up and putting on our crampons. And then we started through
the more difficult country. Having George to help me with
the Sherpas made a tremendous difference, and we made quite
a reasonable speed. But the soft snow made trail-breaking
very tedious, and some of the snow bridges looked rather
fragile and unsafe. The untrusting Tashi Phuta poked furiously at everything with his ice-axe, and gloomy Angje shook
his head and reaffirmed his '*Bohut kharab*' at each of the difficult pitches. As we reached the crest of the icefall, the clouds
were rapidly closing in towards us.

We had expected trouble with the two great crevasses, and
we weren't disappointed. Even with George's expert help, we
had a tough job crossing them. The softening of the snow
had made my routes up and down their steep walls decidedly
unreliable, but George and I got up somehow and hauled the
Sherpas up behind us.

With each moment the snow seemed to be getting softer
and softer. George led off across the murky expanse of the
snow plateau, searching continuously with his ice-axe for
concealed crevasses. And he found them everywhere. We were
startled by a sudden shriek from Tashi Phuta, and turned

around to find only his head visible above the snow. Foolishly, he'd strayed a few feet off George's track and he'd found a crevasse for himself. George was holding him tightly on the rope, and I carefully worked my way over towards him – prodding carefully every inch of the ground. I got close enough to grasp his arm and then we dragged him out of the crevasse. It was only his pack that had stopped him dropping down it like a stone. I peered down the hole he had made, and could see hard green ice disappearing down into a black void. I hastily stepped back and sank to my knee in another hidden crack behind me. Quickly I had to stifle a rising feeling of panic. The Sherpas were frankly scared, and we couldn't afford to let them see that we were too.

We slowly moved onwards, testing the ground with care before we dared step on it. Yet many times we were up to our knees in unsuspected holes, and clumsy Tashi Phuta sank down up to his neck once more before the rope held him. The snow was in such poor condition that snow bridges the full thickness of the ice-axe shaft would collapse and let you through. It was the most dangerous and nerve-racking snow conditions that George and I had ever struck. It was now snowing, and the visibility shrank as the clouds writhed around us. We'd had more than enough, and in desperation we decided to camp. We found a little snowy knoll and tested every inch of it with our ice-axes. Then we pitched our tent and crawled inside. We were a thoroughly demoralised party.

We couldn't understand why the snow had become so soft at over 19,500 feet. The only answer could be the warm monsoon air, and we didn't like the thought of having to weather a monsoon storm in this unsavoury position. I decided to go back with the Sherpas and bring up the rest of the stores that we'd dumped the previous day. Then we'd be able to stand a long period of bad weather.

The Sherpas were understandably reluctant to start again,

but a hot drink put new life into them. George stayed behind
to prepare some food and to guide us back through the mist.
I started off with the Sherpas spread out behind me on the
rope. I'd hoped that we'd found all the concealed crevasses
on our way over, but I was wrong. I hadn't gone fifty feet
before I was up to my waist in a new one. By the time I
reached the first of the great crevasses, I'd had a harrowing
time. We climbed down into it, and then out again and picked
up our loads. Then we started back. I was rather suspicious
of the snow in the bottom of the crevasse, and made the
others stay well behind on the steep wall while I investigated
it. It seemed all right and I stepped carefully forward. Next
moment there was a dull whoomp! and the snow I was on
sank rapidly beneath me into a crevasse. And down I went!
I didn't have much time to think, but I knew the Sherpas
couldn't be relied on for any quick action with the rope. I'd
have to save myself! I threw my legs out and my crampons
bit into the ice on the far wall and, with a jar, my shoulders
jammed against the other one. The snow bridge boomed down
below me into the hidden depths. A few seconds later the
rope came tight.

I was in a precarious position. I estimated I was about
twelve feet below the crest of the crevasse, and felt fairly
certain that the Sherpas would be too frightened to come
down close enough to pull me out. For a moment I gathered
my breath and then, still spanning the crevasse, I shuffled
along on my crampons and shoulders until the gap narrowed
a little. Mercifully I'd held on to my ice-axe, and I was able
to cut a little ledge in the smooth, vertical wall. I managed
to get one of my feet on to it and then, with a supreme effort
that took all my strength, I wriggled myself upright and
swung my other leg across the crevasse and jammed the long
steel points hard into the opposite wall. Gasping for breath,
I chipped out a little step and moved my foot into it. And

there I stood, quite comfortably balanced, with a dark void beneath me and my head only six feet from the surface.

Three feet away was a little snowy ledge attached to the wall of the crevasse. It looked fairly solid, so I slowly worked my way along and levered myself up on to it. On my hands and knees and tensed for any sudden failure, I crawled carefully up it. Then, balancing with my ice-axe against the other wall of the crevasse, I slowly stood up. My eyes came above the edge of the crevasse. I saw three frightened figures spread-eagled on the slopes above – Angje was pulling hard at me; Angputa was pulling hard at Angje; and Tashi Phuta, with terror written plainly on his face, was pulling frantically at Angputa. As the top of my head appeared, the three worried faces shed their fears in enormous smiles, and Angje shouted another relieved 'Bohut kharab, Sahib!'

A strong tug on the rope, a mighty kick from me, and I was out and none the worse for wear. We returned to camp with even more care if that were possible, and were glad to hear George's powerful voice guiding us through the mist. Although his steaming stew did much to soothe frayed nerves, we retired to bed depressed and not a little afraid. The snow conditions were worse than anything either of us had ever encountered. The Sherpas intoned their prayers for half the night.

We awoke very early, to find it was still misty but very much colder. There was quite a chance that there might be a frost to tie the snow together. George and I discussed things; we weren't very optimistic about finding a route on ahead, and we were, in fact, a little doubtful above moving at all until there was a major improvement in the snow condition. But to reach the Nup La had become a challenge that George and I found hard to resist. We decided to go on with light loads. By 5.45 a.m. we'd had a cup of tea and were ready to go. As a special precaution the five of us tied on to a single

200-foot length of rope. This would ensure that at least a couple of us at any one moment would be on stable ground.

We hadn't gone twenty feet from the tent before my foot shot through into a hidden crevasse, and I prepared myself for a continuation of the terrors of the previous day. But the farther we went the harder the surface became, and we started to regain our spirits. We were making our way through an extensive area of gaping crevasses which always seemed to force us in the wrong direction. We were constantly thrusting to the east towards the Nup La and constantly being turned back. At the back of our minds was the fear that the sun might come out and soften the surface, so we drove ourselves as hard as we could. But we seemed to be tied up in an impenetrable tangle of crevasses. And then we came over a crest and saw below us a smooth gully running in the direction we wanted to go. We dropped into it and followed it down. It drained into a wide valley in the ice and, with growing excitement, we saw the slopes on the far side swept in an almost unbroken easy slope to the Nup La.

It would have taken a lot to stop us now. We cut our way into the ice valley and out again the other side. And then we raced up the last slopes. 'We've made it, George!' But it was with almost an air of unbelief that we turned and looked back over the chaos of the icefall. Far below we could see the Ngojumba glacier, and it looked a lifetime away. It was hard to grasp that we'd managed to get through. But I don't think I've ever felt a greater sensation of achievement, and George was bubbling over with excitement.

But great black clouds were boiling up towards us again from Nepal, and we hadn't any time to waste. Just short of the pass was a large flat-topped boulder, and we decided to camp on it. We dumped our light loads and raced back over the winding, twisting route. In an hour we were back at the old camp. We packed everything up into enormous loads, and

then, groaning under the effort, started again for the Nup
La. Snow was falling steadily and we were enveloped in fog,
but we felt our way along our tracks, thankful that they still
remained. It was a great relief to climb up to the boulder and
tie our tent down to its solid rock again.

Late in the afternoon it cleared, and George and I went for
a walk. We climbed up the long easy slopes to the Nup La,
and looked down the great sweep of the West Rongbuk glacier.
And there, glowing in the evening sun, was the massive bulk
of Everest dominating the horizon. It made our efforts seem
well worth while, and we went contented back to bed.

Our first objective was now attained – the reaching of the
Nup La. Our next aim was to see the northern slopes of Everest.

It was beautifully fine next morning when we packed up
and departed. We were away by 7 a.m. and all of us were
carrying heavy loads – the Sherpas about 55 lb. and George
and I 45 lb. each. We climbed up to the Nup La and then
dropped down towards the head of the West Rongbuk glacier.
The glacier swept on smooth and unbroken for many miles,
and we made excellent time down it. At 10.30 we were opposite the peak Lingtren Nup, and we stopped here for a hot
drink. A sharp wind was blowing, so we made a little rock
wall and lit our kerosene cooker behind it. A hot cup of tea
and a snack of biscuits, butter, and jam put new life into us.
Already we were moving into country where all the names
were familiar to us – perpetuated by the stories of the early
Everest Expeditions. George and I were in a continual state
of excitement as we pointed out to each other famous features.
And as Everest got closer and closer it seemed to tower
farther above us, and we could pick out on its rocky flanks
the yellow band and the black band; the rock steps and the
great couloir. All of them so close to the summit – only
another thousand feet of thin cold air and steep rock.

We camped at 2.30 p.m. on the rough moraine just above

the main Rongbuk glacier. The Sherpas were very tired – they'd had a long, tough day – but George and I were in excellent trim. Later in the afternoon we went for a scramble down to the Rongbuk glacier. It was an astonishing sight – row after row of enormous ice pinnacles, some of them as much as two hundred feet high. For an hour we played amongst them, trying to penetrate as far as we could, cutting steps up dizzy ice-walls, and balancing along fragile crests. We didn't get more than fifty feet and admiringly conceded defeat. We returned to camp to do justice to a large and delicious pressure-cooked stew. We crawled into our sleeping-bags feeling very contented.

I didn't have a very comfortable night. My air-mattress kept deflating and, anyway, I think I was too excited. Soon after midnight I poked my head out of the tent door, but I couldn't see very much, for we were down in a hollow. It was very dark and the stars were shining with a cold steady light. My thoughts dwelt on the Swiss. 'I wonder how far they've got? The weather hasn't been too bad and they should have put in their attack by now. I hope we don't get caught over here on the north side with some heavy monsoon snow. It would make the Nup La pretty unpleasant . . . I'm not looking forward to going back over it, anyway!' I tried to compose my mind and sleep, but the same question kept pushing in – 'I wonder what the Swiss are doing?'

It took us three hours next day to go down the Rongbuk glacier and find a place where we could get through the ice pinnacles. We had to cut a way through, but it didn't take us long and we had our lunch on the moraine wall on the far side of the glacier. It was a pleasant place. There was a little lake and even some green grass, and we idled away a couple of hours in the warm sun. We had a remarkable view down the valley and we could see the Rongbuk monastery about ten miles away.

We turned the corner into the East Rongbuk valley – the old pathway to Everest. On the far side of the valley we could see a few stone walls rapidly falling into disrepair. We crossed over and examined them. This was Camp I. It gave me an eerie feeling to look at it, as though the ghosts of Mallory and Irvine and Smythe were still flitting amongst the ruins. The only sign of habitation was the corroded remnant of an old battery. Everything else, every tin and every piece of rubbish, had been destroyed by the weather or been transported down to ornament a Tibetan home.

We continued on up the East Rongbuk glacier – a desolate heap of rock and rubble. We found the scenery disappointingly dull and the peaks monotonous lumps of snow-capped shingle. We couldn't help comparing them with the wonderful ice spires and pleasant valleys of Nepal. We camped at about 18,500 feet on a lump of moraine beside a clear glacial pool – the only oasis we could find in this sad and gloomy valley.

But when we turned the corner next morning the old thrill returned. There was Everest again, proud and aloof against a wind-streaked sky. And the East Rongbuk glacier was a shining pathway of clear blue ice sweeping up to the foot of the mountain. It didn't take us long to reach the site of Camp II, but we could see no sign whatever that anybody had ever lived here. At 10 a.m. we branched off up the small Changtse glacier. A very strong, cold wind was blowing and conditions were most unpleasant. Our Sherpas told us that they were weak and cold and appealed to us to camp. But we persuaded them to go on. 'Only a little farther,' we said. *'Toro! Toro!'* (Little! Little!), they entreated. We found a little snow hollow at nearly 21,000 feet and dug out a platform for our tent. Then we crawled inside out of the wind and cold.

We were hoping to attempt Changtse – the north peak of Everest, 24,730 feet. This was rather a wildly optimistic plan,

and we realised now that we had hardly the equipment or
forces to do it. But at least it was worth a try. If only the
weather held for a few days we might have a chance. Our
limited food supplies would allow no waiting. Our ambitious
hopes, nurtured in the comfort of Namche Bazar, were
starting to fade a little, for the likelihood of the Nup La route
deteriorating was a constant nagging worry.

During the night it snowed steadily, and next morning our
decision had been made for us. It was quite fine, but obviously more bad weather was brewing. We had no hope of
reaching the summit. As a parting gesture, we climbed about
500 feet above camp, but found the snow crusted and
dangerous. We decided to throw it in. We raced back down
the Changtse glacier at great speed, and descended the East
Rongbuk glacier in steadily falling snow. We passed the sites
of Camp II and then Camp I, and finally turned the corner
into the main Rongbuk valley. We camped on the terrace
beside the tarn, and the sun broke through and warmed us.
But the peaks were shrouded in black and threatening clouds,
and they were closing in on us again as we went to bed.

We had a poor morning after a windy, snowy night. But
at this lower altitude we'd had a deep refreshing sleep and
felt prepared for anything. It was miserable all day – gusts
of driving wind and continual falling snow. And everything
seemed to go wrong. We crossed the Rongbuk glacier, but
got lost in the ice pinnacles and the enormous mounds of
moraine. The fog and snow ruined the visibility and our sense
of direction became confused. For hours we stumbled blindly
over miles of sliding rubble and I wished vehemently for the
grassy valley. We were still carrying heavy loads, and they
sapped our strength and our enthusiasm. We camped in the
early afternoon well up the West Rongbuk glacier. Luck had
been with us and we'd been going in the right direction all
the time. In the evening it cleared, and when we looked out

of our tent for the last time, it was crisp and cold and the sky was full of stars. Perhaps there was some good weather ahead.

We woke very early and started the Sherpas preparing breakfast at 3.30 a.m. It was still quite dark outside, but the weather looked promising. At 5.30 I crawled out of the tent. We had plans for examining a possible new pass over the range and we wanted to make an early start. I casually looked around and my face fell! 'Hey! George. Come out and have a look. I don't like it!' George scrambled out to join me and silently looked at the heavens. 'Let's get out of here!' 'Looks like the end of the world!' Over Nepal the sky was as black as night. Great ugly billows were surging up and writhing about the summits. It was the most ominous weather sign I had ever seen.

We didn't waste any time. We stirred the Sherpas out of the tent and packed everything. Then we started up the glacier almost at a jog-trot. We couldn't afford to be trapped on this side of the Nup La. It was about six miles to our camp on the far side of the pass – six miles of soft snow at over 19,000 feet – but our fear spurred us on. We reached the dump in just over an hour and a half, as great, rolling clouds blanketed out the icefall. Soon the clouds were around us and snow was steadily falling. We decided to push on. With all the necessities for a camp on our backs, we dropped down into the ice gully and up through it into the maze of crevasses.

The visibility was shocking and we couldn't see where to put our feet. George's snowglasses fogged up, so I took over the lead. It was nerve-racking work. I felt my way from crevasse to crevasse, getting all my direction from the lie of the country. The snow was falling like a wet blanket and clung to our clothes and our hair. And I soon realised that I had no idea where I was. I stopped in desperation and a sudden quick clearing revealed a rock tusk to the left of us – a rock I knew was just above our old camp. The mist had closed in again, but I stumbled on in the new direction. Quite suddenly I tripped over an empty tin in the snow. It was our old camp site.

We debated whether to go on or stop. We knew we'd have a tough job getting down in these conditions, but the thought of spending more days camped in this unpleasant spot didn't appeal to us at all. We decided to continue. I was prepared to have a go at finding the way down, but I wanted George tied on behind me as a safe and solid anchor. The three Sherpas trailed down last.

I headed off across the treacherous plateau. George had me on a tight rope, and I prodded my way across as fast as I could go. The snow was falling heavily and had blotted out all our old steps and concealed many of the crevasses. But it was no place for a faint heart. The only thing to do was to push ahead. When I sank into a crevasse, George pulled me out and we tried somewhere else. The whole plateau had changed in our absence, and we seemed to be cut off from the great crevasses. In desperation I slithered across a frail snow bridge – and it held! Next moment I was beside the first big gap. The others joined me. George was a tower of strength. Calm and competent, he rode through the storm like a great ocean liner. With his strong hand on the rope, I knew I couldn't fall far.

The route through the great crevasse had disappeared, so we set to work to remake it. We lowered the Sherpas over the edge and followed them down. In the depths of the crevasse it was strangely quiet, although over our heads the storm was reaching a new fury. Our Sherpas were going magnificently, dragging their heavy loads through the deep snow. I asked Angje what he thought of it, and he replied. '*Bohut kharab, Sahib!*', although his grin belied the meaning.

There was at least six inches of fresh snow on the icefall and it was increasing every moment. Already on our right we could head the dull boom as fresh snow avalanches swept down off the bluffs on to the glacier. But we couldn't see anything! Straining my eyes to recognise the way, I fumbled downwards; clearing away the snow on the steep slopes and cutting step after step. Often I'd come to an impossible drop or a gaping crevasse and know I was on the wrong route. And then I'd climb wearily back to the last piece of track I knew and try again. Many of the crevasses had windened and many of our snow bridges had gone. But we found a way down.

We reached the bottom of the icefall in an exhausted condition. To see the easy side moraine again brought tears of relief to our strained eyes. Even the deep snow and the howling blizzard didn't worry us any more, because we knew we were safe. We struggled down a little way to a flat place and decided to camp. The Sherpas wouldn't let us help. Respectfully but firmly they sat us down while they pitched the tent. They laid out our sleeping-bags and put us in them. And before long they were thrusting hot mugs of delicious tea into our hands. We all sat around sipping and laughing like the bunch of old friends and comrades that we were. The storm raged on, but we had forgotten it.

CHAPTER SIX

The Swiss Attack

FOR TWO DAYS WE rested beside a little lake near the Ngojumba glacier. It was calm and peaceful here, and we slept almost continuously. We had obtained some fresh food, and we ate enormous meals of potatoes and butter and yak curds. But we couldn't keep the old question out of our minds. 'What did the Swiss do?' It was now June 5th, and they should be coming off the mountain with their story of success or failure. We decided to go and see them and find out for ourselves.

Between us and the Khumbu glacier was a high pass. This had been crossed from east to west in 1951, and we planned to use it. On June 6th we moved off from our rest-camp and crossed the Ngojumba glacier to the side glacier leading up to the pass. There were six of us altogether – George and I, Angputa and Tashi Phuta, and two tough old specimens we'd recruited down the valley, Pemba and Angpemba. Angje had gone directly down to Namche Bazar with all our excess gear. On the side glacier – the 'Guanara' the Sherpas called it – we found a pleasant and easy route in the trough behind the left-hand moraine wall. It was a quiet and protected place, and the flowers were blooming in profusion. The air was warm and heavy, but George set a cracking pace. We soon drew well away from the Sherpas, so stopped in a grassy hollow and slept for an hour in the sun. Life felt exceedingly good, and the green grass and bright flowers were like a balm to our thin, ragged bodies and tired nerves. But when we camped on the glacier at the foot of the pass snow was falling again.

We awoke at 3.30 a.m. to find it was fine and clear but very cold. Angputa lit the stove and started cooking breakfast. We'd run out of tea, so we had hot water, milk, sugar, and *tsampa*, and followed it with the luxury of fried potato chips. We didn't get away until 5.40 a.m., and then we crossed the glacier to a series of sharp explosions as pieces of ice around us shattered with the cold and the vibration of our passing. It only took us an hour to the foot of the pass, and we started climbing up steep, loose rocks. It wasn't particularly difficult, but there was a considerable danger that one of us might dislodge a rock on to the head of someone behind. So we all kept close together. The Sherpas were going magnificently, and Tashi Phuta, who had generally to be coaxed over the difficult portions, was calmly leading our two new recruits like an Alpine guide.

The first 300 feet was a little dangerous, but after that it was magnificent scrambling – steep but safe. The two old Sherpas were finding the going a little hard, so I remained behind with them, supplying a judicious push on the steeper sections. We were climbing quite a steep pitch when Pemba stopped and picked something off the rock. Obviously greatly excited, he showed it to Angpemba. Feeling somewhat curious, I asked them what it was all about. They placed in my hand a tuft of long black hairs – thick and coarse, they looked more like bristles than anything else. '*Yeti, Sahib! Yeti!*' I couldn't help being impressed by their conviction, and it did seem a strange place to find some hair. We were well over 19,000 feet and the Abominable Snowman was obviously no mean rock climber. I called to George and showed it to him. We discussed it with enthusiasm. It would be quite an achievement to bring back for scientific examination the hair of the Abominable Snowman. But, scenting our intentions, Pemba leaned forward and his gnarled old hand snatched the tuft away and threw it far over the bluff. *'Bohut kharab, Sahib! Bohut kharab!'* Our scientific interest wasn't sufficiently great to make us climb down a couple of hundred feet to find it.

We crossed the pass and descended rapidly towards the Khumbu glacier. Everest was dominating our view now and the sight of it stimulated our desire for information. 'Has it been done?' We reached the Lake Camp and were astonished to find it deserted. Only some faint remaining warmth in the ashes of a fire amongst those rock walls of the Swiss Base Camp showed signs of recent life. We felt annoyed and frustrated. Dropping our packs, we went on up the glacier. It was calm and still. Only the rumble of moraine sliding into an icy pool or the dull boom of a great avalanche stirred the heavy afternoon air. The glacier was deserted and so was the icefall. The Swiss had gone!

We camped that night at the Lake Camp, and I didn't sleep very much. Somehow the answer to our question seemed so important now, and I was determined to find out tomorrow. The Swiss had been a very strong party and a very confident one. They'd had the best of equipment and plenty of it. They'd had oxygen. And, most important of all, the weather had been no worse than you can expect on Everest. 'Had they been able to do it?'

We had to go a long way the next day before we met a human being. Just outside the village of Phalong Karpo we found an old Sherpa watching over his grazing yaks. 'Ask him if Everest has been climbed, Angputa.' For a few long moments they chattered in their Sherpa language, and then Angputa gave us the news. 'Sahib! The old man says that seven Swiss climbers reached the summit of Everest!' My heart sank into my boots. Seven of them had got on top – what a stupendous effort. And then I looked at the doddering old man and wondered . . . Seven sounded rather a lot. I think for the first time I was really admitting to myself quite honestly that I didn't want the Swiss to climb Everest. Let them get very high – good luck to them in that – but not to the summit! I wanted it left for a British party to have a crack at next year. But now it looked as though they might have done it, and the Everest story would be finished. We were very quiet as we went on down the valley.

At 2 p.m. we arrived at the village of Pangboche and were welcomed into one of their fine homes. A huge plate of boiled potatoes was placed in front of us, and we attacked it with vigour. Outside we heard a clattering of boots and next moment Shipton burst into the room. We jumped to our feet and rushed towards him . . . 'What about the Swiss?' 'Lambert and Tenzing reached 28,000 feet. They didn't get to the top!' Relief and admiration chased through my mind. My word, they'd really had a good go at it! But Everest was still unclimbed . . .

We sat Shipton down in front of another plate of potatoes and we all talked furiously. Shipton wanted us to come with him over into the Barun valley and then out to the Indian border by an unexplored route. Evans had already gone into the valley to do some initial exploration. The rest of the party were at Namche Bazar preparing to return to India by various other ways. George and I looked at each other. This was the end of our plan to rest for a week and eat enormously of fresh meat and vegetables. But it was too good a trip to miss. First of all, we had to do something about all our gear down at Namche. I decided to continue on down the same afternoon to sort it out and then return the next day.

There was still the problem of Angputa and Tashi Phuta. We'd promised them a good rest at their homes, and we knew they were looking forward to it. I called Angputa and explained it all to him. He was my personal Sherpa, and we had built up a strong tie of affection. I made it quite clear that he could return home if he wished and we'd pay him off. His reply was immediate: 'If the Sahib goes . . . I go!'

I arrived at Namche Bazar in the evening and saw a hotch-potch of different-shaped tents pitched on a terrace in a scrappy formation. I thought it was the Swiss, but this was an unjustifiable insult – it was the rest of our own party. Later on in the evening I visited the neatly laid out lines of the Swiss Camp with the remainder of our team. We were entertained to coffee after dinner, and we talked and exchanged experiences well into the night.

They had a fascinating story to tell, but they were obviously a weary and dispirited body of men. They had found the icefall a difficult and dangerous obstacle, but they'd made a way through it. Then they'd attacked the slopes leading up to the South Col. And here they appeared to have made one of their greatest mistakes. Instead of using the route suggested by Shipton up the Lhotse glacier, they followed a long, steep rock and snow ridge they called the Geneva Spur. A party of climbers and Sherpa porters struggled up this with great courage and determination, but an enforced night out without anywhere to pitch their tents had sapped their strength and they reached the South Col in an exhausted condition. It seemed that they were so weak that their chances now of reaching the summit were non-existent. But although their strength had gone, they still had plenty of courage. The guide, Lambert, and the Sherpa leader Tenzing had struggled upwards and established a lonely camp at 27,000 feet on the south-east ridge. They didn't have any sleeping-bags, and they had no effective means of melting snow for water. But they spent the night there. In the morning they dragged themselves slowly up the ridge. Their oxygen sets proved difficult to operate, and soon these two fine climbers reached

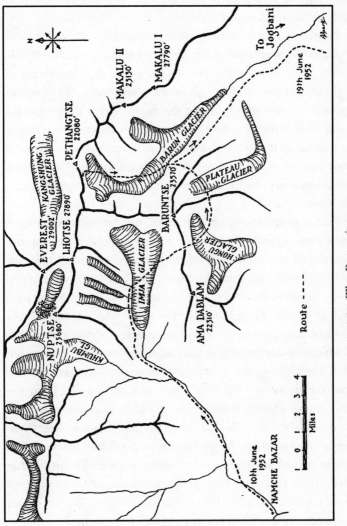

1952. The Barun journey.

the inevitable end. At a height of about 28,000 feet they were too exhausted to go any farther, and only barely struggled back to their camp and safety.

Lambert was a strong and impressive character, and appeared less affected both physically and mentally by his efforts than most of the rest of the party. But the strain of high altitude was showing in all their faces. They'd had enough . . . all they wanted at the moment was the peace and comfort of home. I didn't get the chance to meet Tenzing – he was away doing some task – but I went back to my tent with my mind swimming with the courage and daring of these men, who had unquestionably thrown everything into the fray.

I returned next day up to Pangboche and rejoined Shipton and Lowe. They had recruited a large group of women and children to carry our gear up the Imja valley, as all the men were carrying loads for the Swiss. On June 11th we camped in the south branch of the Imja glacier, underneath the pass leading to the Hongu valley. Here we paid off the weaker carriers. For the next ten days we revelled in the type of life of which Shipton is such an outstanding exponent. We crossed from the Imja to the Hongu valley, and there met up with Evans and his two Sherpas. And then we crossed from the Hongu up on to the Barun plateau, a high unexplored icefield at over 20,000 feet. In two glorious days we climbed three fine peaks, and then plunged down to the Barun glacier itself. The monsoon struck in earnest when we were camped at the head of the Barun, and we struggled down in a foot of fresh snow. Great avalanches boomed down off the steep faces, and we knew our climbing for the season was finished.

On June 19th we descended into the lower Barun valley, and we came into a paradise of flowers. We waded along in acres of blazing red dwarf rhododendrons. The monsoon rain had transformed the landscape, and myriads of tiny blossoms of every colour were bursting through the arid soil. The air was thick and strong, and we breathed it deeply into our starved lungs. But we were now in a world of rain – hundreds of waterfalls drifted gracefully down the mighty rock bluffs of our valleys, and the heavy clouds would only split for a moment to reveal some startling summit before closing in again with torrential rain. But I enjoyed every moment of it, for it was the most beautiful valley I had ever seen. And when, several days later, we climbed up out of the valley, I knew I wasn't likely to forget its soaring peaks or its rugged beauty. And I knew that, given half a chance, I'd come back again to see its flowers and sparkling streams and to accept the challenge of its unconquered mountains.

In the Barun we split up our party. Evans, with dogged independence, disappeared off to the east with two stout Sherpas. His plan was to cross some lesser passes and reach civilisation at Darjeeling. Shipton, Lowe, and I were returning to the railhead at Jogbani. Shipton was filled with a fiery sense of urgency. He felt it was his duty to return to England as soon as possible to help organise the 1953 British attack on Everest. And already time was getting short. He drove our porters into long hard days. We crossed a 14,000-foot pass out of the Barun, and for two days plunged dizzily downwards into the heat and leeches of the Arun river. Tracks were overgrown, bridges were washed away, and the paths were deep in water and mud. And the cruel, muggy heat hit us like a blow after the clean cool air of the mountains. But we plugged onwards, and on June 23rd we crossed the Arun river by a long slender bridge of bamboo and reached the main path back to India.

By this time George Lowe and I were thoroughly tired of any sort of walking. And slipping and sliding along grassy tracks in our rubbers from dawn until dusk had long ago lost its novelty. Even the lovely scenery as we walked for days down beside the great torrent of the Arun river failed to cheer us up. All we wanted was a long, long rest and plenty of comfort. On June 26th we passed through the village of Tumlingtar and descended down to the great tributary river – the Sabeiya. It was several hundred yards across here, but with a slow steady current. Shipton and Lowe and I swam in the cool water and washed off the perspiration and dust of our travelling. Just for the fun of it I inflated my air mattress and paddled my way slowly across. This was the way to travel, cool and effortless, letting the stream do all the work. Why didn't we try it on the Arun? Certainly there had been far too many rapids farther up, but as far as I could remember, from now on it swept along smooth and untroubled. I suggested this to George, and he agreed enthusiastically . . . anything to get us off our feet. We decided to have a practice run before we camped.

We inflated both our air-mattresses and tied two poles across the front and back with a nylon rope. There was a gap in the middle of nearly two feet between the air-mattresses. We picked a couple of branches for paddles and then launched ourselves into the river. It was marvellous! We each sat astride one of the air-beds, and although they buckled a little and we were up to our waists in water, the whole raft was remarkably steady, and we swept down the swift-flowing Arun in great style. We were rapidly gaining on Shipton and the Sherpas, and when they picked a camping spot for the night we swept up to the bank with a flourish of our rough paddles and dragged our craft ashore. Our minds were made up . . . tomorrow we wouldn't walk a step – we'd raft all the way down on the Arun.

It was a hot steamy night, but in the early hours of the morning it became pleasantly cool. We woke up at 4 a.m., and by 4.30 Shipton had left with all the porters. George and I set to work in the dark to reassemble our raft. We made a very careful job of it. We used good stout poles and plenty of nylon rope. And we blew the mattresses up full and hard. The previous evening we'd made some proper paddles for ourselves. As the black of the night turned to the grey of early morning, we were ready to go.

There was no doubt that our enthusiasm had evaporated a little. The great swift-flowing river looked decidedly danger-ous in the dim light, and it was only our pride that made us carry our masterpiece over to the bank and gently lower it in. And then we sat on top of it. As the cool water crept un-comfortably up my body I berated myself for being such an idiot . . . sitting in the water at five o'clock in the morning! George was very quiet, and there was a certain reluctance in his movements which showed his thoughts were similar to my own. But there was nothing for it – we had to go now!

We pushed off into the swift current and the bank started drifting by at great speed. At first we kept close to the shore, but as the light improved and our confidence grew, we paddled out a little and our speed increased. Everything started to seem sensible again. Here we were, shooting along much faster than you could walk, and with literally no effort at all.

'This is the life, George?'

'Too right! We should have thought of it before.'

'How's your new paddle working?'

'O.K., but do you think we should keep closer to the shore?'

'No! The river goes on like this for the next ten miles.'

In half an hour we must have covered over two miles of the river – equivalent to at least three on the twisting track on the cliffs above. It was marvellous. And then, 'Can you hear anything, George?' We listened again. A dull, powerful roar came drifting up the valley. 'Let's get to the side!' We paddled frantically, but our ungainly craft was in the grip of the increasing current and we made little headway. Below us now we could see a great series of bluffs thrusting out into the stream. And high up on the bluffs was the figure of Eric Shipton, waving furiously. We redoubled our efforts with the paddles, but with a feeling of panic we realised that we were helpless.

We could now see what we were coming to. The whole great river was smashing headlong against an enormous bluff. The majority of the water was swept violently into a little smooth-walled bay and formed an enormous whirlpool from which it flushed periodically into the foaming channel below. It was an ugly sight. The roar of the river was now deafening. 'Hold on to the raft whatever happens, George! It's our only chance!' And then we were hurled, on the crest of a wave, at the smooth rock wall.

We were quite helpless. In a vain effort to cushion the blow we thrust our legs out in front. But as the wave crashed on the rocks our buoyant little craft slid sideways off it around into the racing waters of the whirlpool. The whirlpool must have been a good hundred and fifty feet across, with a nasty gaping hole at its centre. We paddled madly to try to reach the bluffs, but the current was far too strong. Around we went, out into the main stream of the river, hurled against the bluff and then back into the whirlpool again. Travelling around with us were masses of small branches and great logs. One log, a foot in diameter and fifteen feet long, was dragged into the centre and sucked down almost out of sight into that evil eye. When it was released it shot into the air like a cork out of a champagne bottle.

Around we went! It was obvious that there was little we could do, and as long as our amazing craft stayed together we would come to no harm. One swirl threw us right into the gaping centre so that the racing water on the rim of the whirlpool towered over our heads. Our dangling legs were sucked greedily down, but the great buoyancy of our little craft saved us and we were expelled to the outer edge again.

1952. The Whirlpool in the Arun River.

After four round trips we were becoming almost hardened
to it, but we still hadn't thought of any way of getting out
of the whirlpool.

'Let's have a bit of your chocolate, George.'

'We'd better be careful with it. I've worked out that we
should last about two days on it.'

'I'm all for a dull life, myself. Let's try another paddle.'

But round we went again out into the stream, smashing
against the bluff, and back into the writhing, plucking depths
of the whirlpool. I blessed the care we'd taken with the raft
an hour before. Only an hour? It seemed like a lifetime!

Shipton was climbing down the steep cliffs, held on a rope
by the Sherpas. As we started for the sixth round I saw him
step down on to the last little ledge above the water. And
then I lost sight of him – I was too absorbed in the gyra-
tions of our craft. There seemed to be a new force in the river
this time and we hurtled at the bluff on an enormous wave.
We rode up it for ten feet into the air as it struck the rock,
and then, when I'd given up hope, we slid off again and were
thrown to the outermost edges of the whirlpool. Desperately
I reached out and caught the rocks at the side. The raft almost
split in two. I had a scissors grip on my air-mattress with
my legs, and I was pulled out straight as I fought with the
current to hold our craft in place. I was about to let go when
the tug lessened, the other end of the raft was washed in,
and George got his hands on to the rocks. We couldn't get
out here, for above us was sixty feet of vertical, holdless rock.
We must try to drag ourselves along the twenty feet to the
ledge where Shipton was standing!

With straining muscles we battled with the current,
making an inch at a time. Fortunately we found enough holds
on the water-polished rock, but at times we were almost
plucked off. Something struck me in the face and Shipton's
voice rose above the roar of the waters. It was a rope. I took

a solid grip on it and Shipton towed us along with powerful tugs. We were dragged up to the ledge and crawled thankfully out.

Four days later we were back in India. Amongst the first news we received was that the Swiss planned to throw another powerful attempt on to Everest in the autumn. Nothing was to be spared; new oxygen had been developed, and a party composed mainly of famous Swiss guides had been chosen. Lambert was to be in charge of the actual attack on the mountain, and Tenzing was to be the Sherpa sirdar. To our prejudiced minds it almost seemed unsporting. They'd had a fair go . . . why didn't they give us a chance now? But, after all, Swiss Himalayan prestige was at stake, and we realised that in similar circumstances we'd have done much the same ourselves.

Shipton flew off to England, and George and I started the long sea trip back to New Zealand. I arrived home in Auckland to find a letter waiting for me from Shipton. Apparently he had agreed, somewhat reluctantly, to take on the leadership of the 1953 British attempt on Everest. He wanted George Lowe, Harry Ayres, and myself to join his party. Nothing could have stimulated more my interest in the Swiss autumn attempt. Every day I scanned the newspapers for their meagre scraps of distorted, inaccurate information. News was slow in coming. One report said the Swiss had camped 120 feet from the top. But finally the facts emerged – they'd failed again! The icefall had proved rather easier and they'd carried tons of stores up the Western Cwm. Benefiting from their previous experience, they didn't use the Geneva Spur, but hacked a route up the Lhotse glacier along the line recommended by Shipton in 1951. After tremendous efforts of routemaking, they established several camps on this great face and ultimately reached the South Col. They had with them this time a greatly improved oxygen set. But they'd left their attack until too late. Winter was approaching, and the bitter cold and strong winds drove them off the South Col without their having reached more than 500 feet above it. Once again the formidable partnership of Lambert and Tenzing had been the spearhead of the attack.

The Swiss parties had been strong ones, well equipped and well organised – and yet they had failed. It is not necessary to find excuses for not climbing Everest – the mountain will supply these in abundance. But if we were to have any chance of success, our expedition would need a high degree of well-acclimatised technical skill; it would need the best in modern equipment and oxygen; and it would need first-class organisation. But more than anything else, it would need its share of good luck.

CHAPTER SEVEN

Everest 1953 – The First Barrier

Everest Expedition Office,
Royal Geographical Society,
1 Kensington Gore,
London, S.W.7.
16*th October,* 1952

DEAR HILLARY,

I believe that Eric Shipton has written to tell you about the change in the leadership of the 1953 Everest Expedition; you may, in any case, have seen press reports. I expect that you must be feeling puzzled and disappointed that this should have come to pass; it is most unfortunate that it should have happened in this way, and very bad luck on Eric Shipton.

However, you will, I am sure, agree with me that there is only one way of looking at it – we must go ahead with the planning with a firm determination to get to the top.

This is an interim letter to tell you that I am busy with the selection of the party and that I very much hope that you and Lowe will be ready to join the party; the proposed team will be approved by the Himalayan Joint Committee at the end of this month, and formal invitations will be sent through the New Zealand Alpine Club. Don't be too disappointed if we cannot take more of your contingent. You will appreciate that it is very difficult to finalise the list; in principle I regard it as very important indeed to have met the individuals before making a final choice. Meanwhile your other recommendations are being seriously considered.

I am looking forward immensely to getting to grips with this problem with you.

Yours sincerely,

JOHN HUNT

This letter was my first introduction to a man who was to play an outstanding part in the final success on Everest. I already knew and disapproved of the Himalayan Joint Commitee's decision to change leaders in mid-stream and felt a tremendous disappointment that Shipton was being superseded. 'Everest without Shipton won't be the same' was my thought; 'And anyway, who is this chap Hunt? – I've never heard of him! I wonder if he's any good?'

Evidence of Hunt's calibre was not long in appearing, for the post brought a series of detailed plans which I reluctantly had to admit seemed to hit the nail on the head every time. Lowe and I were awaiting the announcement of the rest of the party with considerable interest and were very pleased indeed to hear of the inclusion of Evans, Bourdillon, and Gregory of the Cho Oyu Expedition, and Ward of the 1951 Reconnaissance. The climbing team also included Wylie and Noyce, both of whom had excellent Himalayan records; and Westmacott and Band, who had done some fine climbing in the European Alps. The non-climbing members were our movie-cameraman, Stobart, and our old friend Dr Griffiths Pugh, whose inclusion indicated physiological torture for some unwary climbers. Separated as we were from the rest of the party, there was little that Lowe and I could do to help except give advice, but it was quite obvious that organisation was going ahead at great speed and that our equipment was to be the best that could be obtained. This was going to be

The party at Dingla in 1951. Eric Shipton, Bill Murray, Tom Bourdillon, Earle Riddiford, with Michael Ward, and me in front.

Tom Bourdillon working on the final slope at the top
of the Khumbu icefall during the 1951 reconnaissance.

Top of the Khumbu icefall, October 1951. Four of us were traversing above this break when the slope avalanched. The crevasse split the glacier from side to side and stopped us on the threshold of the Western Cwm. Nyima, Ward, and Riddiford are in the picture.

Everest from the Pumori Ridge where Shipton and I saw the possible route up the mountain from the south. We could also see part of the old route up the north side. It looks ahead, straight up the Khumbu icefall to the secret valley of the Western Cwm. While several prewar expeditions had glimpsed the cwm from the frontier ridge, no one had yet seen so far into it.

The photo shows, for the first time, the distant snow face at the head of the cwm, leading directly—and apparently quite straightforwardly—to the South Col (just obscured by the band of white cloud). I am just visible on the lower right.

Our sherpas descending from the Tesi Lapcha, a difficult pass we crossed on November 5, 1951, after the reconnaissance of the southern route.

After successfully finding a route up the Khumbu icefall, the 1951 team ranged far and wide over the mountains around Everest. Here, we are exploring the lower part of the complex Nup La icefall leading toward the Tibetan border. The following year, during the Cho Oyu training expedition, George Lowe and I trespassed right over the pass, into Tibet, and right up to the old prewar Camp III on the East Rongbuk Glacier.

Above: Everest, 1952. Scenes from the leisurely approach to Cho Oyu.

Below: Settled down with a book for the midday halt (above). At night we slept in local houses. Here George Lowe and I settle in at a yak shelter in Okhaldunga.

Eric Shipton

Michael Ward

George Lowe

John Hunt

Above: At Lake Camp, April 17, 1953.

Below: High camp on the "Island Peak" during the acclimatisation period in April 1953.

Assisting Sherpas with supply loads in the Khumbu icefall. Over three tons of stores were ferried through the icefall by thirty-four porters, all of whom were properly equipped and clothed for climbing at high altitudes.

Above: Camp II about halfway up the icefall at 19,500 feet.

Below: Tenzing and I crossing the 18-foot bridge over the crevasse on the lip of the Western Cwm.

The second summit party ready to move.
Note the summit flags wrapped around Tenzing's ice-axe.

Above: 26th May. South Col. George Lowe, Tom Bourdillon, Charles Evans, John Hunt and Tenzing. Taken in the late afternoon when Tom and Charles arrived back from the South Summit climb.

Below: At 27,500 feet on the Southeast Ridge. Below Tenzing is the windswept area of the South Col.

Tenzing Norgay on the summit of Mount Everest at 11:30 A.M. Tenzing waves his ice-axe on which are strung the flags of the United Nations, Britain, Nepal, and India.

Above: Tenzing and I at Camp IV the day after reaching the summit.

Below: John Hunt, Ed Hillary, Tenzing, Ang Nyima (in front), Alf Gregory, and George Lowe, taken at Camp IV shortly after arriving from the South Col.

an oxygen attack, and vast amounts of effort were going into the development of two different types of sets for our use.

The whole expedition gathered together in Kathmandu in the early days of March and I met John Hunt for the first time. I was immediately impressed by his dynamic energy, his organising ability and his charm of manner. I thought he summed his own character up very well for me when we had our first talk; Hunt told me that he intended to 'lead the expedition from the front'. Although I had only known him a few minutes, I was sufficiently impressed to think that he probably would! Here, too, I met Tenzing for the first time. Of strong and sturdy build, he had a quiet air of confidence that quickly picked him out from his fellow Sherpas. Tenzing soon became a valued member of the party and endeared himself to us with his charming smile and natural gentility.

On March 10th we left Kathmandu to start a leisurely march to the foot of Everest. For seventeen days we walked up hill and down dale across the lovely Nepalese countryside in almost perfect weather. We swam in all the rivers, ate enormous meals, and slept out under the stars. By the time we reached the Monastery of Thyangboche we were a very fit party and, as was obvious by now, a very happy one. It was a tremendous thrill to see once again the great bulk of Everest thrusting high over the Nuptse-Lhotse wall, and we were eager to get to grips with it.

At Thyangboche we set up a temporary Base Camp, and here we unpacked all our equipment and spent some days testing it out and gaining experience in using it. Bourdillon, in particular, gave us all a lot of valuable instruction in the use of our various forms of oxygen apparatus. Our plan was to get fit and accustomed to the higher altitudes by carrying out exploration and climbing trips in the many glaciated valleys around Everest. Our first acclimatisation period was from March 30th until April 6th, and during this period we split up into smaller groups of three or four and disappeared off into different valleys. We all regrouped at Thyangboche on April 6th, and everyone seemed to have had an excellent trip. All of us had climbed peaks of around 20,000 feet in height, and we'd carried out some useful exploration. Altogether it had proved a very satisfactory start to the expedition.

A second group of acclimatisation trips was planned to start in a few days' time. It was a great thrill to me when Hunt asked me to take my party up the Khumbu glacier to reconnoitre the icefall into the Western Cwm. My party was to consist of Michael Westmacott, George Band, and, at my special request, George Lowe. I knew the icefall was going to be a tough job and felt particularly keen to have my old companion along. For two days we plotted and planned; sorted out tents, ropes, cookers, pitons, and karabiners; organised our food and worked out the right amount of fuel; checked the equipment of our Sherpas, and signed on a band of coolies to carry for us up the Khumbu glacier. Pugh and Stobart decided to come along with us, and this meant more equipment, more food, and more coolies.

On the morning of April 9th, the six of us set off from Thyangboche, accompanied by five of our high-altitude Sherpas and thirty-nine Sherpa coolies, of whom about half were women. We wandered in a leisurely way up the Imja valley, passed through the village of Pangboche, and turned off up the Chola valley. Dark and threatening skies spurred us to greater effort, and we camped at the deserted village of Phalong Karpo in a flurry of snow. We awoke next morning to a white world. Even in the fields around our tents there was more than four inches of snow, and higher up it was a great deal deeper. Ama Dablam was a tremendous sight sheathed in fresh snow and with its long wind-plume gleaming in the early morning sun. I was greatly puzzled what to do. We were all tremendously keen to get up the valley and attack the icefall without delay, but our coolies had no snow-glasses and we had none for them. If we went on, I was very much afraid they might become snowblind.

But to sit and wait for the snow to melt seemed just too frustrating. Very worried, I talked with our Sherpas. They reassured me that all the coolies wanted to start and were not the slightest bit concerned about the bright snow. 'After all, this is their country and they should know how to look after themselves' was the argument I used to quell my uneasy conscience as I instructed them to start packing. We walked up the valley into a cold fairy-land of shimmering snow crystals. In a childlike exuberance of spirits I threw handfuls of the feathery snow into the air, just to see it twinkle in the soft morning sun. We turned the corner into the Khumbu valley and started climbing up steeply in snow almost a foot deep. The sun was shining fiercely now and the glare was intense. All of those with snow-glasses had put them on, but I could see the rest of our porters squinting painfully in the strong light. With a sinking heart I berated myself for allowing my impatience to overrule my common sense, but then pushed on hard with the determination that the sooner we reached our destination the better. We intended spending the night at Lobuje, a little group of rock-and-sod shelters at about 16,000 feet in the grassy trough beside the Khumbu glacier. I reached there first and gloomily watched the party arriving. And what a sorry bunch they were with their lowered heads and swollen, weeping eyes. I sank into the depths of depression. 'What a leader I am ! Second day out and I get the whole party snowblind !' Later in the afternoon, just to add to my misery, it started snowing again. My companions seemed in an astonishingly cheerful frame of mind in view of this catastrophe, and my old friend George Lowe swept aside my mental agony with the short comment, 'She's jake!' Quite convinced that the whole party would be completely blind for a week, I went morosely off to bed.

But I seriously misjudged the recuperative powers of our hardy Sherpas. In the morning only four of them wished to be paid off, and these only because they were too blind to see at all. The remainder of the party were bleary-eyed but willing. It was obviously impossible to let them start out again into this bright expanse of snow without some form of protection, and I was at a complete loss. The resourceful Stobart came to our rescue. To his vast experience of coping with charging lions in Africa, crashing icebergs in the Antarctic, and luscious film stars in the studio, this problem was undoubtedly small stuff. Some of the party had large panoramic ski-ing goggles with spare celluloid lenses, and Stobart collected these up and proceeded to cut them into small pieces about an inch in diameter. He then produced a large roll of black adhesive tape and some string, and before long the prototype goggle had emerged. It was an immediate success, and the whole party set to work with scissors and adhesive tape to produce large numbers of them. By the time we'd equipped all the Sherpas, we'd made nearly thirty pairs of goggles.

This operation had taken some time, so when we started off from Lobuje the morning was well advanced and the glare considerable. We hadn't gone far before I realised that some of the Sherpas were in worse condition than they had admitted. One girl, in particular, seemed almost blind, but plodded determinedly on with her hand on the Sherpa in front to show her the way. She was in such obvious distress that I decided to be firm and send her down. I took her load off her back and pressed her wages into her hand. It took her a moment to realise what was happening, and then with a wild gesture she threw the money into the snow, picked up her load, and stumbled off after her companions. As I knelt in the snow searching for the coins I reflected that the women here seemed just as illogical as their sisters back home.

After several hours of steady plodding, we reached the rough boulders covering a tributary glacier and started across them. The weather had deteriorated again and snow was falling. George Lowe and I pushed on ahead in order to find a good route while the visibility still permitted, and the Sherpas trailed slowly behind us. We came to the end of the moraine at long last and crossed a snow-covered flat to a camp site beside a lake.

Some of the stronger Sherpas weren't far behind us, but many of them hadn't come into view. George and I went back to give a hand. Far back on the moraine I found one of the women floundering in the snow under a large box weighing over 70 lb. She was almost exhausted and I took her load from her. Her method of carrying it was with a head-band, and as I had no pack frame with me I had to follow suit. My progress at first was exceedingly erratic, but I soon learned to balance the load and found I could make a good pace. In this fashion we collected all the loads and had the last Sherpa in camp by dark. In the dim light and falling snow our camp site presented a miserable picture, but soon camp fires sprang up under every overhanging boulder, and the smell of cooking food and the hearty laughs of the Sherpas brought an air of tired contentment.

We awoke to a beautiful morning, and as we ate our breakfast we couldn't keep our eyes off the wonderful fluted ice of Nuptse, which towered above us on the other side of the glacier. There was a great air of expectancy around the camp, as today we intended to establish our Base Camp and get our first look at the icefall. We were soon on our way and immediately struck out on to the Khumbu glacier. Tedious moraine heap followed tedious moraine heap, but at last we reached the clear ice in the middle and followed up an easy trough between the great ice pinnacles. We were starting to catch glimpses of the icefall now, pouring in a chaotic jumble out of the jaws of the Western Cwm. And floating high above us, almost so far as to be unreal, was the grim black summit pyramid of Everest with its tattered banner of wind-whipped snow streaming out into the thin air. It seemed a long way to go!

We continued on, winding between slender ice spires and impassable cliffs; jumping cold glacier streams and dodging undercut boulders. By midday we had reached the site of the Swiss Base Camp – a barren, rock-strewn expanse of ice with enough flat places to pitch a few tents. We took off our loads and started investigating. A shout from George Lowe brought us hurrying over. He'd found a magnificent pile of juniper wood – enough to keep our fires going for a week. With some regret we paid off our Sherpa coolies and watched them dashing gaily back down the glacier. They'd been a very game bunch and we were sorry to see them go.

Late in the afternoon I set off by myself to find an easy route to the foot of the icefall. I was feeling very keenly the responsibility that John Hunt had given me, and was determined that if it were humanly possible we'd get to the top of the icefall in the half a dozen days before his arrival. Above our Base Camp the Khumbu glacier was a wilderness of ice pinnacles penetrated by winding hollows. I followed up one of these hollows, and it led on into the next – and then the next, until I emerged an hour later at the foot of the icefall. I couldn't see a great deal, for the clouds had closed in, but I immediately realised that the lower portion of the icefall was considerably more difficult than it had been in 1951. But a route up it still looked possible. I returned to camp and told the others what I'd seen. I decided that next day we'd attempt to put a camp as high as we could up the lower slopes. Snow was falling again as we crawled into our tents for the night.

Early next morning we started sorting out equipment and making it up into loads. George Lowe, unfortunately, was ill, but Westmacott and Band looked fit and strong. At 9 a.m., in warm sunshine, the three of us, together with four Sherpas, waved goodbye to George and the others and set off along the track through the ice pinnacles. The whole icefall was now clearly revealed, and the closer we got to it the more depressing it became. It was in shocking condition. Even the easier lower portions were split by innumerable crevasses and menaced by crumbling ice towers. We soon realised there was no point in attempting to establish a camp, so we sent our four Sherpas with all the equipment back to base, while Band, Westmacott, and I set off to reconnoitre a route. Roped together we worked our way carefully over to the left side of the icefall, looking always for a route that could be safely crossed by laden and inexpert porters. At first the going was relatively easy. The large crevasses all had substantial ice bridges spanning them, and we twisted our way in and out with little difficulty. But the angle of the crevasses forced us slowly to the right, and ultimately we were brought to a halt at the foot of an ice-wall.

Westmacott was leading and attacked this problem with vigour. He cut a line of steps across the wall to the left-hand side where it was split into a corner by a crevasse. He then slowly chopped a series of roomy steps up the steep icy corner. After a long effort he reached the top and pulled himself out of sight. A few moments later a hearty call told us he had a good safe stance and that we could come on up. Band followed up slowly. Another yell and it was my turn to go. I crossed over the bottom of the wall to the corner and started climbing up it. It was certainly steep and very exposed, for on the left side I could look straight down fifty or sixty feet into the depths of a crevasse. But Michael Westmacott had done a good job, and I climbed up his steps without difficulty to join

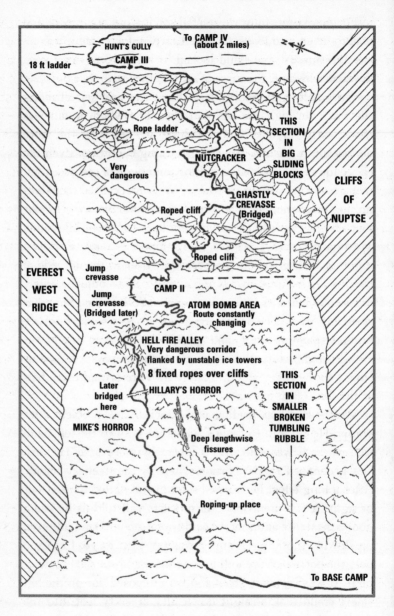

1953. A plan of the route through the Khumbu Icefall.

my companions at the top. 'Mike's Horror', we called this
pitch, and as such it became generally known. Later parties
attached a fixed rope to this section so that the porters could
get up safely.

I now took over the lead. Making every effort to bear left
again, I started searching out a route amongst a maze of
enormous crevasses. Many of the bridges we crossed were
frail, unstable slivers of ice, quite unsuitable for general use
by our porters, but we knew they could be improved later.
After half an hour of slow progress, I came to the edge of
the largest crevasse we'd yet struck. It was about forty feet
across and enormously deep. I searched anxiously for a way
across or around it. The only possibility I could see was a
great chunk of ice which was jammed insecurely across the
crevasse just below the top. It looked as if a decent push
would send it crashing into the depths, but I thought it was
worth a try. Westmacott anchored me firmly with the rope
and I started cautiously over it. I didn't like it at all! I was
sure I could feel it quivering under my feet, and the farther
I went the farther I had to fall. Even when I reached the far
side quite safely, I wasn't out of trouble. The upper lip of the
crevasse was much higher than the bridge and I had a twenty-
foot ice-wall to climb.

From my insecure perch I started cutting some large steps
in the hard ice, and then nicked out some small handholds
above them. When I'd finished them to my complete satisfaction, I climbed up on to the bottom steps and, holding on
like grim death with one hand, swung out directly over the
crevasse. I went on cutting with my free hand, and in this
tiring and uncomfortable fashion worked my way slowly up
the wall. It was a great relief when I was able to stretch my
arm over the lip of the crevasse and drive my ice-axe into
the good snow. A wriggle and a grunt and I was up. And so
'Hillary's Horror' was born. We never liked this place, and

it was only used a few times before a much safer route was
found by doing a long sweep out to the left.

We resumed the familiar pattern through the crevasses
ahead – a cautious examination and then a wild leap if it
wasn't too wide, or for the big ones an anxious search for a
bridge that would hold our weight. And although we were
often stopped, we always managed to find a way round. Finally
we came to a little snowy saddle and sat down for a rest and
a little food. We looked at the route ahead. From here on the
whole nature of the icefall changed. The slopes ahead were
much steeper, and were formed of great unstable blocks of
ice stacked insecurely on top of each other. It was a most
unhealthy looking place, and the remnants of shattered ice
strewing the snow below gave ample evidence that any sudden
move in the glacier sent some of the blocks tumbling down.
The only possible route I could see was up a steep gully
between the ice-blocks, and even this was menaced by overhanging ice on every side. But there was no alternative, so
we'd have to use it. We started off up with a rush, stumbling
over old avalanche debris, whacking steps up ice-slopes, and
plugging on as hard as our straining lungs would let us. Our
one wish was to get out of the danger area as quickly as
possible. We reached the top of the gully panting for breath
and struck immediately out of it to the right. We climbed up
on to a large block that seemed a little more stable than the
rest, and looked back down 'Hellfire Alley', thanking our lucky
stars that we were safely out of it.

But the route ahead didn't look much better. It was just a
jumble of ice-blocks. I started ferreting a way through them.
Sometimes I could squeeze between two of the blocks, sometimes I had to cut a trail over the top, and on mercifully few
occasions I had to make a route almost down underneath
them. It was nerve-racking work and progress was inevitably
very slow. We could now see where the icefall flattened out

slightly and knew that the Swiss had established their camp there, but it was still a couple of hundred yards away and the terrain in between looked quite impossible. Discouraged, tired, and not a little scared, we decided to call it a day, and slowly made our way back to the comforts and safety of Base Camp.

Next day Westmacott and I renewed the attack, accompanied by Ang Namgyal – a safe and steady climber. We climbed back up our tracks, making much faster time now that we knew the way, and we reached 'Hellfire Alley' without a great deal of trouble. Here, however, we had an unpleasant shock waiting for us. Half-way up the gully we found that about twenty feet of our track had been wiped out by shattered blocks of ice that had fallen from higher up during the night. Every block perched above our heads immediately took on a new malevolence, and we hurried up to the top with cold chills running down our spines. We crossed through the maze of ice-blocks and were pleasantly encouraged to find that nothing seemed to have changed there. We had now reached our farthest point of the previous day, and we faced up to the task of getting a bit farther. First of all, we tried a long swing out to the right. Cutting our way over and around the ice-blocks, we hacked a route out for nearly a hundred yards into the depths of the icefall, looking for any sign of weakness in its defences that would enable us to strike upwards. We were effectively stopped by an immense transverse crevasse at least fifty feet wide and guarded by a row of poised séracs. We returned to our starting-place.

It seemed that the only thing to do was to try to get through the impossible-looking country ahead. Just to the right of us were two great blocks of ice forty or fifty feet high, and it struck me that if we could get through between them we might make a little progress. I started cutting a line of steps up their glistening sides, making little handholds in the ice for balance. A long stretch at the top, a quick changing of weight, and I was through. I took a quick look at the difficulties ahead and was able to shout to Westmacott the glad news that some progress was possible. The other two climbed up to me and we moved on again. With a growing air of excitement, we negotiated half a dozen ice-blocks, and then stopped in astonishment at the unusual terrain ahead. There appeared to have been an enormous subsidence in the middle of the icefall, and below us a wide, shallow gully swept smoothly through the icy ruins up to the broad ledge which was our first objective. The floor of the gully was flat enough, but it was split into a jigsaw puzzle of horizontal and vertical crevasses like a pattern of sun-baked mud. And it looked terribly unstable – as though it could sink again at any moment. It was obviously our old 'Atom Bomb' area. But it would take us where we wanted to go, and that was the main thing.

With a familiar tightening of my nerves, I dropped down to the edge of it and started investigations. Westmacott had me on a tight rope, so I dislodged a large piece of ice and pushed it down a crevasse. For a moment nothing occurred, but then a muffled roar came from the subterranean depths and a distinct tremor shot through the whole area. It seemed a bit shaky, but not too bad on the whole. I decided to push on. The first few crevasses were wide and unpleasant and, although we finally got across them, I didn't like the way they shivered and boomed with every blow of the ice-axe. And then I stepped on to the first piece of the jigsaw puzzle, and was relieved to find that it felt fairly stable, although there was clear evidence of recent movement. We continued on, stepping over the small crevasses from piece to piece until we came to the last of them. The gully narrowed and only two crevasses separated us from the snowy shelf ahead. It was a gloomy spot. On either side were great cold ice-walls and a threatening finger of ice stretched out above our heads. We didn't waste any time, and though the crevasses were wide and uphill, we gathered all our strength and leapt across them and came out into the sun and open space of the shelf.

We were now more than half-way up the icefall at a height of about 19,400 feet. We started looking around for a camp site. The shelf was quite extensive, but on closer examination there proved to be few places that weren't in some danger of avalanches from above. Finally we found a suitable spot up on a small ice rib. Only a short distance behind it was an enormous, tilting sérac, but we estimated that, even if it did fall, it shouldn't give the inhabitants of the camp anything more than a bad fright. After a brief halt for lunch, we started off down again. We wanted to improve the track and make it safer, so we started an orgy of ice-cutting. Great steps were hacked in the ice at tricky points, overhanging ice was chopped away, and a safe route was carved down steep ice-slopes and over difficult ice-blocks. We could do nothing to improve the unstable nature of the country, but at least we could reduce the length of time it was necessary to be in the danger zone. We returned to Base Camp in a glow of virtue and our day's adventure lost nothing in the telling.

In the evening we had a long discussion. Although we had established a route well up in the icefall, I was far from happy about its constant dangers. I didn't want to waste any time unnecessarily, but our job was to find the best route possible so that our porters would be subjected to no unnecessary hazards. We decided that next day we'd explore the centre of the icefall and see if we could find a safer route. We had hardly settled down to sleep when Westmacott became violently ill. Continuous and painful vomiting soon weakened him, and although after several hours the worst of the attack had passed, it was quite obvious that he was going to be out of action for a few days. Westmacott had worked magnificently on the icefall, but we suspected that unaccustomed altitude had caught up with him at last. Fortunately George Lowe had by now recovered from his indisposition, so our climbing strength could be maintained.

Lowe, Band, and I set off early in the morning for the centre of the icefall. I'd had a couple of strenuous days and was taking it very quietly, but the others were now going well and did all the hard work. We reached the foot of the icefall without a great deal of difficulty and examined the possibilities ahead. For some distance the icefall climbed up rather steeply, but it was in a far less shattered condition than our other route. Band and Lowe set to work to find a way up these steep pitches, and we gained rapid height as they chipped long flights of steps. On either side of us the slopes were lined with particularly unstable looking séracs, and we took good care to keep well out of their line of fire. We had just climbed up a very steep section on to the crest of an ice bump when, with a suddenness and speed that was quite frightening, a tall sérac only fifty feet to our right split in half and swept past us in a relentless grinding mass of ice-blocks. It was a sharp warning against carelessness. It was becoming obvious now that this route, despite its promising start, was soon to peter out. We climbed over an ice-strewn slope to find a line of teetering séracs barring our way. There was a gap between two of the most unstable ones, but even this was menaced by a block of ice perched above it. None of us was game enough to give it a go, and without further ado we headed down towards camp. We felt now that our route on the left, with all its disadvantages and dangers, was the only possible one.

We arrived back at base and crawled into our warm sleeping-bags. Snow was already falling once again, but it couldn't subdue our feelings of comfort as we lay there drinking large mugs of hot tea and idly discussing the day's activities. I was almost drifting off to sleep when an unfamiliar shout brought me back to consciousness. Next moment the flaps of the tent parted and a cheerful Sherpa face appeared, bringing with it a shower of fresh snow. I was handed a note from the 'Burra Sahib'. Apparently John Hunt was already camping down at the lake with Noyce and Ward, some days ahead of schedule. This information filled us with consternation. We had set our hearts on reaching the top of the icefall before Hunt turned up, and we looked on his early arrival more as a disaster than anything else. 'I suppose they all want to be in on the fun' was my grumbling thought. We decided to push ahead with our plans to establish Camp II. Westmacott was still incapacitated, so we agreed that Lowe, Band, and I would camp on the icefall shelf the following night. Pugh and Stobart had been leading a quiet life in an attempt to assist their acclimatisation, but they now decided to accompany us for the day.

We were away at 9.30 next morning, with three Sherpas to carry some of our gear. The fresh snow had concealed most of our tracks, but we had flagged the route and had no difficulty in following it. Stobart was determined to get some good coloured movies, so for a while he directed us with good effect and 'Mike's Horror' and 'Hillary's Horror' became the authentic location for some gripping scenes of battling with death and destruction. If only a really attractive blonde could have screamed for help within range of his camera, Stobart's cup would have been full. We finally tired of this diversion and set off up the mountain. I had already noticed how, by its very familiarity, the route was appearing a good deal easier and safer. Even 'Hellfire Alley' looked calm and peaceful under its layer of fresh snow. But the Sherpas were far from happy. Though their loads were barely heavier than ours, they were making very hard work of the ascent, and missed no opportunity of telling us how much more dangerous it was than in the previous year with the Swiss party. However, with frequent rests and a good deal of persuasive talking, we managed to keep them going through the ice-blocks and over to the 'Atom Bomb' area.

George Lowe was in the lead as we approached it. When he came to the first crevasse he stopped and eyed it with obvious dislike. 'You didn't cross this bridge, did you, Ed?' he shouted back. I assured him that that was the way we had gone. Completely unconvinced, he gave the bridge a jab with his ice-axe before trusting his weight to it. To his astonishment – and mine – the bridge suddenly dropped out of sight, and a moment later the whole area quivered and shook with a fierce tremor. When everything had quietened down a little, I could feel George's accusing eye on me, so guiltily muttering something about 'heavy handed shoves that would knock the Sydney Harbour Bridge over', I started off on the tedious business of finding another place to get across the crevasse.

Fifty feet out to the left I found another bridge, and this time a more substantial one. We crossed it cautiously and rejoined the old route, then made our way across to the jig-saw puzzle. In our two-day absence a marked change had taken place – some of the blocks had dropped a few feet and some of them had been forced up, but it was still possible for us to step from one to the other and so up to the final crevasses. These, too, in our absence seemed to have widened a little, and it was impossible to jump them with a load on. I took my pack off and leapt safely across. George Lowe was already tying the loads on to a line, and he threw the end over to me. I pulled them in hand over hand. We belayed the Sherpas carefully from both sides and then persuaded them to jump over too. Before long we had all the gear on our camp site and were chipping away the ice to make a level platform for the tents. Once the tents were pitched, we conducted the Sherpas back over the last two crevasses, and left it to Pugh and Stobart to get them safely back to Base Camp.

Lowe, Band, and I settled down in our two small tents. We soon had our cooker going and were sniffing enthusiastically as the aroma of chicken soup wafted through our tents. Even the resumption of our daily snowfall couldn't subdue our feelings of contentment. Later on in the evening, we crawled out of our tents to find that three or four inches of snow had fallen, but the sky was now clear. We were in a most impressive spot completely surrounded by a tumbled ruin of ice. Even the enormous sérac behind the camp seemed to have moved a bit closer in the dim light. And it was very cold and still. But if you stood quietly for a moment your ear attuned itself to the hidden life of the glacier – you heard a soft creak or a sharp snap; or a faint crash as a distant sérac tumbled to its doom; or a sudden roar as an avalanche swept off the hanging ice-cliffs of Nuptse. And always in the background there was a roar like surf breaking on the shore, and you knew that the wind was playing its wild tune amongst the summit rocks of Everest. Yes. Camp II was an impressive place, but we never learned to like it!

It was bitterly cold when we awoke in the morning, though we were warm enough inside our double bags. We started the stove going and had our breakfast, but we didn't dare move outside until the sun was striking the tents. We tied our crampons on and roped up. In the clear morning air the way ahead looked extremely difficult, for from here on the whole nature of the icefall changed completely. Below Camp II the ice-blocks had been broken into moderate size – few of them were more than thirty feet high – but above us they were enormous in extent. Square cut, with cliffs a hundred feet high, they surged over the crest of the Cwm, and like great icebergs ground their way slowly and relentlessly to the bottom. The only way was to try to climb up between them; to clamber over the shattered ice at their feet and to keep clear of the overhanging bulges which periodically split from their sides and devastated the slopes beneath. It looked pretty hopeless, but we knew we had to try. We started off from the tents and climbed steeply up a long gully, jumping a few small crevasses and slowly warming up to our work. We emerged at the foot of the first ice-cliff and eyed it with considerable trepidation. It was obviously very much alive. The steep slope in front of it was littered with splinters of ice, a good deal of it of recent origin. The only way to get past this cliff was to traverse along the slope to the right. We clambered quickly along, always trying to keep a large lump of ice between us and the threat from above. Panting hard in the thin air, we reached the end of the slope, and dropped down off it into a snowy hollow which seemed free from danger.

We sat down for a rest. Band seemed to be acclimatising rather slowly and was making heavy weather of it. There only seemed to be one route out of this hollow, and it led over the top of a tilting sérac. With a resigned shrug, I headed off for it. Half a dozen steps in the sérac's steep side and I was on top, with an airy drop a few feet to the right. Wasting no time, I crossed sérac to the crevasse which divided it from the more stable ground above. On either side of the crevasse I cut a comfortable platform, and then stepped easily across.

George Lowe now took over the lead. He'd only gone a few yards when he stopped and stood still for a moment, looking ahead. Then he waved us up to him. We climbed up and looked over the edge. 'This is the worst yet' was my immediate thought. For the next hundred feet was split by innumerable crevasses, jagged and fresh, and menaced on every side by poised ice-blocks or undercut séracs. There was a brief silence. 'Well, we can only give it a go,' said George,

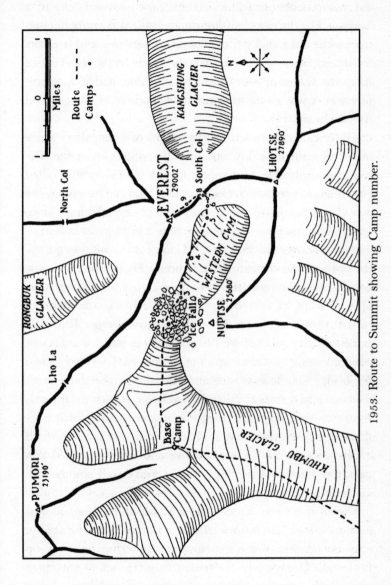

1953. Route to Summit showing Camp number.

and started cutting a line of steps down towards the first crevasse. For the next half-hour his ice-axe was going unceasingly as he cut a shaky trail around, in between, and over the crevasses. The last crevasse was the worst of the lot. The ice on either side of it was loose and unstable, and if anything gave way it was going to bring down a pile of blocks perched insecurely above.

The only way across it was by means of a thin sliver of ice which projected weakly out into the middle. George was understandably reluctant to use it. 'Go on, George!' I yelled with the courage that comes from being on the far end of the rope. 'I've a first-class belay.' George sent one scathing glance behind him, then took a deep breath and light as a feather simply flew over the crevasse – I don't think he was on the piece of ice long enough for it to break. He climbed up a few feet and then brought the two of us across on a tight rope. This sliver of ice served very satisfactorily for a week or so until fifteen-stone Tom Bourdillon came along. Tom was immensely strong, and we often heard his puzzled comment that something 'just came apart in my hands'. Tom approached this bridge for the first time and gave it a 'slight shove' with his ice-axe to test its stability. Whereupon, shaken to the core, it gave up the ghost and disappeared silently into the depths of the crevasse. After that we had to bridge it properly with an aluminium ladder. George Lowe and I always called this place the 'Ghastly Crevasse', and it pretty well summed up our feelings towards it.

Ahead of us was a vast series of ice-cliffs. They looked absolutely hopeless, but we felt there simply had to be a route – we couldn't have the expedition foundering half-way up the icefall. Desperately we tried thrusting out to the right towards the hanging glaciers of Nuptse. For the next hour, with the cold hand of fear gripping at our stomachs, George Lowe led us through a purgatory of fractured ice. We knew we shouldn't be there, but we had to break through somehow. And always another ice-wall turned us back. As a last chance, we tried getting around to the left. We had almost given up when we found a way. Cramponing up steep slopes and forcing a track amongst the snow-covered debris of fallen séracs, we made gradual height, and finally emerged on the crest of a little snowy saddle. We sat down for a rest and munched a little food.

I was looking pessimistically at the route ahead when I suddenly felt a surge of excitement. 'Hey, chaps! That's the edge of the Cwm up there; if we can get up that cliff, we're right!' But the cliff looked as impossible as all the rest of them had. 'Perhaps it's better around the corner,' I said in desperation. But between us and the corner was the usual conglomeration of ice-blocks and crevasses. We set to work to cross them. I dropped down off the saddle, and with a slash of my ice-axe I knocked a lump of ice out of the way and it fell into a crevasse. Next moment the ground quivered and shook. 'Another shaky patch,' I called back. 'You'd better let the full rope out.'

We gathered at the corner. Our way was blocked by a series of small séracs, and George tried to make his way over the top of them. With each blow of his ice-axe they moved visibly, so we decided it wasn't worth it. Right on the corner were two long thin slivers of ice standing upright, with a gap of a couple of feet between them. I looked through and could see reasonable terrain on the other side. But it wasn't much of a place to go through, and if those ice slivers came together when you were between them . . . well, you'd know what a nut felt like in a nutcracker! I mentally shrugged and started cutting steps on each wall. The ice rang hollow, but the slivers didn't move. I climbed inside them and went on cutting. Soon I was able to reach out and drag myself to safer ground. I took in the rope and the others hastily followed me through.

I moved out a few yards to get clear of the corner and then examined the ground ahead. It didn't look too promising. The ice-wall was certainly lower, but I couldn't see a break anywhere in its uncompromising defences. I started along the bottom of the cliffs, examining them closely. In one place the upper portion sloped back at a climbable angle, but the bottom fifteen feet was overhanging and I couldn't see any way of getting up it. I moved on around another corner. Ahead of me an ice buttress leaned lazily against the cliff. My eye followed up it, but it ran out against the vertical face. Then my interest quickened. The top part of the face was split by a vertical crack — the end of a crevasse. If I could get inside that crevasse, I might scratch a route up to the top. Lowe and Band agreed it was our only chance.

I started cutting a track up the buttress. It was very steep, and the hard, smooth ice always seemed to be thrusting me out of the steps. I reached the top of the buttress, and pressed against the cold wall above as I regained my breath. I didn't like the look of the next few steps towards the crevasse. The bulging ice would be pushing me out almost beyond the limits of balance, and there was a long drop underneath. If I could only get one of the other chaps up on to the buttress to belay me with the rope, I might give it a go. I thrust around with my ice-axe and managed to jam it firmly in between the buttress and the wall. I looped the rope around it and it seemed quite a good belay. Band started moving slowly up the steps and I took in the rope. He was soon just below me and was able to jam his ice-axe in beside mine. He looped the rope firmly around it, and then I was ready to move. I reached over carefully and cut a step inside the crack on one of the walls. Then, without stopping to think, I stepped quickly around the bulge and into the gloom of the crevasse. It was like moving into another world — a world of soft green light and cold slippery walls. I balanced in my step and looked up.

The top was only twelve feet above me. I started cutting a line of steps in each wall and the ice-chips tinkled merrily down into the depths below. Wriggling and straining, with a foot against each wall, I climbed up on to the steps and cut some more. I reached up and cleared the snow away from the top of the crevasse and then moved up a bit farther. Next moment I had an arm over the edge, and a few seconds later I was out. With a yell of relief and pleasure I called to the others to come on up. I couldn't see them, but as I took in the rope I could follow their progress by the subterranean noises they were making. Finally an arm and then Band's head popped up above the crevasse, and he scrambled out to join me. George Lowe wasn't far behind.

We stood looking around us. There was no doubt about it – we were on the edge of the Western Cwm. The block on which we were standing looked as though it might start its trip down the icefall at any moment, but it was connected to the area above by an excellent snow bridge. With renewed energy we charged across it, climbed a small slope and stood looking down into a pleasant snowy hollow. It was the ideal spot for Camp III – safe and with plenty of room.

We returned down the icefall in a glow of excitement and looked with scorn on its dangers. We wriggled down the crack, squeezed through the 'Nutcracker', and hastily crossed to the little saddle. By doing a long traverse, we found a reasonably direct route down to the 'Ghastly Crevasse'. A quick step and we were over it and into the maze of crevasses beyond. We climbed down off the tilting sérac, skirted the first ice-cliffs and started dropping down the last gully towards Camp II. We could see the tents now, and to our surprise there were two figures standing beside them. We waved and hurried on down. It was John Hunt and Ang Namgyal, and it was good to see them. Hunt was tremendously pleased at our news, although he was far from happy at the dangerous nature of the route. He'd come up all the way from Lake Camp in his restless desire to get first-hand knowledge of what progress was being made. I took Hunt back up our route as far as the 'Ghastly Crevasse' to give him some idea of what it was like, and then we rejoined the others in Camp II.

I didn't envy John Hunt his task of deciding whether we should use this route for porters. It certainly had its dangers, but George Lowe and I were convinced it was the only way. The alternative was to abandon the attack altogether, which was unthinkable. Hunt agreed, as we knew he would, that we'd have to use this route, but he emphasised that we must spare no effort to reduce its dangers to a minimum. We all roped up and, carrying our personal gear, started off down. We carefully crossed the 'Atom Bomb' area, wound our way through the ice-blocks, hastened down 'Hellfire Alley', and reached Base Camp in a surprisingly short time, feeling rather tired but well satisfied with our efforts.

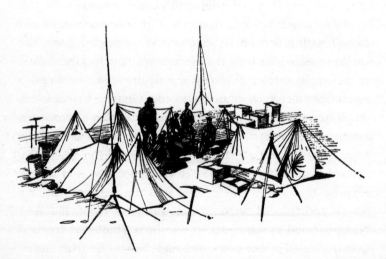

CHAPTER EIGHT

The Second Barrier

IN HIS CAREFULLY PLANNED scheme of acclimatisation, Hunt had allowed for rest periods at lower altitudes after a spell of hard work. Some of us didn't feel particularly like a rest, but Hunt wisely insisted that we take it. We all descended to Lake Camp, and although it snowed heavily every afternoon, we spent quite a pleasant time resting, writing letters, and mending our gear. Several days later we returned to the attack. Our first task was to make the icefall route sufficiently safe and easy to enable our band of porters to get up it. Some of the party, working from Base Camp, concentrated on the lower portion. Long pine poles had been brought up from the valleys, and these, together with sections of our aluminium ladder, were used to bridge the more difficult crevasses. Fixed ropes were placed on 'Mike's Horror' and 'Hillary's Horror', and some of the more threatening of the séracs were cut away. But, despite all this work, the route never really became either easy or particularly safe. The daily falls of snow continually wiped out the tracks, and the 'Atom Bomb' area usually managed overnight to provide a new crevasse or widen an existing one. The icefall was in constant movement, so it needed constant attention.

Meanwhile, another group was working on the upper icefall. Westmacott and I established Camp III, and from it we improved the route below. We bypassed the difficult 'buttress and crack' route by fixing a long rope ladder over the lowest part of the ice-cliff, and we put a fixed rope through the Nutcracker. Westmacott seemed to have fully recovered his strength, and one evening, just to show how well acclimatised he was, he produced a *Times* crossword puzzle and proceeded to work the whole thing out – a feat I was incapable of emulating even at sea-level.

Although Camp III was at the entrance to the Western Cwm, we were still cut off from it by an enormous crevasse – the same one that we had stopped at in 1951 and the one that gave the Swiss so much trouble in 1952. We examined it very closely, but we couldn't find any bridge over it. In one place it was only fifteen feet wide, which meant that we could probably bridge it with our aluminium ladder. On the morning of April 25th Westmacott and I tried to force a route through the middle of the crevasse. After a long period of hard climbing, we reached the far wall where a crack ran to the top. I thought we could probably get up it, but it was a hazardous and difficult route. We decided that it was out of the question for laden porters and returned to camp.

In the afternoon a big party arrived – Hunt, Evans, Noyce, Gregory, and Tenzing, together with a large number of Sherpas. It was the first big lift up the icefall, and everything seemed to have gone very well. It was also Tenzing's first trip above Base Camp for this year, so I asked him what he thought of the route and he seemed quite happy about it. A large camp was quickly erected, and the equipment and food were put into piles and covered up. Mike Westmacott then gathered together all the extra porters and led them off down to Base Camp. Soon after midday it started snowing heavily and before long the tents were sagging under the weight of it. But by four o'clock it was clear and cold. Hunt's thought was concentrated on overcoming the last barrier and getting into the Western Cwm. He immediately suggested we use the rest of the day in bridging the great crevasse. Hunt, Evans, Noyce, Tenzing, and I set off across the soft, new snow, carrying three six-foot lengths of our aluminium ladder. On the edge of the crevasse we bolted them strongly together and then lowered the eighteen-foot ladder carefully into place. It spanned with a couple of feet to spare, but it looked a frail link across the deep gash. I crawled over it to try it out, and although it swayed a little it seemed stable enough. Despite the late hour, Hunt's blood was up and he was eager to push forward into the Cwm. Someone had to go back to answer the five-o'clock radio call from Base Camp, so Noyce reluctantly returned, accompanied by Tenzing.

Hunt crawled across the bridge and Evans and I followed him. Our main aim was to find a route leading to the right into the centre of the Western Cwm, away from the avalanches that swept with great frequency from the hanging glaciers on the West shoulder of Everest. But as we worked our way forward we found we were slowly being forced towards them. Crevasse followed crevasse, but all had substantial snow bridges – all, that is, except one, and Hunt, who was not in the mood to be stopped, cut a line of steps down into it and out again on the other side. We were now close under Everest, and our way to the right was still barred by impossible crevasses. The only escape was to pass quickly over the avalanche-strewn slopes close into the cliffs and then head directly into the Cwm and out of danger. Hunt didn't hesitate. He plunged on over the ice-blocks and avalanche snow, and then shot directly to the right. I didn't really feel happy until the hanging ice was well behind us. Hunt's enthusiasm was becoming infectious and we pushed rapidly on. Ahead of us the Lhotse face and the South Col were becoming exciting realities . . . another challenge to meet and another defence to shatter. Winding amongst the long crevasses, scrambling up snow bumps and sliding down the other side, we swept on towards them, feeling like giants as we strode up the Western Cwm. Common sense finally called a halt. We were already well up the Cwm and night was fast approaching. Ahead of us there seemed to be no obvious problems, so with a great feeling of jubilation we turned back. We returned into a world of indescribable beauty. In the soft evening light the great peaks around were glowing like balls of fire against the background of a dark velvet sky. It seemed a fitting finish to an exciting day.

April 26th dawned fine and clear. It was to be our first big day in the Western Cwm. Hunt, Evans, Tenzing, and I were to go ahead and complete the route as far as the site of the Swiss Camp IV. Noyce and Gregory were to follow behind with half a dozen laden Sherpas. Hunt and Evans tied on to one rope and Tenzing and I on to another. This was the first time I had climbed with Tenzing, or indeed even seen him climbing, and I was very interested to watch him in action. Tenzing on his part was obviously viewing the day's activity with considerable enthusiasm, as up to this time he had been necessarily confined to Base Camp with the numerous duties involved in his important task of helping to organise the Sherpas.

Hunt and Evans led off along our old tracks and we followed behind. We crawled over the bridge, crossed Hunt's gully, and wasted no time in passing under the threatening cliffs of Everest. As we moved out into the Western Cwm, Tenzing pointed out the site of the Swiss Camp III and mentioned that they'd left a little food there. Hunt agreed that we should make an investigation, so Tenzing led off on the track towards it. We found a few boxes and sacks buried under the snow, and opened them with enthusiasm. But alas for our hopes of tinned fruit-juices and Swiss delicacies! The food was nearly all uninteresting pemmican. We made a pile of it and then chased off after the others.

The sun was now very hot indeed, and as its rays reflected fiercely from every snowy slope, the Western Cwm became an absolute inferno. The combination of heat and altitude produced a lassitude that was hard to overcome. We caught up to Hunt and took over the lead. The snow was deep and loose and making a trail was tiring work. I was feeling particularly fit and pushed on hard, but Tenzing was eager to do his share. We crossed many crevasses, some of them well concealed and decidedly tricky. After a long and hot battle with the deep snow, we climbed the last small slope to Camp IV. Once again a pile of snow-covered boxes and bags greeted our eyes. We started digging around, and a considerable amount of useful food came to light. Biscuits, cheese, porridge, bacon, jam, and other odds and ends were produced in sufficient quantity to make a pleasant change in diet for our voracious appetites. Hunt and Evans arrived – Hunt looking drawn and tired. But we were already getting accustomed to his habit of driving himself to the limit with the inevitable reaction at the end of the day. The astonishing thing was how he recovered overnight and pushed on as hard as ever the next day.

With considerable interest, we examined the Lhotse face. It seemed to tower above us, and we could see the wind whipping the snow off the South Col. Hunt felt confident that we could climb to the Col in two or three days, but Evans and I were much more pessimistic – at least a week was our bet. After a couple of hours Tenzing and I started off down, as we were going right back to Base Camp. We raced down the Cwm and caught up to Noyce and Gregory and their Sherpas, who had dumped their loads about half an hour from Camp IV. At Camp III we met Bourdillon and Ward, who had brought up a band of laden porters. The icefall lift seemed to be on in earnest.

We dropped quickly down to Camp II and found George Lowe in residence with another group of porters. For a few moments we swapped stories and then we turned to leave. 'I'll say "hello" over the radio link-up at five o'clock,' I commented idly. 'That'll be the day,' said George, who knew this meant getting down to Base in the unprecedented time of less than an hour. This seemed a good enough excuse to hurry, and I set off at a run with the unfortunate Tenzing running behind. I jogged through the 'Atom Bomb' area, noticing a few changes there as I did so, and approached its last crevasse. Not waiting to cross the bridge I took a mighty leap in the air and landed with some force on the far side. It was too much for the overhanging lip, and with a sharp crack it split off and descended into the crevasse with me on top of it. I didn't have much time to think. I only knew that I had to stop being crushed against the ice by the twisting block, and I threw my cramponed feet hard against one wall and my shoulders against the other. Next moment the rope came tight and the block dropped away underneath me. Tenzing's reaction had been very quick. I cut my way to the surface without too much difficulty, and thanked Tenzing for his capable handling of the situation. He seemed to regard it as a rather good joke. Berating myself mentally for being so foolishly careless, I started on again. But human nature being what it is, I reached Base Camp just in time to say a breathless 'Hello' to George.

I had found Tenzing an admirable companion – capable, willing, and extremely pleasant. His rope work was first class, as my near-catastrophe had shown. Although not perhaps technically outstanding in ice-craft, he was very strong and determined and an excellent acclimatiser. Best of all, as far as I was concerned, he was prepared to go fast and hard.

For the next few days, despite deplorable weather, the lifts of gear through the icefall and up the Western Cwm went on continously. Heavy falls of snow each day meant that the track had to be daily remade, at much cost of energy and breath. Apart from this tedious and often dangerous work, the main interest in the expedition had turned to the reconnaissance of the Lhotse face. Hunt had decided that, in order to give the closed-circuit oxygen set (our rather radical new type) a thorough testing out at higher altitudes, it should be used on this reconnaissance. Bourdillon and Evans, the formidable 'closed-circuit' team, were to be the spearhead of the attack, and Hunt himself was to be one of the support group.

The attack on the Lhotse face exerted a powerful fascination on the members of the expedition – we felt it was the key to the summit – and all of us who weren't taking part in it looked with envious eyes on those that were. I'd already had more than my share of the enjoyable jobs on the expedition, but I racked my brains for some excuse that would let me get in at least on the ground-floor of the reconnaissance. At last I thought of something with sufficient merit not to be turned down. I proposed to Hunt that two of us should do a long and severe test of our open-circuit oxygen apparatus. I'd gone to some pains to become thoroughly conversant with the mechanics of this set, but had only used it for half an hour on an acclimatisation trip. As there had been no need for oxygen at the moderate heights of the icefall and Western Cwm, the open-circuit set had not really been fully tested out. My suggestion was that if the set stood up to a rigorous test and enabled us to do a longer, harder day, then our confidence in it would be enormously increased. And confidence was going to be a vital factor when we used oxygen at great altitudes. I thought that if two of us could go from Base Camp to Camp IV and back in one day – a full two-day trip without oxygen – we would have shown its worth. Hunt, happily, agreed to this suggestion and to Tenzing accompanying me.

On May 1st most of the party were on the icefall or up in the Western Cwm, and it was very quiet at Base Camp. I knew that on the following day the closed-circuit team would be attacking the Lhotse face for the first time and I was eager to be at Camp IV when they returned. All afternoon I worked, preparing the two oxygen sets and anxiously watching the weather. My heart sank when soon after lunch the clouds swept over and the perpetual snow started falling again. But this time we were lucky – hardly more than a couple of inches had fallen before the skies cleared and our prospects looked more promising.

We awoke very early to find it clear and cold. We had a quick breakfast and then lifted our oxygen sets on to our backs. I connected Tenzing's up and turned it on and then did the same to my own. At 6.30 a.m. we were away. I knew that our oxygen would be completely exhausted by 11.30, so I set a hard pace. We surged up through the lower icefall and the 40 lb. on our backs seemed like nothing at all. 'This oxygen is certainly the stuff' was my thought as we walked into Camp II after less than an hour and a half's going. Everyone was in bed and it was bitterly cold. A stove was lit and a cup of coffee produced, and then we moved on again. I suggested to Tenzing that he take a lead, but he smiled and waved me on. Refreshed by the hot drink, we found the two inches of fresh snow on the track no problem at all and walked into Camp III after fifty minutes of steady plodding. We had a pleasant chat and another hot drink, and continued on. We crossed the long bridge above the camp and started moving out into the Western Cwm. To our annoyance we suddenly struck deep, soft snow. Obviously the snowfall had been much heavier here and the track was completely wiped out. We plugged grimly on in snow that was sometimes up to our knees. The sun was beating down and the heat and glare were terrific. But I knew we couldn't afford to rest. Taking turns, we drove ourselves on with determination, and finally dragged ourselves into Camp IV at 11.30 – two hours of travelling from

Camp III. We took off our empty sets and crawled into one of the tents for a rest. Considering the efforts we had put in, we recovered remarkably quickly, and were soon taking a keen interest in food and drink. I had a pair of binoculars with me and I searched the Lhotse face for some sign of the assault party, but I could see nothing.

The afternoon passed quite pleasantly. First of all, Wylie and Ward arrived up with heavy loads, and after them came six Sherpas. Before long a much bigger camp had been established. But time was passing and there was still no sign of the others. We were seriously contemplating a rescue party when they appeared in sight, moving very slowly down towards us. From their frequent rests, it was obvious that they'd had a tough day. We went out to meet them. Evans and Bourdillon were very tired, and Hunt looked absolutely exhausted. I was helping him down the slope when he produced a classic of understatement: 'You know, Ed, for the first time I really feel a bit done in!' They told us how they'd managed to reach about 500 feet up the Lhotse face, but how the great heat and heavy loads had more than outweighed the advantages of the oxygen. But they still felt confident that, given suitable conditions, the closed-circuit set would be a powerful contribution to success. Hunt had planned to descend with us, but he was too tired to leave. At 4.20, travelling light without any oxygen, Tenzing and I dashed off into a gathering storm.

We'd only gone a quarter of a mile before the wind and snow swooped down on us with unbelievable fury. In ten minutes our deep upward tracks had been completely wiped out. Our widely spaced flags were, for most of the time, invisible. With only my memory of the lie of the land to guide me, I felt my way down through the driving mist, groaning with the effort of plugging every step again. As each flag suddenly appeared in front of me or beside me, I looked on it as an old friend and searched anxiously for the next. Already great avalanches were booming down the tremendous cliffs of Everest and Lhotse, and sweeping out into the Cwm. At times I had to stop and wait for a few moments, leaning into the wind, until a slight clearing enabled me to see a little ahead through the murk. And then I'd plug on. Our pace seemed to be funereal, but somehow we fumbled our way down. It was a great moment when I found the bridge above Camp III. We crawled across it and in bitter, driving hail made our way slowly to the camp. With a shock I realised there were no tents up. I'd forgotten that they had all been moved up to Camp IV. There was nothing to stop for, so we staggered on.

Now, despite the lack of visibility, I was on familiar ground. But the heavy snow had concealed every hole and small crevasse. I ploughed my way down, spending at least half of my time waist deep in hidden holes and the other half crawling out of them. The light was rapidly fading, but a sudden easing of the heavy snowfall improved the visibility and we made a desperate dash for Camp II. There was no one there. There were tents and sleeping-bags and food, but as I looked at their cold misery I thought of the warm comfort of Base Camp. 'What do you think, Tenzing? Shall we push on down?' Tenzing looked into the gathering dusk and shrugged his shoulders: 'Just as you like!' I thought of the complicated track ahead of us and the deep snow. 'I'm sure I can find the way down the icefall to the glacier. Do you think you can get us home from there?' Tenzing thought he could. I decided the risk was worth it and that we'd go on. I started down into the 'Atom Bomb' area. In the dim light and under its blanket of snow, it was an eerie and frightening sight. The track seemed to have been engulfed; dark holes gaped on every side of us; ghost-like séracs leaned over our heads. For one awful moment I completely lost my sense of direction and searched frantically for the route. I was fighting off a feeling almost of panic when I suddenly recognised the shape of a piece of ice and knew we were on the right road. To cross its last crevasse was like a reprieve to a doomed man.

It was now almost dark and the tumbled mass of ice-blocks all looked the same. It was impossible to try to follow any winding track, so I took a line across country from flag to flag. And when I couldn't see a flag I just kept going the same way and hoped for the best. We went with a wild rush in our race against the light – climbing up on to ice-blocks and slithering down the other side into waist-deep snow, then on over the next boulder. For a period we seemed to be lost. We were still going down, but I could recognise nothing, for the darkness and the blanket of snow made everything the same. It was hard work making the trail in the deep snow and I had to let Tenzing have a go at it. As soon as he got in front of me his figure and the long rope made the whole slope come into perspective. I started recognising parts of the route again. I shouted to Tenzing to move farther to the right. Next moment we slid down a steep slope into 'Hellfire Alley'. It was pitch dark when we crossed the last bridge in the icefall. It wasn't dangerous any more, but we had no torch so couldn't see a thing. We fumbled our way along, falling down snow slopes, running into invisible walls, and tripping over occasional rocks. The lights of Base Camp were a welcome sight, and as we walked up the last slope towards them we were pretty tired. 'Well, we've made it,' I thought, 'and I expect we've proved something. But at the moment I've no idea what it is.'

Next day most of us descended down valley to a rest-camp at Lobuje. To see the grass and flowers again was itself a tonic, and we lay around idly in the sun laughing and talking. Our appetites grew even larger, and we could almost feel the flesh going back on to our lean frames. When we returned to Base Camp three days later, we felt greatly refreshed and eager to get on with the assault. The Lhotse face reconnaissance party was there when we arrived and we noisily cross-questioned them. Apparently they'd met many difficulties but had established Camp V at 22,000 feet and Camp VI at 23,000 feet. In a last thrust, Evans and Bourdillon had reached to over 23,500 feet. They had two main conclusions – firstly, that the Lhotse face was going to be a tough proposition, and secondly, that the closed-circuit oxygen apparatus worked extremely well.

Most of the night John Hunt's light was shining and his typewriter was tapping. But when he called Evans and myself together for a conference next morning, May 7th, he was his usual drawn-faced but positive self. He invited our comments on a list he'd drawn up apportioning certain tasks in the assault to certain people. We agreed with all his selections. We crossed over to the large tent where the whole expedition was gathered, and as we went inside it was impossible not to feel the air of suppressed excitement and anticipation. Hunt started talking, and there was a sudden hush in the tent as everyone concentrated on his words. He explained his view of the problems ahead; the Lhotse face, the establishing of a substantial camp on the South Col, the putting in of a very high camp at 28,000 feet and finally the two assaults with different types of oxygen apparatus. There was nothing new about this, and on every face I could read the same thought, 'Hurry up, John! Tell us what job you've given to me!' John Hunt picked up his list and started reading, and as each name appeared with its selected task, I could hear tense lungs relaxing with a quiet hiss of satisfaction.

The tough problem of the Lhotse face had been given to Lowe, Westmacott, and Band; the vital job of getting a large number of Sherpa porters to the South Col to Noyce and Wylie; the first assault party, using the powerful closed-circuit oxygen apparatus, was to be Evans and Bourdillon; Hunt and

Gregory were the support party to establish Camp IX at 28,000 feet; Tenzing and I were the second assault party using the open-circuit oxygen set.

Tenzing was in the tent with us, and Hunt explained to him in his fluent Hindustani the details of the plan and the allocation of tasks. When Hunt came to his name, Tenzing smiled as though well satisfied. In fact, I think there was general satisfaction except perhaps for poor Mike Ward, who had been asked to act as a reserve. He was finding the responsibilities of being medical officer an unhappy restriction on his climbing activities.

We didn't waste any time putting the plan into operation, but right from the start the Lhotse face party became depleted. Band developed a cold and had to return to Base, and Westmacott, though he tried again and again, seemed unable to drive himself much over 22,000 feet. So the burden of the task fell on the shoulders of George Lowe. By May 11th George was established in Camp VI at a height of 23,000 feet. His only companion was a tough, strong Sherpa, Ang Nyima. In shocking weather conditions these two men worked under great difficulties, cutting innumerable steps on the steep ice-slopes, putting in fixed ropes on the more dangerous stretches, and generally transforming this highly technical route into one that a heavily laden man could follow.

We were getting decidedly worried about the weather. For six weeks not a day had passed without a snowfall, and it seemed to be getting worse. We feared that the monsoon might have arrived already and that our attempts on the summit were doomed to failure. I was working in the Cwm conducting parties of Sherpas from Camp III to Camp IV and back again. For five successive days we had particularly heavy snowfalls, and for five successive mornings I had to break trail up the Cwm in fresh snow a foot to eighteen inches deep. It was most disheartening. But despite the weather the work went on. The majority of our stores had been lifted through the icefall and were well on their way up the Cwm. By May 14th most of us had moved up to live at Camp IV, and George Lowe had succeeded in pushing the route through to 24,000 feet, and found a site for Camp VII.

On May 15th I had my first close look at the Lhotse face. Noyce and I with three Sherpas took loads up to Camp VI. George was there, as he was having a rest-day, but despite his long spell at this considerable height without oxygen, he still looked fresh and fit. I sorted out some gear – a tent, a cooker, some food, and fuel – and divided it up between the three Sherpas and myself. Then we carried it up to Camp VII. Carrying a load and making a trail was hard work at this altitude, and we weren't using oxygen. It was a great thrill to me to arrive at 24,000 feet, as this was the highest I'd been, and I was greatly encouraged to find that I could, if necessary, have gone on a great deal farther. I returned to Advance Base, with a vivid impression of the steepness and difficulties of the route and a great admiration for the work Lowe and Ang Nyima had put in on it.

There now commenced the most frustrating period that the expedition was to experience – a period during which it appeared at times as if the whole attack was breaking down. From our grandstand seat at Advance Base we could watch all the activities on the Lhotse face with binoculars, and every morning a worried line of climbers would be looking anxiously upwards. And none was more anxious than John Hunt.

> '*May* 16*th*: . . . George Lowe and Wilf Noyce started from Camp 6 for 7, but after going half-way returned. George had taken a sleeping pill with disastrous effect and kept falling asleep . . .'

A vital day lost!

'*May* 17*th*: . . . George and Wilf reached Camp 7 and did a short reconnaissance above . . . Wilf then returned to Advance Base with Sherpas and Mike Ward and Da Tenzing stayed with George . . .'

'*May* 18*th*: . . . George, Mike, and Da Tenzing went for a short distance above Camp 7 and then returned to camp. They hadn't gone as far as the previous day . . .'

The excitement at Advance Base when they started off was intense. Hunt was looking more hopeful than he had for a week. We saw their tiny figures moving slowly on the great expanse of the upper Lhotse face. It really looked as if they might get to the top of the Lhotse glacier and traverse across towards the South Col. Perhaps they might get to the South Col itself? And then they suddenly stopped and turned back. Our disappointment was bitter.

'. . . Apparently windy and cold, but it seemed to us at Camp IV that there was a certain lack of drive . . .'

I argued strongly with Hunt. The whole Lhotse attack was too weak; George Lowe had done a good job, but he'd been up there too long and no longer had any punch; if we didn't crack the route to the South Col pretty soon, we might as well go home; we were all sitting down here doing nothing while the expedition was crashing in ruins about our ears. Why couldn't some of us go up and finish off the job?

But our leader, worried as he was, refused to be hastened into any ill-considered action by such wild arguments, however true they might be. His whole purpose was to keep his assault teams fresh for their vital tasks, and he didn't intend to expend them on the Lhotse face. But I could see he was aching to be up there himself.

'*May* 19*th*: . . . We watched Camp 7 with great eagerness but there was no sign of activity. A strong wind
was blowing but this eased about 11 a.m. Still no signs
of life. John very depressed at lack of progress. Band
made a bit of a comeback and took a group of Sherpas
to Camp 7 with loads and reported George's opinion
that it was too windy and cold to start . . .'

Valuable time was passing and our progress up the mountain was virtually at a standstill. Obviously some drastic
action was called for. John Hunt made a strong and coura-
geous decision. He decided to commence immediately the next
phase of the operation – the carrying of equipment and food
up to the South Col. The route there wasn't completed, so
these men would have to make it for themselves. Noyce, who
was leading the first group of Sherpas, had the enormous
responsibility of seeing that they got there. On May 20th he
and his nine Sherpas climbed slowly up to Camp VII. Later
on in the day, George Lowe and his companions returned to
Advance Base. Despite his long spell of ten days on the Lhotse
face without oxygen, George looked astonishingly fit and
declared himself quite ready to return to action after a few
days' rest.

We were out of our tents unusually early on May 21st, for
we knew it was probably our most crucial day. 'Would the
Sherpas start?' was the question we kept asking ourselves.
For a long time nothing happened and a general feeling of
depression spread through the camp. Then, at 10 a.m., there
was a shout from someone and we looked up to see two dots
climbing above Camp VII. The Sherpas had refused to start,
so Noyce and stout-hearted Annullu were trying to get
through by themselves, using oxygen. Our excitement was
intense as we watched them climb steadily up the Lhotse
glacier and then strike out strongly to the left across the

great traverse leading to the South Col. With every hundred feet they gained our spirits rose accordingly.

On the lower slopes, Charles Wylie and the second group of nine Sherpas were making their way slowly up towards Camp VII. With all our South Col Sherpas crowded into Camp VII, our limited supplies of food and fuel up there would be quickly consumed. Either the whole party would have to get to the South Col tomorrow or descend instead into the Cwm, and this would delay the attack by perhaps a week. They must be persuaded to go on!

With a glance at the two figures climbing higher and higher towards the South Col, I went over to John Hunt's tent. Evans was already there. I pleaded with Hunt to let me and Tenzing go up and add a boost to the next day's effort. I knew that by using oxygen, we could easily go from Camp IV to VII in the afternoon and that Tenzing's presence alone would probably be sufficient to inspire his Sherpas to action. I was equally convinced that we were fit enough not to be seriously affected by this effort. To my surprise John readily agreed – I think he'd probably decided on the same course himself; but he stressed the importance of our not going above Camp VII unless it was absolutely necessary.

I rushed off to tell Tenzing the good news and then hastily helped Bourdillon prepare two oxygen sets.

We reached Camp VII at 4.30 p.m., and Noyce and Annullu returned half an hour later. They'd done magnificently and had reached the South Col. I felt they'd broken the spell which seemed to be holding us back. In the evening Tenzing was invaluable; he and Wylie organised all the loads and allocated them to the Sherpas so that we could have an early start. As we crawled into our tents for the night, the general morale in the camp was excellent, and remembering Hunt's instructions I asked Tenzing if he thought the Sherpas could get to the South Col without our going along. Tenzing thought they wouldn't. Wylie was quite prepared to take the whole group up, but he agreed that to ask one man to look after fourteen Sherpas was expecting a bit much. I decided we'd have to go on.

The morning was fine but cold, with a bitter wind. We commenced cooking at 5 a.m., but didn't leave until 8.30. Tenzing and I went on ahead, kicking and cutting a route, while Wylie coaxed and helped the Sherpas along. By the time we reached the top of the Lhotse glacier, the Sherpas were already tired; on the traverse many of them were lying down to rest and crawling on their hands and knees. But somehow they kept on, and thirteen stout-hearted Sherpas climbed the last few hundred feet and dropped their loads on the South Col. It was a great triumph. It meant that our second problem had been overcome; the grim defences of the Lhotse face had been defeated and the South Col had been stocked. The way was now open for the assault.

As Tenzing and I climbed wearily down off the Lhotse glacier towards Advance Base, we met a heavily laden party on the way up. It was the 'closed-circuit team', Evans and Bourdillon, and Hunt himself. In two days they'd be camping on the South Col. The attack was on!

CHAPTER NINE

South Col

I WAS RUNNING FOR my life! Leaping from ice-block to ice-block and frantically jumping crevasse after crevasse, I sought to escape from the monstrous pile of ice that was crashing down behind me. But dodge as I could it was getting closer and closer . . . Suddenly a gigantic crevasse loomed in front of me – I was trapped! In desperation I looked around at the grinding ice surging towards me . . .

I awoke to strangely mixed feelings of discomfort and anticipation. My air-mattress had deflated during the night and my hip was resting on the inhospitable ice. Reluctantly, to escape a rather too realistic dream, I opened my eyes and looked around the familiar surroundings of Camp IV. Our large tent presented a depressing scene in the early morning light. Scattered around the icy floor were the silent, sleeping bodies of my companions, all hidden in the depths of their sleeping-bags. A chaotic mass of oxygen apparatus, rucksacks, spare clothing, ropes, pitons, crampons, and ice-axes cluttered up the remaining room. With a feeling of uneasy distaste, I closed my eyes again. It was just another morning at Camp IV! Life at over 21,000 feet didn't leave you feeling too full of joy and happiness. Suddenly my mind cleared, and I remembered that this was far from being an ordinary day. Probably for me it was the most important day of all, for it was our turn to start on the long slow upward grind that might, with luck, end on the summit of Everest.

My frozen hip brought me back to realities. With a grunt I reluctantly moved an arm from the warmth of the sleeping-bag and fumbled round for the valve of the air-mattress. With some repugnance at the thought of the numerous other mouths that had already chewed on it, I placed it between my lips and began to blow steadily. Slowly I was raised from my chilly proximity to the ice. Not moving from my sleeping-bag, I dragged myself over to the door and looked out. Above me loomed the Lhotse ice-face, every ice-cliff and crevasse standing out clear and hard. Already the morning sun was sharply etching the jagged summit of Lhotse 7,000 feet above us, but the South Col looked grim and foreboding. I thought of Hunt and Evans and Bourdillon in their lonely camp – 'My God! They must be cold up there!' A soft, freezing wind drifted down the Western Cwm, and I shivered violently, then muttered through my sunburnt lips, 'It's fine! We're right – it's fine!' I was spurred to sudden action – 'Thondup! Thondup!' A faint reply and sounds of movement from our cook's tent satisfied me, and with a pleasant glow of virtue I dropped the tent flap and snuggled deep within my sleeping-bag, determined to make no further efforts of will until a hot drink made me at least half human.

In half an hour a cheerful Sherpa face appeared at the tent door, and soon we were grasping large mugs of hot tea. Or perhaps calling it tea is too high praise! Only a man with a constitution of iron could face up to such a drink with any pleasure – a brown hottish liquid with a thick scum of fat, tea leaves, lumps of milk powder, and the remnants of last night's stew. 'High-altitude tea' we called it, and looked on it as a grim necessity that must be forced down into an uneasy stomach at all costs. With loathing I consumed half of it, and then, stimulated by its warmth, dragged myself out of my sleeping-bag. I felt terribly weak, and for one moment the unpleasant thought flashed across my mind that perhaps the altitude was affecting me at last. But reason intervened when I reminded myself that we always felt like this in the morning, anyway. Dressing was a simple process involving merely the pulling on of my boots, but it seemed to take a long time. I dragged myself heavily to my feet and lurched out of the tent. The sun was now fast approaching our camp, and with some eagerness I looked high up the mountain to see what the wind was doing. It looked most encouraging! The usual long plume of wind-driven powder snow was absent, and the long ridge of Lhotse, usually tormented by the wind, looked peaceful and quiet. With my rubber soles sliding on the icy surface, I moved cautiously over the snow to Tenzing's tent and shouted a greeting to his recumbent body. His cheerful grin soon showed he understood my optimistic forecasts, and he crawled out of his bag. I started preparing our oxygen sets, testing the bottles for pressure, carefully examining the tubes and valves and economiser. I turned on all the valves and listened carefully as oxygen rushed from the face-masks in a series of hoarse pants. It seemed all right, but we couldn't afford to have anything going wrong now.

The whole camp stirred to activity as Thondup appeared with breakfast – porridge, tinned bacon (which was generally disliked), and, best of all, fresh eggs which had been collected from the villages some days away in the valleys and carried laboriously up to our camp. I was feeling much better and attacked the food with vigour. The fine weather and the exciting thoughts of what lay ahead were effectively subduing the lethargy of altitude. Into a light cloth bag I forced a sleeping-bag, an air-mattress, and all my spare clothing, and then attached it to my oxygen frame. I looked at the time – it was 9.15 a.m. At Camp V, a thousand feet above us, we could see Lowe and Gregory, with eight Sherpas, winding slowly out on to the Lhotse face. They were to support us in our assault, and had gone up the previous evening to Camp V in order to reduce their climb to Camp VII. Tenzing and I heaved our heavy loads on to our backs and put our oxygen masks on our faces. In order to maintain our strength, we were using oxygen all the way from Camp IV. I carefully checked Tenzing's oxygen set. At one period Tenzing had asked to be allowed to go to the South Col without oxygen, as his experience of the previous year with the oxygen set of the Swiss Expedition had given him little confidence in its value. Now, through extra experience and practice, he fully realised its benefits. But the Sherpas, whose life in the main is a simple one completely devoid of mechanical and scientific gadgets, cannot understand the complicated operations of an oxygen set. It was always necessary to prepare the set for them, to connect up the necessary tubes, to turn it on, and in fact to make sure that it is working at all. Even Tenzing was no exception to this.

Both our sets seemed to be working well. We tied our nylon rope around our waists, mentally checked to see we had left nothing behind, and then, with a wave to the party, and their good wishes and a final 'See that you get up!' ringing in our ears, I led off up the Western Cwm. The trail was beaten hard by the passage of many feet and wound up the easy snow slopes ahead like a giant snake, bending gracefully to avoid impassable or dangerous crevasses. We moved steadily upwards. The weather was perfect with scarcely a breath of wind. Around us towered the tremendous rock and ice-walls of the Western Cwm, and higher still was the incredibly deep blue of the sky. But lovely as the scene was, we seemed cut off from it by the barrier of our oxygen masks. In the thin air every step required a conscious breathing effort, and it demanded most of our attention. I was now feeling in excellent form. Far above us, Lowe and Gregory with their Sherpas were climbing up a steep portion of the Lhotse ice-face. The thought 'I wonder if we can catch them up' drifted idly into my mind, but I shrugged it off as impossible. Almost unconsciously, however, I increased my pace. My 45-Ib. load was dragging uncomfortably at my shoulders as we moved quickly onwards. I glanced back at Tenzing. He seemed to be going well. The track crossed an unstable snow bridge, swung to the right to dodge an impassable crevasse, climbed a steepish slope, and suddenly we were at Camp V.

A deserted camp is always a depressing sight, and this was no exception. Three or four sagging tents with an area of dirty trampled snow between them and in every direction empty containers, ranging from bully-beef tins to oxygen bottles. We took our loads off and had a brief rest. Our view down the Western Cwm was superb! Guarding the entrance to the valley were the great ice-clad buttresses of Nuptse and the West ridge of Everest, while framed between them was the shapely peak of Pumori – the Tibetan for 'daughter peak', and so named by Mallory after his own daughter. Above us the first party was going well and had nearly reached Camp VI. After ten minutes' rest, we resignedly heaved our loads on to our shoulders again, turned on our oxygen and moved on up.

We were now climbing rather more steeply, but the route was still straightforward. Long, gradual traverses helped to make the gain in height easier. We were approaching the first great ice-cliffs of the Lhotse face, and laboured steadily up towards them. We cautiously crossed a dangerous-looking crevasse, climbed up a short but steep snow bump, and then reached a little terrace at the foot of the ice-cliffs. We took off our loads, disconnected the oxygen and removed our masks, and everything seemed to come back into focus as the fresh, cool air played over our heated countenances. We sat on the snow, breathing slowly and deeply, and enjoying the wonderful sweep of glacier and ridge and peak before us.

There was hard and difficult work ahead of us. We strapped our crampons on to our boots, checked the rope tying us together, and replaced our oxygen sets. Then we started up the first really steep slope. A great stairway had been hewn in the hard green ice, and as we climbed slowly up it we were thankful to use a long fixed rope as a handrail. With increasing consciousness of the great drop beneath us, we shuffled across a narrow ice-ledge over a vertical ice-wall. Above us stretched a steep and narrow gully. I had never liked this gully, for at the bottom of it was a large crevasse bridged by a most unstable-looking snow bridge – a snow bridge which with every crossing sagged farther and farther towards some gloomy depths. And to make things worse the gully was dominated by an evil-looking, tottering ice pinnacle which gave the strong impression that it might crash at any time and sweep all before it. There was no escaping it; we must go up. Gingerly I crossed the snow bridge, and in imagination felt it give beneath my feet. Spurred on by my fears, I raced up the gully keeping one apprehensive eye on the ice above until the rope suddenly came tight and the unfortunate Tenzing was almost dragged off his feet. 'Come on, Tenzing!' But now I was out of danger and could relax on an easy snow shelf as Tenzing hurried up to join me.

Ahead of us we could see a long rope hanging down a very steep ice-slope. This was undoubtedly the most difficult part of the Lhotse face. Above us now was a slope, about 400 feet long, of hard, green ice. I moved to the bottom of it and took a firm grasp on the rope, and gave it a great tug to make sure it was firmly attached. Reassured, I critically eyed the approach to the ice-slope. A rickety route ran for twenty feet up an unstable, almost vertical ice-cliff. Like an old hen, I grubbed around with my ice-axe trying to scratch out a few steps in the crumbling ice. Then I resigned myself to the inevitable, took a firm grip on the suspended rope, and with a rush clawed my way to the top. Tenzing scrambled energetically up behind me and we moved on again. With an instinctive tensing of muscles and nerves, I traversed steeply up the ice-slope. I placed each step with considerable care, and took every advantage of the fixed rope as the route became more and more exposed. Far below now – almost under our feet it seemed – was Camp V. I glanced back. Tenzing was moving steadily behind me, head down and shoulders bent as he lifted himself determinedly from step to step. The slope went on and on, never ending! Suddenly I could see Camp VI – a tiny ledge under an ice-wall. With a feeling of relief, I climbed up to it.

Ten days before, Camp VI had been the main base for operations on the Lhotse face, but now it was a camp only in name. Some odd pieces of equipment, a few ropes, and some empty tins were the only evidence left of an uncomfortable but essential staging point. We sat down on the ledge and dangled our feet over the slope below. It looked awfully steep! I grasped an empty oxygen bottle lying nearby and dropped it over the edge. With horrifying rapidity it slithered down the ice, going faster and faster. It shot into the air above a great precipice, and then seemed to float gracefully down for an unbearably long time before glancing crazily off an ice pinnacle and disappearing into the depths of a crevasse. With a hollow feeling inside, I dragged myself a little farther on to the ledge. This was certainly not a place to fall off.

We moved on again, winding in and out amongst crevasses and climbing some steep but short ice-slopes. A long traverse to the left gained us considerable height and took us to the foot of a great line of broken ice-cliffs. We moved along the foot of them, scrambling in and out amongst broken debris, and then climbed sharply up a long and steep slope to reach a little ledge of snow – the first flat place since Camp VI. Only a short distance above us now were the stragglers

from the first party, making slow and heavy work of it. Lowe
and Gregory had already disappeared behind the ice pinnacle
concealing Camp VII. Feeling a little like an express train
overhauling a slow freight, we caught up with these men and
made sure that they were capable of reaching the camp.

We started up the last few hundred feet; a careful move
along a narrow ice-ridge with a deep crevasse on the left, a
slow and cautious climb of a steep ice-bluff, and we were at
the foot of the final slopes. We had climbed 3,000 feet and
were a little tired. With the pleasant feeling of a job nearly
done, we slowly surmounted the last line of steps, climbed
around the side of an ice pinnacle and emerged just below
the tents of Camp VII. I glanced at my watch – it was only
12.30 p.m. We'd done it in 3 1/4 hours – easily the fastest time
yet. With a glow of ill-concealed satisfaction, I strode up to
the tents and cheerfully greeted Lowe and Gregory.

That afternoon at Camp VII was the finest we'd had for
six weeks. The sun beat down with considerable warmth and
there was hardly a breath of wind. We really felt that the
weather was taking a turn for the better, and it looked as
though we had a chance of getting the few fine days that
were essential if our attack on the summit was to have any
hope of success. In unaccustomed fashion we strolled around
outside our tents, enjoying the view and taking numerous
photographs. We prepared everything for the next day – loads
were made up for the Sherpas and oxygen sets supplied with
full bottles. Eight Sherpas were spending the night with us
at Camp VII. Three of these were specially picked men with
good records whom we had kept in reserve to carry loads for
the camp we planned to establish at about 28,000 feet. The
other five were a magnificent group of men who had all
carried loads to the South Col for us before and who had
volunteered to do it a second time.

The sun disappeared behind a distant peak and freezing

cold descended. But we were comfortably inside our sleeping-bags sipping at a mug of hot soup and munching a few biscuits. Lying here in our cosy sleeping-bags, surrounded by cheerful companions, we were hardly conscious of our 24,000 feet, and life wasn't too bad. In order to guarantee ourselves a good and restful sleep, we were on this occasion using sleeping oxygen. This meant breathing oxygen at only a very slow rate of flow, but because of our inactivity at night it had a considerable effect. We connected up our oxygen and then settled down for the night. Soon Tenzing's deep and rhythmical breathing showed he was fast asleep, and after I had run over in my mind the plans for the following day, I quickly joined him.

I awoke feeling cold and uncomfortable. Our oxygen had run out and the whole camp was frozen and still. I glanced at my watch – it was very early, but I knew it would take a long time to prepare our breakfast and depart. I stirred the sleeping Tenzing, and then bellowed out across to the other tents to wake the Sherpas and get them to start up the kerosene stoves. They were understandably reluctant to respond, but when Tenzing joined in we produced a duet that would have wakened the dead and finally achieved a weak acknowledgment of our summons. Soon we heard the familiar rattling sounds of the stove-lighting operation. Any task at this altitude takes a long time, as the brain and body, affected by the lack of oxygen, have little co-ordination or concentration. It was at least an hour and a half before we managed to get a lukewarm mug of tea, and with this we munched a few biscuits. We'd all had a reasonably good night, thanks to the oxygen, but it took a tremendous mental effort to drag ourselves out of our warm bags and pull on our boots.

Tenzing crawled out of the tent first, and I crawled after him. It was another lovely morning at Camp VII, though high on the mountain a cloud of powder snow was being blown off the ridge. But it didn't look too bad. I was joined by Lowe and Gregory, and we optimistically discussed our prospects. Meanwhile Tenzing was hastening the other Sherpas in their preparations. We issued out the loads. On one rope we tied the three 'high-altitude' Sherpas, and on another the five who were only going to the South Col. Lowe and Gregory roped up together and so did Tenzing and I. A final check to see that we had everything and we moved out of camp. There was no initial easy going to enable us to get warmed up to our task, for our first move was to cross a large crevasse by a difficult and dangerous snow bridge. Climbing cautiously but rather clumsily, we belayed each other across on the rope, and then followed the line of steps cut across the steep ice-slope above.

The upper Lhotse face continued in a succession of steep and difficult ice-walls. Nowhere was there a place where we could really relax. I led off upwards. Despite my usual early morning feeling of debility and general disinterest, I could feel my uncomplaining leg muscles taking the load easily as I forced myself upwards. I must be going well! Pausing only to clear any fresh snow out of the ice-steps, I continued up, feeling a certain fierce joy in throwing myself against the barrier of altitude and beating it. I didn't need to worry about Tenzing. I knew he'd be plugging up behind, climbing safely and with determination. We were now in the sun and our spirits lightened accordingly. We were steadily drawing away from the rest of the party, and I knew we'd have to stop and wait for them. But first we had to cross a last crevasse and reach the top of the Lhotse glacier. This crevasse had almost stopped us getting up the mountain. Deep and wide, it stretched right across the Lhotse face. And there was no snow bridge, so we were being forced to cross by a way none of us liked. We moved up and gloomily eyed it. The upper and lower lips of the crevasse were overhanging the icy depths and stretched to within three feet of each other. By stepping on to one overhanging lip and stretching across to the other we could cross – as long as neither step gave way. I signalled to Tenzing to hold the rope tight and then, stepping as lightly as I could, I shot across, getting a vivid impression of unpleasant depths below. I brought Tenzing across on the rope, and we moved up a few feet to a safe spot before settling down in the snow to wait and rest.

Our view was most impressive. In front of us the Lhotse face dropped 4,000 feet to the Western Cwm, making us very conscious of our height. We were at 25,000 feet, and on our left we could just see over the top of the fantastic ice pinnacles on the crest of the great mountain wall enclosing the Western Cwm on the southern side. Beyond these pinnacles was a vista of cloud-filled valleys and jagged ice-peaks, seeming to stretch for hundreds of miles across Nepal. A murmur of voices and some grunts of effort told us that the others were crossing the crevasse, and they soon appeared, moving laboriously, and with each step a slow and studied action. With gasps of relief the Sherpas sank down beside us. Our five South Col 'tigers' looked cheerful and fit, but Lowe told us that the three high-altitude 'specials' were not going at all well. This was rather a worry, as we were expecting to get a good deal of help from them.

I was munching a little chocolate when a shout from George Lowe attracted my attention. I looked in the direction he was pointing and had one of the greatest thrills I have ever experienced. High above us loomed the South Summit of Mount Everest, joined to the South Col by the long South-east ridge. And moving on to that ridge were two tiny figures – it was the first assault team, Evans and Bourdillon. Excitedly we watched them. They were going well, very well! We knew that their primary objective was to reach the South Summit, but our hopes were high that they might have sufficient time and energy to go on towards the top. Then we noticed two more figures a little distance behind, and going rather more slowly. According to our plans, this should have been John Hunt and two Sherpas carrying loads of equipment and oxygen up to the ridge for the second assault party to use when we established our camp. But apparently only one of the Sherpas had started. Evans and Bourdillon were going in great style, and the gap between the two parties was steadily widening. Feeling very excited, we loaded ourselves up again and started out on to the great traverse leading to the South Col. The Sherpas, fully convinced that the two men were going to reach the top, were in a cheerful and noisy frame of mind, but Tenzing, in reply to my enthu-siastic comments, seemed strangely silent. The reason for this we found later, for when we reached the South Col and before we knew how far Evans and Bourdillon had gone, Tenzing confided to John Hunt that he considered a Sherpa should have been in the first party to reach the top.

Lowe and Gregory had the responsibility of getting the Sherpas to the Col and had to stay with them, but I was keen on getting up there quickly and giving any assistance that was needed to the first party. The route lay across the tremen-dous slope which runs in one great sweep from the summit of Lhotse to the Western Cwm. I headed on to this great traverse with a rush. The tracks made by the previous party were largely intact and little work was necessary. This was a pleasant change from the previous time I'd crossed this slope, when we had to kick and cut steps the whole way across. Moving steadily and rhythmically, taking no rests at all, I soon became almost oblivious to our surroundings. The wonderful views opening up all around us, the terrific depths underneath, meant nothing. My whole life was encompassed by the next step and the next breath. Forcing my lungs to the utmost, I sought to draw in the maximum of life-giving air – to relieve the dreadful feelings of deadness in the limbs and pain in the chest. My whole body was crying out for rest, but I knew it was just a weak delusion of the flesh that had to be ignored. 'South Col or bust!' – that was the story! Ruthless in my determination, I looked around at the luck-less Tenzing. But I need have no worries. Head down, he was matching me step for step with dogged determination. We were gaining height rapidly. High up, the wind was rising and the South-east ridge was enveloped in cloud. But as we strained our eyes upwards, the ridge suddenly cleared, and we could see Evans and Bourdillon still climbing strongly and now half-way up to the South Summit. Already they were nearly as high as men had ever been. John Hunt and his companion had stopped a little way up the ridge and were going no farther. The clouds closed in again and we concen-trated all our attention on the slopes ahead.

In order to reach the Col, we had to climb to the top of the rocky Geneva Spur at 26,000 feet, and then drop down a slope on the other side. We came to the end of the great traverse and started climbing a steep snow gully. Kicking steps in the loose soft snow, we dragged ourselves upwards, taking advantage of any rock ledges we could find for a firm foothold. We scrambled up a mixture of rock and snow, and then finally to the top of the Geneva Spur. Towering above our heads was our mountain, looking depressingly steep and formidable. Clouds were streaming off it under the strong wind, and we could see no sign of Evans and Bourdillon. Several hundred feet below us was the South Col – icy, barren, and windswept! Down there in a little lonely group were three small tents, their canvas bucking and thrashing in the wind. Lowe, Gregory, and the Sherpas were out of sight and well behind us, so without waiting for them we moved down the slope and approached the tents. In response to our shouts the door of the middle tent opened and a face slowly emerged

– the face of Sherpa Balu! I have never seen anyone looking more ashamed of himself. Balu was a big, strong, swanking chap who had thrown his weight about a good deal lower down, and had been recommended by Tenzing as one of the special high-altitude men. But on the South Col his nerve had cracked and he had refused to go any higher. Looking now thoroughly shifty and unreliable, he greeted us sullenly and then withdrew into his lair. We turned our oxygen off and removed our loads. My eyes strayed irresistibly back to the great slopes above us, and I suddenly noticed two black dots on the snow, moving slowly and painfully down towards us. It must be John Hunt and Da Namgyal! I asked Tenzing to prepare some hot drinks as quickly as possible, but knew this would take some time. Without bothering to use any oxygen, I started up the icy slopes.

Hunt and Da Namgyal were moving at a funeral pace. They seemed only able to walk fifty feet before slumping down on the ice for a rest. Spurred on by their obvious distress, I made rapid height, and was encouraged to find how quickly I could move without oxygen at this altitude. As the others came closer, I could tell by their stiff and clumsy movements just how tired they were. I reached them just as an exhausted John Hunt dropped to the ice once more. It was good to see them again and to feel I could help them. Hunt told me how he and Da Namgyal had carried their heavy loads up on to the South-east ridge as high as they possibly could. When they couldn't go a step farther and couldn't even crawl on their hands and knees, they left their loads in a little pile and struggled down. Hunt was terribly tired, for in his unselfish urge to leave supplies of oxygen as high as possible on the mountain, he had left his half-used bottle of oxygen up there and had come down without it. He was obviously going to need assistance down to the tents. I looked at Da Namgyal. Faithful and strong, he is a magnificent type of

Sherpa, and as he had looked after me in the earlier part of the expedition, I had a particular affection for him. His cheerful and determined smile showed he still had a little strength in reserve.

I put John Hunt's arm over my shoulder and held him firmly around the waist and started down the ice-slope again. We were going very slowly and frequent rests were necessary. When John slipped down on to the ice once more, I realised that something more drastic was required. I left him sitting on the ice and raced back down to camp. I still had some oxygen left in my set, so I heaved it on to my back and returned. John was sitting slumped over on the ice and didn't seem to have moved. I put the oxygen mask on his face and turned on the maximum flow. It had an immediate effect. Soon he was able to drag himself to his feet and, with my assistance, move slowly down the ice-slope and finally up to the tents. We crawled inside, and as John lay resting on his sleeping-bag, I flooded the tent with oxygen. The door opened and Tenzing thrust in a hot drink to complete the recovery.

Suddenly we heard excited voices. The tent swayed and shook as George Lowe thrust his bearded countenance into the entrance and shouted 'They're up! By God, they're up!' Then an elated George explained how the clouds had cleared for a moment and he'd seen the tiny figures of Evans and Bourdillon moving up on the South Summit. This was wonderful news! The South Summit was 28,700 feet high – only 300 feet from the top – and a lot higher than men had ever been before. To reach it in one day from the South Col was a tremendous effort.

Excitedly we discussed the likelihood of their going on towards the top. It was already fairly late, and we knew it was a long way and their oxygen might be running short. They were going to have a difficult decision to make up there on the South Summit. Automatically my thoughts drifted back a week to Camp IV when we'd been discussing the possibility of the first assault party having to make this same decision. Tom Bourdillon, in his slow and steady way, had told us not to worry, as both he and Charles Evans were pretty sensible chaps with a keen desire to go on living. I felt quite happy about Charles – he was just about the most sensible chap I knew – but I wasn't quite so sure about Tom. I had a great respect for Tom's bulldog determination, but I didn't feel too sure that it mightn't at times influence his judgment. I spoke to John Hunt and found that exactly the same conversation and the same reaction had been drifting through his mind. Well, it was no use worrying! We could only wait and see!

I crawled out of the tent. It was bitterly cold. The wind was blowing strongly and the mountain was enveloped in cloud. The Sherpas who were carrying loads to the Col for us for the second time had just arrived. Looking fit and strong despite their exhausting carry, they cheerfully answered our inquiries after their welfare, and told us they were quite capable of getting down to Camp VII again. As they were our most experienced Sherpas, we thought it safe to send them down without escort. They deposited their loads, had a quick drink, and then couldn't resist a hasty souvenir hunt amongst the remnants of the Swiss tents before setting off back along their tracks, accompanied by a cheerful Da Namgyal and a sullen Balu, both of whom wanted, understandably, to get down into the Western Cwm as quickly as possible.

Clad in every bit of our clothing, George Lowe and I set to work to make the camp shipshape. We had three tents; a two-man Meade with A poles at each end; a larger pyramid developed from an Arctic type; and a small light dome. All these tents were flapping furiously in the wind and their guy-ropes needed tightening. George and I commenced prising boulders out of their icy beds and carrying them to the tents as anchors. We found that many of the guy-ropes had almost frayed through. As the consequences of this could have been rather unpleasant, we prevented any likelihood of a recurrence by cutting short lengths of nylon rope and attaching them to the tents as guys. We then anchored them securely around a number of big boulders. After a great deal of work and periodic visits to our sleeping-bags to get numbed hands back to life, we had the tents organised to resist the worst of weather.

Our thoughts and attention had never strayed far from the ridge above, but we had seen nothing further of Evans and Bourdillon. More worrying, perhaps, was the non-appearance of our three Sherpa 'specials'. It was a great relief to us when they came over the Geneva Spur and descended slowly down towards us. Our plans required all three of them to carry loads for us higher on the mountain, so we were a bit worried to see that Ang Temba was weaving his way down the slope like a drunken man. As he approached the tents, he stumbled and fell slowly on to his face and lay there – dead to the world! On the South Col you become hard – my only thought was 'Blast it! That's one less to carry a load tomorrow!' We put Ang Temba inside the tent, out of the wind.

A cry from the observant George Lowe told us he'd caught sight of Evans and Bourdillon. Eagerly we looked where he was pointing. The clouds had cleared for a moment and there they were – still at over 27,000 feet, but now crossing from the ridge into the steep snow couloir which leads down to the long slopes above the South Col. They seemed to be going very slowly! Just as the clouds blotted out our view, we saw them start down the couloir. 'Thank God, they are safe!' We saw nothing more for ten minutes until the wind again relented and swept the clouds aside. We picked them out again. To our surprise they were already at the bottom of the couloir. They seemed to have got down it extraordinarily quickly. Now they were going very slowly indeed. We could see they needed help. George grabbed his movie-camera, and then the two of us started up the slopes towards them.

The two men were an awe-inspiring sight! Clad in all their bulky clothes, with their great loads of oxygen on their backs and masks on their faces, they looked like figures from another world. They moved silently down towards us – a few stiff, jerky paces – then stop! Then a few more paces! They must be very near to complete exhaustion. With a lump in my throat, I climbed up to where they now stood waiting, silent and with bowed shoulders. From head to foot they were encased in ice. There was ice on their clothing, on their oxygen sets, and on their rope. It was hanging from their hair and beards and eyebrows; they must have had a terrible time in the wind and the snow! Feeling more emotional than I thought possible, I threw my arms around their tired shoulders and muttered some familiar abuse. Charles Evans thumped me weakly in the ribs, and his calm lilting Welsh voice broke the spell and everything seemed to come back to normal.

George Lowe had conscientiously filmed our meeting, but now he joined us and lightened the air with a vigorous greeting. Despite their exhausted condition, the two men were carrying in their hands two bottles of oxygen – oxygen which the Swiss had jettisoned at the bottom of the couloir the previous autumn. Bourdillon had thought they might be useful for sleeping purposes on the South Col. We took the bottles from them and started helping them slowly down the hill. Soon we were met by Hunt and Gregory. And then Tenzing arrived with hot soup. He gently wiped the ice off their beards and held the steaming mug of soup to their lips. It took a long time to get up the small slope to the tents.

Evans and Bourdillon had a great deal to tell. Their original plan was to leave very early in the morning, but they had experienced great trouble in getting their complicated closed-circuit oxygen sets to work. The valves kept icing up, and at times it seemed they wouldn't be able to start. At 7.30 they managed to get their sets going, and they set off from the South Col. They were breathing almost pure oxygen and this gave them great vigour, so they were able to climb quickly up on to the South-east ridge and make rapid height up it. At 28,300 feet – already higher than any men had ever been before – they reached the bottom of the long, very steep slope running up to the South Summit. They could see that ahead of them were few, if any, places to rest, so they decided to change over to a fresh bottle of oxygen, even although their first bottle was not completely exhausted. They couldn't take the risk of having their oxygen run out while they were doing some difficult or dangerous climbing. Leaving their nearly empty bottles behind them on the ridge as a reserve, they started off again. It was immediately apparent that something was wrong with Evans' set. Despite frantic efforts to fix it, they were never fully successful. It must have been terribly frustrating to Bourdillon, who had put so much work and faith into the closed-circuit oxygen. Impatient to be on, Bourdillon continued up the severe slopes ahead, with Evans trailing behind and having considerable difficulty with his breathing. It was a wonder that he could keep going at all!

After a grim struggle, they reached their primary objective – the South Summit – and were the first men to look along the ridge towards the top. They told us that the ridge looked a very formidable barrier indeed.

They then had to make a difficult decision – should they go on or turn back? They had only a limited amount of oxygen left, they were tired, and the ridge ahead was harder than anything up which they'd yet been, but to balance these factors was the tantalising thought that their life's ambition was almost within their grasp – the summit of Mount Everest! Evans was of the view that they had neither the strength nor oxygen to continue safely, while Bourdillon thought he might have a chance if he went on alone. After some discussion, a reluctant Bourdillon agreed to turn back. Their trip down the ridge must have been a nightmare. Too tired to climb safely, they stumbled down with frequent slips and falls, and only a kindly fate saving them from disaster. As Charles Evans rather wryly put it later, 'We yo-yoed our way down on the rope!' Their quick descent of the couloir was now explained – they'd fallen down it, and only the good fortune of some soft snow at the bottom had saved them from injury or worse. But they had got down – that was the main thing – and after a feat of courage and endurance as great as had ever been performed by men at high altitudes. We felt terrifically elated and encouraged by their efforts.

We sorted ourselves out for the night. The three Sherpa porters were together in the little dome tent; Hunt, Evans, and Bourdillon, in an unselfish effort to give the second assault any little extra comfort which might maintain their strength, crowded into the two-man Meade tent; Lowe, Gregory, Tenzing, and I were in the larger pyramid tent. Hunched over against the wind, I made a final check to see that all our guy-ropes were intact, and then crawled into the pyramid tent. I looked into a scene of utter confusion. Gregory was lying stolidly full-length in his sleeping-bag on top of his air-mattress and seemed to fill half of the tent. Lowe was struggling with a half-inflated air-mattress, a sleeping-bag, and some bottles of oxygen, in a determined effort to get enough room to lie down between Gregory and the wall of the tent. Tenzing, sitting cross-legged, effectively occupied the rest of the room as he watched with an inscrutable air a vast yellow flame, three feet high, which was surging from a kerosene stove between his knees. (None of the Sherpas ever seemed to grasp the fact that it was necessary to prime the stove thoroughly with spirit before it would go effectively.)

There didn't seem to be any room for me! With a hearty cry of 'Hold tight! Here I come!' I forced my way inside, keeping a wary eye on the flaming cooker and giving a few helpful suggestions as to how to get it going properly. I decided, somewhat reluctantly, to sleep between Tenzing and the other wall of the tent, so after I'd inflated my air-mattress – nearly knocking the cooker over in the process – I pushed it down into the minute space still left for me. Leaving all my clothes on, I wriggled down inside the sleeping-bag, and then collapsed, panting furiously after the effort. As a result of Tenzing's patience or my encouraging advice, the cooker was now going properly and was melting some snow for soup. We were all feeling hungry, which was a very good sign, so we spent the next few hours getting a satisfactory meal out of our limited resources: biscuits, jam, honey, sardines, dates, chocolate, cheese, tinned fruit, and hot soup were the main ingredients, but we probably got the majority of our energy requirements out of mug after mug of hot water flavoured with lemon crystals and sweetened with vast quantities of sugar. Sugar was our main standby, and each of us ate nearly a pound of it a day. The honey was a rather unexpected delicacy, as we hadn't carried any up with us. But on the Col we had found two pots left by the Swiss the previous autumn, and the contents were still in excellent condition.

With the meal completed, Tenzing turned off the cooker, and then squeezed down into his sleeping-bag between us. We were going to use sleeping oxygen in order to try to get some rest during the night, so, panting and grunting, we rolled an oxygen bottle into position between each pair of us. Tenzing and I were using the same bottle. I connected up the necessary tubes and reducing valves and attached our face masks. I then turned the tap on and tested each mask to see that the oxygen was flowing freely by the simple method of holding a lighted match in front of it. If the match flared up and burnt fiercely, it showed oxygen was present. All seemed well, so I handed Tenzing his mask and watched him as he put it on. I then adjusted my own and crawled deep into my bag. George Lowe blew out the candle.

As our familiar but uncomfortable little world faded into darkness, the harsh reality of our situation flooded into my mind. I could hear the wind roaring menacingly as it flowed in a mighty unrelenting stream over the inhospitable wastes of the South Col. In response to it our tent was flapping in a tormented fury and seeking to wrench itself from its moorings. It didn't seem possible for the material to stand such a thrashing, and, in imagination, I could see us lying exposed and unprotected amongst the ice and boulders. Crammed immovably between Tenzing and the quivering wall, I could feel the icy breath from outside penetrating through my sleeping-bag, through my down clothing and right into my bones! I felt a terrible sense of fear and loneliness. 'What was the sense in it all? A man was a fool to put up with it! And for what?' Shuddering with the cold, I tried to put such unprofitable thoughts aside, and compose my mind so that the time might pass a little more quickly. Under the merciful effects of the oxygen I drifted into a half-world of noise and cold and sleep—but above all, of sleep . . .

That night on the South Col was just about the most unpleasant I had ever experienced. I didn't have enough room to stretch out to my full length, and jammed tight as I was, turning over was a task that required a good deal of thought and a lot of effort, and always resulted in a spasm of panting. The tent was constantly thumping me in the ribs to remind me of what the wind was like outside. My face felt sticky and clammy under the oxygen mask. But, worst of all, the cold made life a dull misery. All during the night as I dozed and tossed and turned, I kept one eye on the luminous dial of my watch and prayed for the hours to pass more quickly. I must have slept a good deal. At four in the morning I came back to full consciousness with a bump and found that our sleeping oxygen had run out. My air-mattress had deflated and my frozen hip was resting on the ice. Outside, the wind was reaching a new crescendo of fury and our chances of starting up the mountain seemed non-existent. But we must be ready in case the wind dropped. I jabbed the uncomplaining Tenzing in the ribs, murmured a few words about the cooker, and then snuggled back into the depths of my sleeping-bag.

Breathing quickly and audibly Tenzing sat up and commenced to light the burner. Under the drag of altitude all his movements seemed slow and languid, and it was a long time before the burner was going properly. I blew some air into my collapsed mattress, and as the temperature of the tent rose a few degrees life became a little more bearable. I was feeling quite hungry. I started rummaging around for food and disturbing my companions, but soon all of us were munching biscuits in the flickering light of the stove. I had put a thermometer against the wall of the tent, and it showed the temperature was 25 degrees below zero Centigrade, 45 degrees of frost Fahrenheit. Time passed quite pleasantly as we ate and drank and told each other what a miserable night we'd had. George Lowe, in particular, had had an unenviable time. Through a tiny hole in the tent wall he'd been bombarded all night by a stream of freezing air and powder snow – his sleeping-bag was white with frost. It was now quite light, and it was astonishing to see how our fears had vanished with the darkness. Lowe, Gregory, and I discussed the weather pessimistically. It was quite obvious that if we started we wouldn't get a hundred feet above the camp unless the wind dropped. The only thing we could do was wait. I decided to go over to the other tent and discuss the matter with John Hunt.

Getting dressed was a simple matter. I had slept with all

my clothes on, including boots, so I just had to pull myself
out of my sleeping-bag and I was ready to go. I rolled over
to the tent door and started fumbling with the tapes which
tied it up. They were covered with ice and were very stub-
born. They came loose with a rush, and as the door gaped
open a stinging shower of powder snow swept into the tent.
The view outside was miserable in the extreme – a chaos of
ice and rocks veiled by a driving maelstrom of snow. A chorus
of complaints from my companions spurred me to unhappy
action. I crawled out of the tent and staggered weakly to my
feet. Next moment I was on my knees again – blown there
by the bitter wind. Twenty yards away was the other tent. I
didn't try standing up again, but crawled across the ice and
rocks on my hands and knees. High above us a great trail of
snow and cloud was streaming off the mountain.

I reached the Meade tent and shouted hoarsely to its
inmates. The door opened and I crawled thankfully inside.
The congestion was frightful, and all I could see of Hunt,
Evans, and Bourdillon was a confused mass of faces, arms, and
bodies. I sat down on some unidentified legs and we discussed
the weather. They all agreed that no upward move was
possible. It was essential, however, in order to conserve our
supplies and because of the danger of their deteriorating physical condition, that Evans and Bourdillon must go down. All
three of them, in fact, looked very weak after their exhausting
experiences of the previous day and the unpleasant night, and
I felt rather worried as I crawled back to the pyramid tent
to impart my fears to Lowe and Gregory.

Half-way through the morning the wind started to ease a
little and John Hunt moved into our tent so that Evans and
Bourdillon could have sufficient room to get themselves ready
for the trip down. I went over to see if I could give them any
assistance, and found them still lying there, quietly talking.
They were discussing the view they'd had of the final ridge

running from the South Summit to the top, and trying to compare it with other ridges they knew in the Alps. They couldn't remember anything they'd seen quite like it, and the only comparison they could make was to say that it must be very similar to the descriptions Lowe and I had given of some of the great snow and ice ridges in New Zealand. Our New Zealand tales had lost nothing in the telling, so I was rather appalled by their comparison. Would we be able to cope with that sort of ridge at nearly 29,000 feet? Poor Tom was still berating himself for not having gone on alone from the South Summit, and seemed to be living in a vague mental depression from which he'd emerge every now and then with a new set of figures and times to prove that he could have done it. We were only thankful he hadn't tried, as Charles Evans and the rest of us were convinced that he would never have returned.

Towards midday they emerged from the tent and started strapping their crampons on to their boots. Ang Temba was going down too, as he'd been sick all night. I helped them to rope up, and then watched them start off towards the slopes leading to the Geneva Spur and the Western Cwm. Ang Temba went first, with a glassy stare of complete incomprehension in his eyes; then Tom Bourdillon; and finally Charles Evans as anchor-man. They were going very slowly indeed. To conserve supplies for the assault, they weren't using oxygen, and they seemed pitifully weak without it. As I watched, Tom Bourdillon bent gradually forward, and then, to my horror, fell full length on to the ice. For a moment he didn't stir, while the others waited helplessly. Then he dragged himself on to his elbows; then on to his knees, and finally to his feet. Swaying slightly, he stood for a few moments gathering his strength, and then took a few slow paces upwards. The effort was too much for him and he crashed forward once again. To see Tom's great body sprawling on the ice brought home to me, as nothing else had, the dangers of high altitude – the narrow margin between survival and extinction. With visions of the immense labour involved in carrying Tom's fifteen stone down the mountain, I hurried up the slope towards them. Tom was still down on the ice and seemed incapable of moving. We decided we'd have to use some oxygen. Charles and I returned quickly to the tents, prepared an oxygen set and carried it back up. Tom was now on his hands and knees. Charles put the mask on his face and turned the oxygen on full strength. It brought life back into Tom's body and he was able to get to his feet. Still breathing oxygen, he started up the slope at a snail's pace.

I returned to the tents feeling very worried. I crawled in with John Hunt and George Lowe, and told them of what had occurred and of my fears that the three men would never get down. I thought that someone should go down with them. John immediately agreed that this was essential, and suggested that George was the man to do it. This hardly worked in with George's plans – or mine for that matter – and George didn't hesitate to suggest that John should go down himself. But John's whole thought was bound up in the main assault, and his responsibilities were weighing heavily on him, so he felt he must stay and see it through. George pointed out rather forcibly that John was by now physically incapable of giving any assistance other than moral support, but John was adamant – he felt he couldn't go down at this crucial stage. A very disgruntled George prepared to leave. And then John came to a sudden decision! It had suddenly penetrated into his tired mind that our carrying strength was so depleted that if George went down it might prejudice the whole attack. Immediately casting aside all his deep-seated feelings and worries, he decided to descend himself. I have never admired him more than for this difficult decision.

George Lowe started up the slope carrying Tom Bourdillon's pack, and I helped John to get ready. As John gathered together his few personal articles, we talked. He told me of his deep belief that we had a duty to climb the mountain if we could. That so many thousands of people had pinned their faith and hope on us that we couldn't let them down. 'And so, Ed, the main thing is to get down safely, but I know you'll get to the top if you possibly can!' In a rather shamefaced and uncomfortable Anglo-Saxon way, he handed me a small envelope and asked me if I'd leave it on top. I opened it and found in it a small white crucifix. John had received it in the post, with a little note requesting that it be left on the summit. The idea had instinctively appealed to his idealistic nature. I put it in the pocket of my wind-proof.

I offered to carry John's pack for him to the top of the Geneva Spur, and we left the tent together. I knew that John was in a fairly weak condition after his three nights on the South Col, but until I started walking behind him I didn't realise just how serious it was. With frequent stops for breath, he dragged himself up the slope, weaving groggily from side to side. But the worrying thing was that all the time he kept saying how well he was feeling and how he'd get the other chaps down safely. I don't think he had any idea how weak he was. We arrived at the top of the Geneva Spur in time to see Bourdillon, despite his oxygen, flat on his face in the snow. This was the last straw! Charles Evans seemed the only rational member of the party. I whispered in his ear – 'For God's sake, Charles, keep an eye on John! He's out on his feet but doesn't realise it!' Charles turned on me his warm and friendly smile and said, 'Don't worry, Ed – I'll get them down!' It is some indication of the vast respect I had for Charles that I felt a slight easing of my worry at his words. The four of them moved off. Four tired men – most of them with only the vaguest idea of what they were doing, and the technical difficulties of the great traverse and the Lhotse ice-face in front of them! I felt pretty disheartened as I stood there with George Lowe, watching them disappearing out of sight – the blind leading the blind! As we descended back to the tents, I gave vent to my worries and berated George for not having gone down with them. 'It will be your fault, George, if they don't get down! Not that that will be much consolation!' Poor George had already had much the same thought, and spent the rest of the day castigating himself. One isn't very logical on the South Col!

The party did get down safely, but not without a grim struggle. They had nearly reached Camp VII when Ang Temba fell off a snow bridge into a crevasse and hung there upside down on the rope. The other men stood there help-lessly, as they didn't have the strength to pull him out. Fortunately Wilfrid Noyce and Michael Ward were in Camp VII and dragged the unfortunate Ang Temba to the surface and helped the weary men into camp.

I spent most of the afternoon on the South Col preparing our oxygen sets and making up loads for the following day. I tested masks, adjusted flow rates, connected up bottles, and generally took three hours to do what I could have done in half an hour at sea level. George Lowe and I ventured on one little reconnaissance and braved the wind to cross on to the east side of the Col, and had a wonderful view down on to the great east face of Everest. In previous years, George and I had visited every side of Everest except this, and it was a tremendous thrill to look down on to the Kangshung glacier 8,000 or 9,000 feet below us, and mentally link up this last stretch of country with that we already knew. We had to struggle back to our tents in the teeth of the wind, and arrived back with frozen cheeks and watering eyes. We were greatly encouraged to find how fit we still were and how freely we could work and move at 26,000 feet without oxygen.

We decided to reorganise ourselves for the night. Gregory had lain inactive in his sleeping-bag in the pyramid tent for most of the day, so we left him there. George Lowe stayed with him while Tenzing and I moved into the relative comfort of the Meade tent. Ang Nyima and Pemba were in the dome tent. Our supply of oxygen was quite good, so we decided to use some again at night, making use of the two Swiss bottles that Bourdillon and Evans had carried down from the couloir. They were rather small bottles, but the two of them could give sufficient oxygen for Lowe and Gregory to sleep on. With a large spanner I screwed the adapters into place, and fitted them up with reducing valves for our sleeping-masks. All day I had been wandering around with a large spanner in my hand, and George commented, rather despairingly I thought, that I looked more like a mechanic than a mountaineer. The wind was still blowing in full force as we settled down for another night.

As I turned the oxygen on and blew out the candle, I wasn't feeling very optimistic about our chances. The wind was showing few signs of abating, and Evans and Bourdillon had been rather depressing about the difficulties of the summit ridge. Evans had gone so far as to tell George Lowe that he doubted whether we'd be able to get up it. Shrugging these thoughts off, I rolled on to my side, taking care not to crush the oxygen tube underneath my arm. With only two of us in the tent, I had enough room to curl up into a ball, and felt a good deal warmer and more comfortable than I had the previous night. Accidentally my head touched the end wall of the tent and the thrashing canvas pummelled it like a pneumatic drill. My thoughts drifted to Hunt and Evans and Bourdillon somewhere far down below us, and I wondered anxiously if they'd reached the safety of Camp VII. I dozed off into an uneasy sleep. Periodically during the night I awoke cold and stiff to find that my air-mattress had deflated, due to ice getting into the valve, and with a muttered curse I'd struggle in the dark to poke a pencil into the valve and get it to operate again. But the time passed!

CHAPTER TEN

Camp Nine

I AWOKE WITH THE feeling that something was wrong. It took me a moment to understand what it was, and then I realised that everything was deathly quiet – the wind had dropped completely. And then I heard it approaching again like an express train emerging from a tunnel, and soon the tent was rocking and wrenching in familiar fashion. But the fact that the wind had stopped, even for a moment, was the first hopeful sign we'd had since I'd reached the South Col. I glanced at my watch – it was just after four o'clock, so I stirred Tenzing, and we started our long, slow preparations for breakfast. By 7.30 the wind had started to ease a little, and I crawled out of the tent and conferred with Lowe and Gregory in the Pyramid. We decided to start. All six of us were to carry substantial loads of oxygen, food, and equipment, and the previous day we'd carefully made them up so as not to have a pound of unnecessary weight. I was checking oxygen loads when a shout from George Lowe attracted my attention, and he came over to me with a very worried look on his face. Apparently Pemba had been ill all night and didn't feel capable of leaving. We went to see Pemba. It was absolutely vital, we thought, that he should carry a load for us up the mountain. But one look at him shattered our hopes. Poor Pemba was a sad sight. He'd been vomiting all night and looked pale and spiritless. This was a sad blow. We had left now only one Sherpa porter – the stalwart Ang Nyima – and a bare minimum of supplies had to be carried up the South-east ridge if we wanted to establish a high camp and have any chance of reaching the top.

Standing out in the wind, with the mountain towering above our heads, Lowe and I discussed our desperate situation. There seemed to be only two alternatives – to abandon the attempt or to carry all the gear ourselves. To abandon the attempt was unthinkable. With great care I went through all the loads again, removing anything that wasn't absolutely essential. Regretfully, Lowe left his movie-camera and film behind. Lowe, Gregory, and Ang Nyima were to leave first and pioneer the route up to the South-east ridge, so that Tenzing and I could conserve our strength for the following day. At 8.45 they tied on the rope, heaved their loads on to their backs, and turned on their oxygen. George Lowe had three light alloy oxygen cylinders and a few pieces of equipment, making a load of about 45 lb. Gregory was using an oxygen set containing a large, heavy, wire-wound steel cylinder, and this, together with a primus cooker, some solid emergency fuel, and some food, came to about 40 lb. Ang Nyima had 41 lb. of light alloy oxygen cylinders. With a cheerful wave, George led off from camp – he seemed to be in great form. As I watched them leave, it struck me that, despite their slow and almost laboured pace, there was an air of relentlessness about them as their great bulky shapes started to move up the icy slopes towards the mountain.

I turned away and started to pack my own load. Into a light cloth bag I forced a sleeping-bag, an air-mattress, spare socks and gloves, down socks, a spare pullover, two spanners for the oxygen sets, two masks and tubes for our sleeping oxygen, a pencil and paper, two boxes of matches, and some sticking-plaster. Then, because I heartily disliked the majority of the assault ration which had already been carried on ahead, I added to my load some food that I was sure I would like – two packets of dates, two tins of sardines, a half-used carton of honey, a few small packets of lemon crystals and, most precious of all, a tin of apricots in syrup. I had carried the majority of this food up from Camp IV, and had kept it carefully concealed from the ravenous eyes of my companions. My cloth bag was almost bursting at the seams under this load, and although cold reason told me that most of this food wasn't really essential, I couldn't summon up the courage to part with any of it. I had already checked my oxygen set with its two light alloy cylinders of oxygen, and on to this I tied my bulging bag. I eyed it all gloomily. Including my camera and exposure meter, it must weigh nearly 50 lb. – it didn't look as if I was doing much strength-conserving today. Tenzing had also been making up his load, and his personal gear and more food must have given him a substantial 43 or 44 lb.

We didn't plan to leave until ten o'clock, so with a glance up at the first party, who were gradually gaining height up steep snow slopes, we crawled back inside the tent and tried to get some life back into our hands, which had become frozen as we packed our gear. In a strange mixture of English and Hindustani, Tenzing told me of the miserable time the two Swiss Expeditions had spent on the South Col the previous year, of how cold they were, and how their solid fuel had proved too inefficient to heat enough water for their moisture-starved bodies. And through his story it was impossible not to notice the vast respect and admiration which he held for the Swiss guide Lambert who, in choosing Tenzing as his companion, had given him such an opportunity to prove his courage and ability. Tenzing told me that after the two Swiss Expeditions he had decided that he had had enough of Everest, and he had been reluctant to return with the British party. But now he felt fit and strong and was keen to try to reach the summit.

It was nearly ten o'clock, so we crawled out of the tent and tied up the entrance. I spoke to the prostrate Pemba and asked him to keep an eye on the tents. We heaved our loads on to our backs and I felt my shoulders sag under the strain. We put on our oxygen masks, and I turned Tenzing's set on and checked to see that it was going properly. I then turned on my own. As the oxygen flowed into my lungs, my load seemed to lose half of its weight. I searched the slopes above for the first party and quickly picked them out – three black dots a third of the way up the great snow couloir leading towards the South-east ridge. They seemed to hardly move at all. With sinking feelings I wondered if it was proving too much for them. I glanced at Tenzing – a formidable figure in his bulky garments and great burden – and his nod showed he was ready to leave.

With an automatic reaction I checked the nylon rope tying us together and then led off from the tents. I dropped down the slopes to the lowest point of the South Col, and then slowly commenced ascending the ice-slope leading towards the mountain. As the slope steepened, I could feel the drag of altitude which even the oxygen couldn't banish, and I set myself grimly to the task ahead. Soon the dreadful weakness disappeared from my legs, and I achieved a slow, laborious yet rhythmical pace that carried me steadily upwards. Work at these altitudes can rarely if ever be a pleasure – every step demands so much conscious physical and mental effort. And yet, when I could look back and see the South Col tents dwindling beneath us, I experienced a glow of achievement that made all this effort seem worth while. We had been cramponing up this great ice-slope – bare and hard with all the snow blown off by the continual winds – for about half an hour when Tenzing gave a tug on the rope to attract my attention.

When I looked around he was pointing towards an object on the ice about a hundred feet away towards the right. He shouted 'Swiss oxygen!' We traversed over to investigate it, more from curiosity than anything else. It was an oxygen set with two bottles attached and the whole thing was frozen into the ice. Tenzing wrenched it free and it seemed in a surprisingly good state of repair. We checked the bottles, and they both apparently contained a good supply of oxygen. However, it was of no use to us as we had an ample supply for our assault, so we left the set lying in its icy grave.

We laboured on again, bodies bent well forward to counter our burdens, and every step a conscious effort of will. Only a short distance ahead of us and cutting right across the slope was a great crevasse. As we came up to it we noticed with relief that its lower lip was flattened out, and there was ample room to sit down and have our first good rest since leaving camp. We turned off our oxygen and removed our masks, and sat there quietly drawing in great long gulps of cool fresh air. My eyes wandered to the great bulk of Lhotse on the far side of the South Col, but a long inspection only served to confirm our views that this mountain, the fourth highest in the world, is an exceedingly formidable opponent. I looked upwards. The other party was now two-thirds of the way up the couloir, and I could just distinguish an ice-axe swinging rhythmically in the hands of George Lowe. Apparently they were striking a lot of hard going which was demanding a bout of step cutting. This seemed rather bad luck, as the previous party up the couloir had experienced quite easy snow conditions. We reluctantly got to our feet. Above the crevasse the ice-slope steepened considerably in the 300 feet still to go to the foot of the couloir. We crossed the crevasse without a great deal of difficulty by a substantial ice bridge, and then started tackling this slope. We could just pick out on the hard ice the marks made by the crampons of the other party.

As the angle of the slope increased, we found it impossible to climb it direct with our heavy loads, and instead zigzagged our way upwards in order to give some relief to overburdened legs and lungs. But we were gaining height relatively quickly. Ahead of us the slope changed from ice to snow, and we hoped to find easier going. But the snow had been packed by the wind into such a hard surface that we obtained little relief. The angle steepened still more, and I was just about to start chipping some steps to give our ankles a rest when I came on a fine line of steps already made by George Lowe. I grunted with satisfaction and started cramponing up them. Technically, the climbing was steep but not particularly difficult. All the same, the cumbersome loads on our backs made it hard to maintain good balance in the small steps. I couldn't help glancing down the long hard slope underneath us and mentally assessing the consequences of a slip. 'Well, I don't think you'd kill yourself, but you wouldn't be feeling too bright by the time you hit the bottom' was my estimate. Pushing the thought out of my mind, I concentrated more carefully on the route ahead. The line of steps rose in a series of great zigzags to the foot of the couloir, and we climbed slowly but steadily upwards. Every thirty or forty steps, we'd stop and rest, with our chests on our bent knee to give our backs and lungs a chance to recover. Time seemed to have lost its meaning, and although I knew we'd gained considerable height, I couldn't have guessed how long we'd been going – the slope seemed endless.

We were shocked into attention by a new problem. There was an ominous whirr from above, and we instinctively ducked and hunched our heads into our shoulders. Next moment we were showered and clouted by a stream of ice and snow chips falling at great speed. Fortunately the bigger ones missed us. I looked up and saw that we had reached the foot of the great couloir, and that high above us George Lowe was cutting another long line of steps. By the time the debris from his ice-axe reached us, it had achieved a decidedly uncomfortable and perhaps dangerous velocity. We hastily retreated along our tracks out of danger. It would be unsafe for us to enter the couloir until the others had finally got out of it. On this steep slope there was no comfortable place to rest, so we chopped out little terraces for ourselves in the hard snow, and then perched on them as best we could, thrusting our ice-axe shafts deeply into the slope to act as an anchor. I checked my watch and found to my amazement that we'd only been going for about an hour and twenty minutes. We turned off our oxygen in order to conserve it for the harder work ahead, and I examined our two sets to make sure they were operating at a constant rate. Everything seemed to be all right. The other party was now trying to get out of the couloir up the rocks to the right so that they could get on to the South-east ridge.

As soon as they were clear of the couloir, Tenzing and I stood up again and tried to loosen up our cramped muscles. We turned on our oxygen and then commenced our slow but steady progress up the steps. The couloir was an impressive place with vertical rock bluffs towering over it on either side, and the hard, packed snow demanded constant care and attention. Underneath us the slope ran in one great sweep of a thousand feet to the tiny flapping tents on the South Col. As we climbed upwards I could readily pick from the shape and spacing of the steps the stretches when Gregory, and on one occasion Ang Nyima, had been giving George Lowe a change with the step cutting. George is an adept with the ice-axe, and when we went off his steps it was just a little like turning off the main highway on to a rather bumpy side-road – you got along it all right, but it tended to cut down your speed.

With this great stairway to go up, we made rapid progress and zigzagged our way to the rocks near the top of the couloir.

Following George's route we climbed out to the right on to an easy ledge, and walked along it to a stretch of loose rocks. We scrambled up them to the foot of another steep snow slope and another long line of steps. We reached the crest of the slope to see the other party only fifty feet away sitting on some rocks on the South-east ridge.

Just in front of us was one of the loneliest sights I have ever seen. On a little snow shelf perched the tattered remnants of a small tent. Some of the metal framework and the guy-ropes were still standing, but the majority of the fabric had been torn away by a year of Everest's winds. Nearly everything was frozen rigid into the ice, but a few frayed rags were still flapping pathetically in the breeze. I turned to Tenzing and gestured towards the tent, and he smiled and shrugged his shoulders. He wasn't likely to forget the night he'd spent there with the Swiss guide Raymond Lambert without drink or food or even sleeping-bags. We continued on up to the ridge, turned off our oxygen, took off our loads, and then sat down with our companions.

We were at a height of about 27,000 feet. Happily free of our packs, George and I scrambled around excitedly taking photographs and enthusiastically discussing the wonderful views in every direction – views of mighty peaks, of spectacular Himalayan ice-ridges, of deep valleys and great glaciers, and even, in the distance, of brown and rounded foothills. We were like a couple of novices on our first climb. Even to look down on to the Kangshung glacier which George and I had always had an ambition to visit gave us a particular thrill. It was most encouraging to find how fit we were feeling. Reports from previous expeditions indicated that at over 27,000 feet, whether you were using oxygen or not, you'd feel listless and weak with little or no reserves. Even John Hunt and Da Namgyal had been up here on oxygen a few days before and had almost reached the limit of their strength.

But moving around even without oxygen we felt strong and active, and confident that we'd establish Camp IX very high on the mountain. We all seemed to have reached our best acclimatisation at the same time.

I checked all the oxygen sets. George Lowe had used up one of his bottles, so we removed it from his set and connected up to one of the other ones he was carrying. Then we all started off again. About 150 feet above us was our first objective – the equipment John Hunt had carried up for us several days before. The ridge ahead rose quite steeply, but it wasn't difficult and we had plenty of good handholds and footholds. But we climbed very carefully for all that. The whole ridge was covered with a light layer of snow, and we often had to feel around for reliable ledges. It was the sort of climbing in which the airy drops beneath, rather than technical difficulties, forced us to take every care. It was a ridge which we knew was going to be a lot more dangerous to come down than it was to go up – the experience of Evans and Bourdillon had shown us that. With our eyes glued on the slope ahead and our backs bent under our loads, we forced ourselves upwards, still feeling a keen satisfaction in our ability to defeat the altitude.

And then we came upon the dump – an impressive pile of oxygen bottles, a tent, food, and fuel, and all of it essential for our high camp. We sat down on the ridge and looked at it. To add all this to our loads was going to give us burdens far heavier than it was thought possible to carry at this altitude, even using oxygen. We didn't even know if we *could* carry it. But weight was not the only problem. There was also the difficulty of attaching this gear to our already bulky loads. There were two particularly troublesome objects – a Meade tent weighing 14 1/2 lb. and a large black oxygen bottle weighing 20 lb. George and I discussed the problem lugubriously. It was obvious that one of us was going to have to carry more than the others because of the peculiar size of the objects. Finally I made up my mind. 'Look, George, I'll take the tent if you'll do the route-making up the ridge.' George quickly estimated that I'd have a load of over 60 lb., and commented that I wouldn't be much use the next day if I carried that much up the ridge. But finally he agreed there was no alternative. The black oxygen bottle was tied on to Gregory's load after we'd taken away most of his food and the cooker; George put a third bottle of oxygen on to his frame, together with Gregory's excess gear; and Tenzing took another oxygen bottle. All of these now had over 50 lb. each. Ang Nyima wasn't going quite so strongly as the rest of us, so we left him with his original 40 lb.

I squatted down and put my arms through the shoulder-straps of my pack, and then gradually eased the weight on to my back. Grunting with the effort, I slowly tottered to my feet. I felt as though I was being crushed into the earth. I'd carried 63 lb. and more many times in New Zealand – it was never any fun, but we did it because we had to – but carrying such a load at 27,400 feet made quite a difference. Experimentally I tried moving around without any oxygen, and although I was heavy and slow it was encouraging to find that I could move at all. I put on my oxygen mask and shouted to George: 'O.K., George, I'm right! You do the work and I'll follow along in the rear.' George grinned and waved cheerfully. Then, bent under his own enormous load, he led off up the ridge. There was no doubt now that our pace had dropped off considerably. Every step had become a separate entity – a major task that was going to require a maximum of effort. Our eyes continually searched the ridge ahead for the next foothold. Instead of striding like giants, we were now stepping like pygmies, and any lift of more than six inches was too much for our straining legs and lungs. Despite this we were making progress – climbing even more carefully, if that were possible, because we knew our reserves were very limited.

Then the ridge came to a short but steep bluff. We climbed it very slowly and with difficulty. Gregory seemed almost at the limit of his strength and was groaning with the effort. Ang Nyima had to be helped up it with a tug on the rope. At the top of the step we rested for a moment, and then George moved on again. This was really a great day for him. The Lhotse face had been a series of frustrations, of infinitesimal progress, and of a constant fight against acclimatisation. But here George was in wonderful form and mastering easily the technical problems along the ridge. The ridge broadened on to a steep snow slope where the snow was firm and hard, and George's ice-axe started swinging again. We were getting desperately tired. Our eyes searched anxiously for a tiny ledge – any place on which we could pitch a tent. And always there was a site fifty feet above our heads, and always when we reached it it would be impossible. We were getting very high indeed, and already, behind us, Lhotse was dropping away. Gregory was putting up an astonishing performance. He'd always been a tough little man and an excellent acclimatiser, but we had never looked on him as much of a load carrier before, and here he was carrying 50 lb. at nearly 28,000 feet. But he appeared at the absolute limit of his strength.

Ahead of us the ridge seemed to level off a little, so gathering up our fast-diminishing energy we hopefully pressed on. George reached it first, and his violent gesture indicated complete disgust. It was far too steep to hope to make a camp. We crowded up together as close as the angle of the ridge would let us and discussed things. In the next 200 feet the way steepened considerably and formed a great bluff with a snowy cap. To go directly up the bluff looked far too difficult – we would have to get around it on the left. We could see no camp site between us and the snow-top and we doubted if we had the strength to reach that. But there was no question of turning back. The only thing to do was to keep going.

With faint hope I asked Tenzing if he remembered the ground from the previous year. To our surprise he told us that he thought there was a place only fifty feet above us, but well out to the left. He and Lambert had noticed it as a possibility, and he thought he could find his way to it. I moved aside to let Tenzing through and he led off to the left. He started over a very steep snow slope which channelled down thousands of feet to the Western Cwm. The snow was powder, deep, and loose. There was no likelihood of a safe anchor, so this was an exposed and impressive pitch. Tenzing ploughed across the slope, throwing all his strength into making a way through hip-deep snow, and with the rest of us following unhappily but hopefully behind. We scratched our way around a rock buttress, and up a very steep little gully from which the powder snow hissed away in a small avalanche. Then a shout and a pointed arm from Tenzing showed that we'd reached his camp site. We climbed eagerly up to him only to have our hopes crushed. His camp site was a little snow saddle – certainly flat – but with barely enough room for two of us to sit, let alone pitch a tent.

Once again we searched the great face above us. Suddenly, George shouted and pointed upwards. About fifty feet up the slope there seemed to be a more promising ledge. We climbed slowly up towards it, having been disappointed too often to be really optimistic. As we got closer my spirits rose. It certainly wasn't by any means flat, but it was extensive enough and sufficiently well protected to give us a chance to make something of it. We'd just about reached the limit of our strength anyway, so this would have to do. I looked at my watch – it was 2.30 p.m. I knew the others had a long trip ahead of them down to the South Col. 'This'll do,' I shouted, and the others were only too eager to agree. Tenzing told us that this was about as far as he'd got with Lambert the previous year.

We disconnected our oxygen, took off our packs, and started to remove the gear that was to stay up here. We'd already used more oxygen than we had planned, so the descending party decided to try to get down with practically nothing. But the three of them were obviously so tired that without oxygen the slopes below could well be their undoing. Gregory still had a little oxygen left in his bottle, but Ang Nyima and George now had nothing. I rummaged around amongst our supplies and found two half-full bottles and, despite George's protestations, I pressed these on them. Just as they were about to leave, Ang Nyima made a parting plea. He asked if he could be allowed to stay up the night with us in order to help us down the next day. This demonstration of loyalty and un-selfishness from a man who was obviously going to have great difficulty in getting down at all affected me deeply and seemed to epitomise all that is best in the Sherpas. With a lump in my throat I thumped him on the shoulder in appreciation and shook my head. A hearty handclasp with them all the Gregory led off wearily down the mountain – a tired but watchful George going down last. Tenzing and I watched them go, and I felt an intense feeling of loneliness as they slowly clambered down the mountain-side, leaving us on our little ledge.

Their trip down the mountain was a marathon of endurance. They found the ridge on descent steep and dangerous, and they had little strength to deal with it. After a long time they reached the couloir only to find that most of their steps had been wiped out by wind-blown snow. By this time Gregory and Ang Nyima had used all their oxygen and were terribly weak. George had to go down in front and cut a new line of steps, but after a hundred feet of this his oxygen ran out too. Fortunately he had enough strength left to complete the line of steps to safety, and the whole party dragged themselves down towards the South Col tents. The indefatigable George, with remarkable enthusiasm, unroped, and went on ahead so that he could film the others coming into camp completely exhausted.

I watched our support party disappear down the ridge, and then turned to examine our camp site more closely. It wasn't really much of a place. Above us was a rock cliff – black and craggy, but at least devoid of loose stones to fall on us. From the foot of the cliff a little snow slope ran at an easy angle for eight or nine feet to the top of the steep and exposed south face of the mountain. This little slope was to be our camp site. It was certainly far from flat, and it was going to need a lot of work on it before we could possibly pitch a tent. We carefully moved all the gear to one side, and then set to work with our ice-axes to remove the surface snow off a reasonably large area. Ten inches down we struck rock, and after half an hour's hard work we had cleared an area about eight feet long and six feet wide. The slope underneath was made up of stones and rubble, all firmly glued together with ice. This was much harder going. With the picks on our ice-axes we chopped away at the slope, prising out the separate stones and scraping away the rubble. But our progress was very slow. We weren't using any oxygen at all, but we found we could work very hard indeed for periods of ten minutes or so. Then we'd have to stop and have a short rest. With the debris we chopped out of the slope we tried to build up the platform on the downhill side, but almost invariably saw it collapse and go roaring down over the bluffs below. At times we were buffeted by wind and snow, yet we worked doggedly on, knowing that our tent was our only chance of survival against the rigours of the night.

By 5 p.m. we had managed to construct two little terraces side by side and each about seven feet long and three feet

wide. But the top one was about six inches higher than the
other. We decided that we had no hope of levelling them up,
and determined to use them as they were. We unrolled the
tent and almost lost the poles over the edge in the process.
Then we started putting it up. We joined the four collapsible
poles together and pushed them into their slots at each end
of the tent so that they formed a rigid ∧. As the poles slipped
readily into place, I blessed the ease with which our Meade
tents could be erected. Then we pulled the tent up so that it
straddled the two ledges and set to work to anchor it. But
this was very difficult to do. There were no large rocks to
which we could tie a guy-line. I tried driving aluminium tent-
pegs into the frozen slope, but they simply bent and refused
to penetrate at all. The powder snow on the slopes around
the tent was far too loose to hold a peg in place. In desperation my eye lighted on some of our oxygen bottles. I carried
several of them a couple of yards away from the end of the
tent on to a steeper slope covered with deep powder snow
and then tried stamping and packing them firmly down. After
a good deal of work they gave the appearance at least of
stability, and I attached the main guy-rope around them and
pulled the end of the tent up. It didn't seem too bad.

I climbed along to Tenzing's end. He had been tackling
the problem in a somewhat different manner. On the bluff
above were a number of smooth fingers of rock pointing
straight outwards – certainly nothing over which you could
hitch a line. But around these jutting fingers Tenzing had
tied a web of rope hoping that friction would keep it in place.
At my look of doubt he gave me the line to tug and even
under a hearty jerk it remained attached. I wasn't too confident that it would withstand hours of battering from the
wind, but it would have to do. In a similar fashion and using
the limited means at hand, we tied down the rest of the guy-
ropes so that the tent stood up reasonably well to the quite

fierce gusts of wind that were already blowing. We put all our personal gear inside, and then Tenzing crawled in to start our stove and prepare some food and drink.

It was now about 6 p.m. and the view in every direction was superb. The great giants, Makalu and Lhotse, were bathed in a warm red light and seemed almost close enough to touch. The valleys were all hidden by a layer of fleecy clouds, with only an occasional icy fang thrusting up above and glowing in the setting sun. Far below us was the Western Cwm, already filling with the gloom of night. And on the South Col I could just pick out the tiny group of tents flapping furiously in the eternal South Col wind. The view spurred me to take a number of photographs. In particular I wanted a photograph of our tent, but I found considerable difficulty in getting into any position on the steep face where I was far enough away to get the tent into my viewfinder. Finally I gave up in disgust. A soft purr from inside the tent showed that Tenzing had succeeded in lighting the kerosene stove. This was good news, for we regarded ample supplies of moisture as a prime essential.

I set to work to check the oxygen supplies. The whole plan of attack was based on Tenzing and me starting off from Camp VIII with two full bottles of oxygen each and using it at the rate of four litres a minute. We thought this flow rate to be the minimum if we were going to have a good chance to get to the top. I sorted through the bottles and my heart sank. I checked them all again – yes, I was right! We had only two full bottles left and two about two-thirds full. I knew we'd used some of the assault oxygen on the way up, but I hadn't realised just how much. Aghast, I did some mental arithmetic – at four litres a minute we had only about five and a half hours of oxygen left. It wasn't going to be anywhere near enough. Then I remembered how well we'd come up with heavy loads on four litres a minute. Perhaps we could go on if necessary on three litres a minute? This would give us just over seven hours' endurance, which might be enough. I decided to adjust the sets to three litres, and set to work putting the necessary bottles in place and connecting up the tubes. I checked the flow from the sets, and then carefully put them between the tent and the rock bluff behind.

I planned to use the large black oxygen bottle that Greg had carried up for sleeping purposes. But when I looked for the special adapter that we had brought up for it, I couldn't find it anywhere. After a thorough search I realised that someone must have carried it down again, and that the oxygen in the bottle was useless to us. I examined the remaining partly filled bottles of oxygen. There were three of them, but there was only enough oxygen in them to give us four hours of sleep at one litre of oxygen per minute. I decided to space this through the night from 9 to 11 p.m. and from 1 to 3 a.m. We had one fact in our favour in respect to oxygen. While Bourdillon and Evans were on the first assault, they jetti-soned two partly filled bottles of oxygen on the ridge about three hundred feet above us. If we could find these and they still contained some oxygen, they'd prove a valuable addition to our limited endurance. It was getting very cold now, so with only a passing glimpse at the scene around I crawled inside the tent.

Despite the uneven floor the tent looked quite roomy. Tenzing was sitting on the upper ledge at the far end with the cooker on the bottom ledge between his feet. A thin cloud of steam was coming from the pot. He smiled and asked me what I'd like to drink. As I settled myself into the tent the tempting aroma of chicken noodle soup surrounded us, and before long we were drinking it down with great relish. Rather astonishingly, perhaps, for this altitude, we were really hungry. Out came all our delicacies – we had sardines on biscuits, fresh dates, and pint after pint of hot lemon drink

Camp IX on the ledge at 27,900 feet.

crammed with sugar. As a special treat I produced my tin of apricots and Tenzing opened it with his tinopener. He tipped it upside down, but instead of delicious fruit and tasty juice flowing out, all that emerged was a solid block of ice. However, a short dose of treatment in a saucepan over the primus soon made it highly edible, and we ate it slowly, lingering over the flavour. But our main sustenance was our hot lemon drink fortified with heaps of sugar. We were both very conscious of the great dangers of dehydration, and were determined to stock our bodies up with an ample supply of water. To this end I was especially pleased with the way our little kerosene stove was operating. I'd taken particular care in testing it down in the Western Cwm, and now, at nearly 28,000 feet, it was humming along with a hot blue flame. When we'd finally eaten all we wanted and drunk all our bodies could hold, we started settling down for the night.

I took a last look outside the tent door and dragged our sleeping oxygen inside. The sky above was completely clear and every star shone with a cold steady light. Only in the deep valleys below could I distinguish any sign of clouds. Our prospects for tomorrow looked excellent. The only worrying feature at the moment was the occasional vigorous gusts of wind which shook and rattled our tent. I didn't feel too confident that our insecure guy-lines could stand too much of it. Tenzing blew up his air-mattress and then laid it on the lower terrace. He spread his sleeping-bag out and started to crawl inside – boots and all. A long struggle ensued before he had pulled his bag up around his neck and settled calmly down to rest. He seemed quite unaffected by the fact that the edge of the tent beside him overhung the tremendous south face of the mountain.

As soon as he was out of the way, I started my own preparations. I blew up my air-mattress and pushed it into the narrow space on the upper ledge. Then I debated what to do

about my boots. During the day my feet had become quite
wet with perspiration, so I changed into dry socks. I didn't
know whether to wear my boots inside my sleeping-bag and
so have an uncomfortable night and warm boots in the
morning, or whether to have a comfortable night and frozen
boots. The flesh was weak and I decided on a comfortable
night. I put on some warm down socks and then wriggled
inside my bag. There wasn't enough room for me to lie flat
out on the upper ledge, so I squatted across my air-mattress
with my head against the wall of the tent and my feet thrust
into the corner of the tent on the bottom ledge, straddling
Tenzing's legs. It wasn't really a very comfortable position,
but I was thankful to have a tent over my head at all. I
connected up an oxygen bottle to our sleeping-masks and
turned the oxygen on. With a lighted match I tested to see
if it was operating properly. Then I handed a mask to the
recumbent Tenzing and he clipped it on into place. I put my
own on and wriggled deeper into my bag. Tenzing turned
out the stove and the tent suddenly became dark.

As I lay there breathing slowly and deeply on our tiny
supply of oxygen, my mind automatically drifted to the next
day. There were so many questions to answer. Would we be
able to climb on three litres a minute and, even at this, would
we have enough endurance? Was the weather going to be
fine? And, anyway, if we did get to the South Summit, would
we be able to make a route along the summit ridge – the
ridge about which Evans and Bourdillon had painted such a
gloomy picture? I didn't know any of the answers and told
myself there was only one way to find out. Everything outside
was still and quiet, and lying in the darkness inside the tent,
warm and comfortable from the food and drink we'd
consumed, it was difficult to realise where we were – camped
on a narrow ledge far higher than anyone had ever camped
before.

All of a sudden I heard a whistling roar from higher up the ridge. I braced myself quickly with my shoulders against the upper wall of the tent and my feet pressed hard against the lower terrace. Next moment a gust of wind hit us like a battering-ram and the whole tent shook and swayed in a most unpleasant manner. Tenzing started up in alarm as the gust reached a crescendo of fury; then, to our relief, it completely died away. But we hadn't liked it at all! Ten minutes later I had to brace myself again as another gust signalled its approach by a roar like an express train high above us. Once again the tent swayed and flapped. With monotonous regularity the gusts thrashed at us. After a time the fact that the tent seemed to be withstanding them reasonably well subdued our worried feelings, and under the beneficent effects of the oxygen we went off into a light doze.

I awoke suddenly with my mind clear and active but my body shuddering with the cold. I realised immediately that our bottle of oxygen must have run out. There was a deathly quiet everywhere, broken only by Tenzing turning restlessly inside his sleeping-bag. 'He's cold too,' I thought. I looked at the dial of my watch – it was eleven o'clock. The wind seemed to have dropped completely – that was a bit of luck. I would have been much warmer with the other half of my double sleeping-bag, but we'd left our inner bags behind to save weight. I asked Tenzing if he were cold and he said 'Yes'. We were spending the next two hours without oxygen and there was no sense in being too miserable. I knew we had a reasonable supply of kerosene, so I told Tenzing that we might as well get the cooker going and try to warm ourselves up with a hot drink. He was only too quick to agree, and before long our faithful stove was steadily melting ice. I was feeling a bit hungry so rummaged around for some biscuits and piled hard, granulated honey on to them. Any form of sugar, as long as it wasn't too sickly, tasted good to me. And then we started drinking again – great mugs of 'lemonade'. In this way the hours passed astonishingly quickly. Soon it was 1 a.m. and time for our second dose of oxygen. While Tenzing put the cooker away, I connected up another bottle, and then we settled down again. I was feeling pretty stiff from lying hunched up against the wall of the tent on one elbow, but the oxygen enabled me to forget most of this and the cold, and I dozed once more.

It was absolutely still outside when our oxygen finally ran out about 3 a.m. I lay there for a long time miserably cold. At 4 a.m. I forced myself to move. I struggled to get my arms and shoulders out of the sleeping-bag and started to undo the tent door. It was frozen stiff as a board, but finally the tapes came undone and I could push it aside. I looked out on to a cold, hard world but an incredibly beautiful one. The early morning light was already tinging the sky and clearly outlining the icy peaks which stretched from horizon to horizon. The valleys below were dark and sleeping. Tenzing was looking over my shoulder and suddenly grunted and pointed downwards – 'Thyangboche'. Sure enough, there in the great wide Imja valley we could see the faint outlines of the monastery perched in its lovely setting on top of a great spur. It was about 17,000 feet below us. Already we knew that the monks down there would be performing their early morning devotions, and perhaps, as they had promised to do, they were at this moment turning their eyes up towards us and praying for our well-being. Our prayers, at least, seemed to have been answered with a fine day and a chance for the top.

I looked at the thermometer leaning against the wall of the tent. It was reading 27 degrees below zero Centigrade. Not too bad really for this altitude. Tenzing was working on the cooker once again, so I hauled the two oxygen sets into the tent. The bare metal was terribly cold, but I knocked the snow and ice off the sets, checked all the connections and the dials, and tested to make sure the oxygen was flowing freely. They seemed in good order. Once again we tackled our food and drink with enthusiasm, trying to get as much moisture into ourselves as we could. The very heavy and quick breathing that such altitudes demand mean the body is expelling a tremendous amount of water vapour in the breath and, unless this is replaced, extreme fatigue and collapse will ultimately result. We were determined that this shouldn't happen to us.

I examined my boots. As I had anticipated, they were frozen iron hard, and it was impossible to get them on to my feet. Obviously drastic measures were called for, so I put the stove between my knees and started to cook my boots in its fierce heat. Refusing to be cowed by the smell of burning leather and rubber, I persisted with this strong treatment and finally ended up with a pair of boots that were somewhat singed but at least were malleable enough now to go on to my feet with ease. I rubbed my face with cream to protect it from the wind and sun, and Tenzing did the same. On our bodies we were wearing all the clothes we possessed – string singlet, woollen shirt, Shetland wool pullover, woollen underclothes, thick down trousers and jackets, and over them all strong wind-proof trousers and jacket with a hood over the head. On our hands we had three pairs of gloves – first silk, then woollen, then windproof. To protect our eyes we wore snowglasses.

For the last time I checked my camera. I had put a new roll of colour film in it the night before, but now I set a stan-dard speed and aperture – 1/100th at f.11. I tucked it care-fully inside my clothes and zipped up my windproof.

We were ready to leave!

CHAPTER ELEVEN

Summit

AT 6.30 A.M. WE crawled slowly out of the tent and stood on our little ledge. Already the upper part of the mountain was bathed in sunlight. It looked warm and inviting, but our ledge was dark and cold. We lifted our oxygen on to our backs and slowly connected up the tubes to our face-masks. My 30-lb. load seemed to crush me downwards and stifled all enthusiasm, but when I turned on the oxygen and breathed in deeply, the burden seemed to lighten and the old urge to get to grips with the mountain came back. We strapped on our crampons and tied on our nylon rope; grasped our ice-axes and were ready to go.

I looked at the way ahead. From our tent very steep slopes covered with deep powder snow led up to a prominent snow shoulder on the South-east ridge about a hundred feet above our heads. The slopes were in the shade and breaking trail was going to be cold work. Still a little worried about my boots, I asked Tenzing to lead off. Always willing to do his share, and more than his share if necessary, Tenzing scrambled past me and tackled the slope. With powerful thrusts of his legs he forced his way up in knee-deep snow. I gathered in the rope and followed along behind him.

We were climbing out over the tremendous South face of the mountain, and below us snow chutes and rock ribs plummeted thousands of feet down to the Western Cwm. Starting in the morning straight on to exposed climbing is always trying for the nerves, and this was no exception. In imagination I could feel my heavy load dragging me backwards down the great slopes below; I seemed clumsy and unstable and my breath was hurried and uneven. But Tenzing was pursuing an irresistible course up the slope, and I didn't have time to think too much. My muscles soon warmed up to their work, my nerves relaxed, and I dropped into the old climbing rhythm and followed steadily up his tracks. As we gained a little height we moved into the rays of the sun, and although we could feel no appreciable warmth, we were greatly encouraged by its presence. Taking no rests, Tenzing ploughed his way up through the deep snow and led out on to the snow shoulder. We were now at a height of 28,000 feet. Towering directly above our heads was the South Summit – steep and formidable. And to the right were the enormous cornices of the summit ridge. We still had a long way to go.

Ahead of us the ridge was sharp and narrow, but rose at an easy angle. I felt warm and strong now, so took over the lead. First I investigated the ridge with my ice-axe. On the sharp crest of the ridge and on the right-hand side loose powder snow was lying dangerously over hard ice. Any attempt to climb on this would only produce an unpleasant slide down towards the Kangshung glacier. But the left-hand slope was better – it was still rather steep, but it had a firm surface of wind-blown powder snow into which our crampons would bite readily.

Taking every care, I moved along on to the left-hand side of the ridge. Everything seemed perfectly safe. With increased confidence, I took another step. Next moment I was almost thrown off balance as the wind-crust suddenly gave way and I sank through it up to my knee. It took me a little while to regain my breath. Then I gradually pulled my leg out of the hole. I was almost upright again when the wind-crust under the other foot gave way and I sank back with both legs enveloped in soft, loose snow to the knees. It was the mountaineer's curse – breakable crust. I forced my way along. Sometimes for a few careful steps I was on the surface, but usually the crust would break at the critical moment and I'd be up to my knees again. Though it was tiring and exasperating work, I felt I had plenty of strength in reserve. For half an hour I continued on in this uncomfortable fashion, with the violent balancing movements I was having to make completely destroying rhythm and breath. It was a great relief when the snow conditions improved and I was able to stay on the surface. I still kept down on the steep slopes on the left of the ridge, but plunged ahead and climbed steadily upwards. I came over a small crest and saw in front of me a tiny hollow on the ridge. And in this hollow lay two oxygen bottles almost completely covered with snow. It was Evans' and Bourdillon's dump.

I rushed forward into the hollow and knelt beside them. Wrenching one of the bottles out of its frozen bed I wiped the snow off its dial – it showed a thousand-pounds pressure – it was nearly a third full of oxygen. I checked the other – it was the same. This was great news. It meant that the oxygen we were carrying on our backs only had to get us back to these bottles instead of right down to the South Col. It gave us more than another hour of endurance. I explained this to Tenzing through my oxygen mask. I don't think he understood, but he realised I was pleased about something and nodded enthusiastically.

I led off again. I knew there was plenty of hard work ahead and Tenzing could save his energies for that. The ridge climbed on upwards rather more steeply now, and then broadened out and shot up at a sharp angle to the foot of the enormous slope running up to the South Summit. I crossed over on to the right-hand side of the ridge and found the snow was firm there. I started chipping a long line of steps up to the foot of the great slope. Here we stamped out a platform for ourselves and I checked our oxygen. Everything seemed to be going well. I had a little more oxygen left than Tenzing, which meant I was obtaining a slightly lower flow rate from my set, but it wasn't enough to matter and there was nothing I could do about it, anyway.

Ahead of us was a really formidable problem, and I stood in my steps and looked at it. Rising from our feet was an enormous slope slanting steeply down on to the precipitous East face of Everest and climbing up with appalling steepness to the South Summit of the mountain 400 feet above us. The left-hand side of the slope was a most unsavoury mixture of steep loose rock and snow, which my New Zealand training immediately regarded with grave suspicion, but which in actual fact the rock-climbing Britons, Evans and Bourdillon, had ascended in much trepidation when on the first assault. The only other route was up the snow itself and still faintly discernible here, and there were traces of the track made by the first assault party, who had come down it in preference to their line of ascent up the rocks. The snow route it was for us! There looked to be some tough work ahead, and as Tenzing had been taking it easy for a while I hard-heartedly waved him through. With his first six steps I realised that the work was going to be much harder than I had thought. His first two steps were on top of the snow, the third was up to his ankles and by the sixth he was up to his hips. But almost lying against the steep slope, he drove himself onwards, ploughing a track directly upwards. Even following in his steps was hard work, for the loose snow refused to pack into safe steps. After a long and valiant spell he was plainly in need of a rest, so I took over.

Immediately I realised that we were on dangerous ground.

On this very steep slope the snow was soft and deep with little coherence. My ice-axe shaft sank into it without any support and we had no sort of a belay. The only factor that made it at all possible to progress was a thin crust of frozen snow which tied the whole slope together. But this crust was a poor support. I was forcing my way upwards, plunging deep steps through it, when suddenly with a dull breaking noise an area of crust all around me about six feet in diameter broke off into large sections and slid with me back through three or four steps. And then I stopped; but the crust, gathering speed, slithered on out of sight. It was a nasty shock. My whole training told me that the slope was exceedingly dangerous, but at the same time I was saying to myself: 'Ed, my boy, this is Everest – you've got to push it a bit harder!' My solar plexus was tight with fear as I ploughed on. Half-way up I stopped, exhausted. I could look down 10,000 feet between my legs, and I have never felt more insecure. Anxiously I waved Tenzing up to me.

'What do you think of it, Tenzing?' And the immediate response, 'Very bad, very dangerous!' 'Do you think we should go on?' and there came the familiar reply that never helped you much but never let you down: 'Just as you wish!' I waved him on to take a turn at leading. Changing the lead much more frequently now, we made our unhappy way upwards, sometimes sliding back and wiping out half a dozen steps, and never feeling confident that at any moment the whole slope might not avalanche. In the hope of some sort of a belay we traversed a little towards the rocks, but found no help in their smooth, holdless surfaces. We plunged on upwards. And then I noticed that, a little above us, the left-hand rock ridge turned into snow and the snow looked firm and safe. Laboriously and carefully we climbed across some steep rock, and I sank my ice-axe shaft into the snow of the ridge. It went in firm and hard. The pleasure of this safe belay after all the uncertainty below was like a reprieve to a condemned man. Strength flowed into my limbs, and I could feel my tense nerves and muscles relaxing. I swung my ice-axe at the slope and started chipping a line of steps upwards – it was very steep, but seemed so gloriously safe. Tenzing, an inexpert but enthusiastic step cutter, took a turn and chopped a haphazard line of steps up another pitch. We were making fast time now and the slope was starting to ease off. Tenzing gallantly waved me through, and with a growing feeling of excitement I cramponed up some firm slopes to the rounded top of the South Summit. It was only 9 a.m.

With intense interest I looked at the vital ridge leading to the summit – the ridge about which Evans and Bourdillon had made such gloomy forecasts. At first glance it was an exceedingly impressive and indeed a frightening sight. In the narrow crest of this ridge, the basic rock of the mountain had a thin capping of snow and ice – ice that reached out over the East face in enormous cornices, overhanging and treacherous, and only waiting for the careless foot of the mountaineer to break off and crash 10,000 feet to the Kangshung glacier. And from the cornices the snow dropped steeply to the left to merge with the enormous rock bluffs which towered 8,000 feet above the Western Cwm. It was impressive all right! But as I looked my fears started to lift a little. Surely I could see a route there? For this snow slope on the left, although very steep and exposed, was practically continuous for the first half of the ridge, although in places the great cornices reached hungrily across. If we could make a route along that snow slope, we could go quite a distance at least.

With a feeling almost of relief, I set to work with my ice-axe and cut a platform for myself just down off the top of the South Summit. Tenzing did the same, and then we removed our oxygen sets and sat down. The day was still remarkably fine, and we felt no discomfort through our thick layers of clothing from either wind or cold. We had a drink out of Tenzing's water-bottle and then I checked our oxygen supplies. Tenzing's bottle was practically exhausted, but mine still had a little in it. As well as this, we each had a full bottle. I decided that the difficulties ahead would demand as light a weight on our backs as possible so determined to use only the full bottles. I removed Tenzing's empty bottle and my nearly empty one and laid them in the snow. With particular care I connected up our last bottles and tested to see that they were working efficiently. The needles on the dials were steady on 3,300 lb. per square inch pressure – they were very full bottles holding just over 800 litres of oxygen each. At three litres a minute we consumed 180 litres an hour, and this meant a total endurance of nearly four and a half hours. This didn't seem much for the problems ahead, but I was determined if necessary to cut down to two litres a minute for the homeward trip.

I was greatly encouraged to find how, even at 28,700 feet and with no oxygen, I could work out slowly but clearly the problems of mental arithmetic that the oxygen supply demanded. A correct answer was imperative – any mistake could well mean a trip with no return. But we had no time to waste. I stood up and took a series of photographs in every direction, then thrust my camera back to its warm home inside my clothing. I heaved my now pleasantly light oxygen load on to my back and connected up my tubes. I did the same for Tenzing, and we were ready to go. I asked Tenzing to belay me and then, with a growing air of excitement, I cut a broad and safe line of steps down to the snow saddle below the South Summit. I wanted an easy route when we came back up here weak and tired. Tenzing came down the steps and joined me, and then belayed once again.

I moved along on to the steep snow slope on the left side

of the ridge. With the first blow of my ice-axe my excitement increased. The snow – to my astonishment – was crystalline and hard. A couple of rhythmical blows of the ice-axe produced a step that was big enough even for our oversize high-altitude boots. But best of all the steps were strong and safe. A little conscious of the great drops beneath me, I chipped a line of steps for the full length of the rope – forty feet – and then forced the shaft of my ice-axe firmly into the snow. It made a fine belay and I looped the rope around it. I waved to Tenzing to join me, and as he moved slowly and carefully along the steps I took in the rope. When he reached me, he thrust his ice-axe into the snow and protected me with a good tight rope as I went on cutting steps. It was exhilarating work – the summit ridge of Everest, the crisp snow and the smooth easy blows of the ice-axe all combined to make me feel a greater sense of power than I had ever felt at great altitudes before. I went on cutting for rope length after rope length.

We were now approaching a point where one of the great cornices was encroaching on to our slope. We'd have to go down to the rocks to avoid it. I cut a line of steps steeply down the slope to a small ledge on top of the rocks. There wasn't much room, but it made a reasonably safe stance. I waved to Tenzing to join me. As he came down to me I realised there was something wrong with him. I had been so absorbed in the technical problems of the ridge that I hadn't thought much about Tenzing, except for a vague feeling that he seemed to move along the steps with unnecessary slowness. But now it was quite obvious that he was not only moving extremely slowly, but he was breathing quickly and with difficulty and was in considerable distress. I immediately suspected his oxygen set and helped him down on to the ledge so that I could examine it. The first thing I noticed was that from the outlet of his face-mask there were hanging some long icicles. I looked at it more closely and found that the outlet tube – about two inches in diameter – was almost completely blocked up with ice. This was preventing Tenzing from exhaling freely and must have made it extremely unpleasant for him. Fortunately the outlet tube was made of rubber and by manipulating this with my hand I was able to release all the ice and let it fall out. The valves started operating and Tenzing was given immediate relief. Just as a check I examined my own set and found that it, too, had partly frozen up in the outlet tube, but not sufficiently to have affected me a great deal. I removed the ice out of it without a great deal of trouble. Automatically I looked at our pressure gauges – just over 2,900 lb. (2,900 lb. was just over 700 litres; 180 into 700 was about 4) – we had nearly four hours' endurance left. That meant we weren't going badly.

I looked at the route ahead. This next piece wasn't going to be easy. Our rock ledge was perched right on top of the enormous bluff running down into the Western Cwm. In fact, almost under my feet, I could see the dirty patch on the floor of the Cwm which I knew was Camp IV. In a sudden urge to escape our isolation I waved and shouted, and then as suddenly stopped as I realised my foolishness. Against the vast expanse of Everest, 8,000 feet above them, we'd be quite invisible to the best binoculars. I turned back to the problem ahead. The rock was far too steep to attempt to drop down and go around this pitch. The only thing to do was to try to shuffle along the ledge and cut handholds in the bulging ice that was trying to push me off it. Held on a tight rope by Tenzing, I cut a few handholds and then thrust my ice-axe as hard as I could into the solid snow and ice. Using this to take my weight I moved quickly along the ledge. It proved easier than I had anticipated. A few more handholds, another quick swing across them, and I was able to cut a line of steps up on to a safe slope and chop out a roomy terrace from which to belay Tenzing as he climbed up to me.

We were now fast approaching the most formidable obstacle on the ridge – a great rock step. This step had always been visible in aerial photographs, and in 1951 on the Everest Reconnaissance we had seen it quite clearly with glasses from Thyangboche. We had always thought of it as the obstacle on the ridge which could well spell defeat. I cut a line of steps across the last snow slope, and then commenced traversing over a steep rock slab that led to the foot of the great step. The holds were small and hard to see, and I brushed my snow-glasses away from my eyes. Immediately I was blinded by a bitter wind sweeping across the ridge and laden with particles of ice. I hastily replaced my glasses and blinked away the ice and tears until I could see again. But it made me realise how efficient was our clothing in protecting us from the rigours of even a fine day at 29,000 feet. Still half blinded, I climbed across the slab, and then dropped down into a tiny snow hollow at the foot of the step. And here Tenzing joined me.

I looked anxiously up at the rocks. Planted squarely across the ridge in a vertical bluff, they looked extremely difficult, and I knew that our strength and ability to climb steep rock at this altitude would be severely limited. I examined the route out to the left. By dropping fifty or a hundred feet over steep slabs, we might be able to get around the bottom of the bluff, but there was no indication that we'd be able to climb back on to the ridge again. And to lose any height now might be fatal. Search as I could, I was unable to see an easy route up to the step or, in fact, any route at all. Finally, in desperation I examined the right-hand end of the bluff. Attached to this and overhanging the precipitous East face was a large cornice. This cornice, in preparation for its inevitable crash down the mountainside, had started to lose its grip on the rock and a long narrow vertical crack had been formed between the rock and the ice. The crack was large enough to take the human frame, and though it offered little security, it was at least a route. I quickly made up my mind – Tenzing had an excellent belay and we must be near the top – it was worth a try.

Before attempting the pitch, I produced my camera once again. I had no confidence that I would be able to climb this crack, and with a surge of competitive pride which unfortunately afflicts even mountaineers, I determined to have proof that at least we had reached a good deal higher than the South Summit. I took a few photographs and then made another rapid check of the oxygen – 2,550 lb. pressure. (2,550 from 3,300 leaves 750. 750 over 3,300 is about two-ninths. Two-ninths off 800 litres leaves about 600 litres. 600 divided by 180 is nearly 3 1/2.) Three and a half hours to go. I examined Tenzing's belay to make sure it was a good one and then slowly crawled inside the crack.

In front of me was the rock wall, vertical but with a few promising holds. Behind me was the ice-wall of the cornice, glittering and hard but cracked here and there. I took a hold on the rock in front and then jammed one of my crampons hard into the ice behind. Leaning back with my oxygen set on the ice, I slowly levered myself upwards. Searching feverishly with my spare boot, I found a tiny ledge on the rock and took some of the weight off my other leg. Leaning back on the cornice, I fought to regain my breath. Constantly at the back of my mind was the fear that the cornice might break off, and my nerves were taut with suspense. But slowly I forced my way up – wriggling and jambing and using every little hold. In one place I managed to force my ice-axe into a crack in the ice, and this gave me the necessary purchase to get over a holdless stretch. And then I found a solid foot-hold in a hollow in the ice, and next moment I was reaching over the top of the rock and pulling myself to safety. The rope came tight – its forty feet had been barely enough.

I lay on the little rock ledge panting furiously. Gradually it dawned on me that I was up the step, and I felt a glow of pride and determination that completely subdued my temporary feelings of weakness. For the first time on the whole expedition I really knew I was going to get to the top. 'It will have to be pretty tough to stop us now' was my thought. But I couldn't entirely ignore the feeling of astonishment and wonder that I'd been able to get up such a difficulty at 29,000 feet even with oxygen.

When I was breathing more evenly I stood up and, leaning over the edge, waved to Tenzing to come up. He moved into the crack and I gathered in the rope and took some of his weight. Then he, in turn, commenced to struggle and jam and force his way up until I was able to pull him to safety – gasping for breath. We rested for a moment. Above us the ridge continued on as before – enormous overhanging cornices on the right and steep snow slopes on the left running down to the rock bluffs. But the angle of the snow slopes was easing off. I went on chipping a line of steps, but thought it safe enough for us to move together in order to save time. The ridge rose up in a great series of snakelike undulations which bore away to the right, each one concealing

the next. I had no idea where the top was. I'd cut a line of
steps around the side of one undulation and another would
come into view. We were getting desperately tired now and
Tenzing was going very slowly. I'd been cutting steps for
almost two hours, and my back and arms were starting to
tire. I tried cramponing along the slope without cutting steps,
but my feet slipped uncomfortably down the slope. I went on
cutting. We seemed to have been going for a very long time
and my confidence was fast evaporating. Bump followed bump
with maddening regularity. A patch of shingle barred our
way, and I climbed dully up it and started cutting steps around
another bump. And then I realised that this was the last bump,
for ahead of me the ridge dropped steeply away in a great
corniced curve, and out in the distance I could see the pastel
shades and fleecy clouds of the highlands of Tibet.

To my right a slender snow ridge climbed up to a snowy
dome about forty feet above our heads. But all the way along
the ridge the thought had haunted me that the summit might
be the crest of a cornice. It was too late to take risks now. I
asked Tenzing to belay me strongly, and I started cutting a
cautious line of steps up the ridge. Peering from side to side
and thrusting with my ice-axe, I tried to discover a possible
cornice, but everything seemed solid and firm. I waved Tenzing up to me. A few more whacks of the ice-axe, a few very
weary steps, and we were on the summit of Everest.

CHAPTER TWELVE

Adventure's End

IT WAS 11.30 A.M. My first sensation was one of relief – relief that the long grind was over; that the summit had been reached before our oxygen supplies had dropped to a critical level; and relief that in the end the mountain had been kind to us in having a pleasantly rounded cone for its summit instead of a fearsome and unapproachable cornice. But mixed with the relief was a vague sense of astonishment that I should have been the lucky one to attain the ambition of so many brave and determined climbers. It seemed difficult at first to grasp that we'd got there. I was too tired and too conscious of the long way down to safety really to feel any great elation. But as the fact of our success thrust itself more clearly into my mind, I felt a quiet glow of satisfaction spread through my body – a satisfaction less vociferous but more powerful than I had ever felt on a mountain top before. I turned and looked at Tenzing. Even beneath his oxygen mask and the icicles hanging from his hair, I could see his infectious grin of sheer delight. I held out my hand, and in silence we shook in good Anglo-Saxon fashion. But this was not enough for Tenzing, and impulsively he threw his arm around my shoulders and we thumped each other on the back in mutual congratulations.

But we had no time to waste! First I must take some

photographs and then we'd hurry down. I turned off my oxygen and took the set off my back. I remembered all the warnings I'd had of the possible fatal consequences of this, but for some reason felt quite confident that nothing serious would result. I took my camera out of the pocket of my wind-proof and clumsily opened it with my thickly gloved hands. I clipped on the lenshood and ultra-violet filter and then shuf-fled down the ridge a little so that I could get the summit into my viewfinder. Tenzing had been waiting patiently, but now, at my request, he unfurled the flags wrapped around his ice-axe and standing on the summit held them above his head. Clad in all his bulky equipment and with the flags flapping furiously in the wind, he made a dramatic picture, and the thought drifted through my mind that this photograph should be a good one if it came out at all. I didn't worry about getting Tenzing to take a photograph of me – as far as I knew, he had never taken a photograph before and the summit of Everest was hardly the place to show him how.

I climbed up to the top again and started taking a photo-graphic record in every direction. The weather was still extraordinarily fine. High above us were long streaks of cirrus wind cloud and down below fluffy cumulus hid the valley floors from view. But wherever we looked, icy peaks and sombre gorges lay beneath us like a relief map. Perhaps the view was most spectacular to the east, for here the giants Makalu and Kanchenjunga dominated the horizon and gave some idea of the vast scale of the Himalayas. Makalu in partic-ular, with its soaring rock ridges, was a remarkable sight; it was only a few miles away from us. From our exalted view-point I could see all the northern slopes of the mountain and was immediately struck by the possibility of a feasible route to its summit. With a growing feeling of excitement, I took another photograph to study at leisure on returning to civilisation. The view to the north was a complete contrast

– hundreds of miles of the arid high Tibetan plateau, softened now by a veil of fleecy clouds into a scene of delicate beauty. To the west the Himalayas stretched hundreds of miles in a tangled mass of peaks, glaciers, and valleys.

But one scene was of particular interest. Almost under our feet, it seemed, was the famous North Col and the East Rongbuk glacier, where so many epic feats of courage and endurance were performed by the earlier British Everest Expeditions. Part of the ridge up which they had established their high camps was visible, but the last thousand feet, which had proved such a formidable barrier, was concealed from our view as its rock slopes dropped away with frightening abruptness from the summit snow pyramid. It was a sobering thought to remember how often these men had reached 28,000 feet without the benefits of our modern equipment and reasonably efficient oxygen sets. Inevitably my thoughts turned to Mallory and Irvine, who had lost their lives on the mountain thirty years before. With little hope I looked around for some sign that they had reached the summit, but could see nothing.

Meanwhile Tenzing had also been busy. On the summit he'd scratched out a little hole in the snow, and in this he placed some small offerings of food – some biscuits, a piece of chocolate, and a few sweets – a small gift to the Gods of Chomolungma which all devout Buddhists (as Tenzing is) believe to inhabit the summit of this mountain. Besides the food, I placed the little cross that John Hunt had given me on the South Col. Strange companions, no doubt, but symbolical at least of the spiritual strength and peace that all peoples have gained from the mountains. We made seats for ourselves in the snow, and sitting there in reasonable comfort we ate with relish a bar of mintcake. My camera was still hanging open on my chest so I decided to put it safely away. But my fingers seemed to have grown doubly clumsy. With slow and fumbling movements, I closed the camera and did up the

leather case. I suddenly realised that I was being affected by
the lack of oxygen – it was nearly ten minutes now since I'd
taken my set off. I quickly checked the gauges on our bottles
– 1,450-lb. pressure; roughly 350 litres of oxygen; nearly two
hours' endurance at three litres a minute. It wasn't much, but
it would have to do. I hastily put my set on and turned on
the oxygen. I felt better immediately. Tenzing had removed
the flags from his ice-axe and, as there was nothing to tie
them to, he thrust them down into the snow. They obviously
wouldn't stay there for long. We slowly got to our feet again.
We were tired all right, and all my tension and worry about
reaching the summit had gone, leaving a slight feeling of
anticlimax. But the smallness of our supply of oxygen filled
me with a sense of urgency. We must get back to the South
Summit as quickly as possible.

I took up my ice-axe, glanced at Tenzing to see if he were
ready, and then looked at my watch – it was 11.45, and we'd
only been on top fifteen minutes. I had one job left to do.
Walking easily down the steps I'd made in the ridge I
descended forty feet from the summit to the first visible rocks,
and taking a handful of small stones thrust them into my
pocket – it seemed a bit silly at the time, but I knew they'd
be rather nice to have when we got down. Then, wasting no
time, I set off along the ridge. Fortunately my steps were all
intact, and we cramponed along them quickly and safely. We
knew we had to hurry and, tired as we were, we drove
ourselves hard. In what seemed an astonishingly short time,
we were climbing down towards the top of the difficult rock
step. I could see from here the frail fashion in which the
cornice was attached to the rocks, but with the confidence of
familiarity I plunged down into the chimney and wriggled
my way between the rock and the ice to the bottom. Tenzing
quickly followed and we climbed on again. The ridge was
now much steeper and more exposed, so we moved one at a

time, each man belaying the other as he moved. We were going very quickly indeed, but at the same time taking every care. We cautiously shuffled our way across the rock ledge, and then moved on to the steps crossing the last steep slopes. Once again I could see far below us in the Western Cwm the dirty smudge of Camp IV, and I thought how pleased they'd all be at our news. With a feeling of relief I cramponed on to the little saddle at the foot of the South Summit, and then slowly climbed up the generous stairway I'd whacked out in its icy side nearly four hours before. I sat down beside our discarded oxygen bottles, and Tenzing joined me there. It had only taken us one hour from the top.

Once again I checked our oxygen bottles – there was only about an hour's endurance left, but this should get us down to our reserve supply on the ridge. Tenzing offered me his waterbottle and I had a long swig out of it. It was a delicious brew of water, sugar, lemon crystals, and raspberry jam. I looked back up the ridge, and saw that our steps were clearly outlined in the snow, so I got out my camera once again and photographed them. Despite the cold conditions, my camera seemed to be working very well, which was most encouraging, as I realised how important these summit photographs were. Our rest was very short – only a few minutes – and then we were on our feet again and starting down.

The thought of this descent had never been far from my mind throughout the day, and I viewed it with fearful anticipation. It had seemed so difficult and dangerous on the ascent that I was very much afraid that when we came down it tired and much less alert, one of us might slip and precipitate a disastrous avalanche. I was determined to pack the treacherous snow into safe and stable steps as if our lives depended, as they probably did, on not one of them breaking. Tenzing looked as strong and staunch as ever, and I felt I could confidently rely on him as a stout anchor. I started cramponing carefully down the first steep slopes of frozen snow. The wind was now a good deal stronger, and occasional strong gusts made us feel uncomfortably off-balance. I soon reached the first line of steps down the steep ridge at the top of the great slope. Steadying myself against the slope with my ice-axe, I climbed carefully down from step to step. And then I muttered a hearty curse! I'd come to the steps Tenzing had cut on the way up, and which had been all right on the ascent but were too widely spaced for a safe or comfortable trip down. Rather reluctantly I decided to take care and set to work to recut them again. Cutting steps down a steep slope when you are laden with cumbersome gear is always a tedious business, especially in a gusty wind, and I wasn't sorry to move back on to my own steps again and drop rapidly down to where the ridge petered out in the great slope.

Now the unpleasant moment had arrived and we had 300 feet of steep and dangerous snow to deal with. First of all, we had to get on to the slope, and this entailed a traverse over some steep rocks. Tenzing belayed me carefully, and I started across them. Using every meagre handhold I could find I inched my way along, very conscious of the tremendous drops beneath and realising for the first time just how tired I was. To reach the snow slope from the rocks was a tricky move, but with a long step I lowered myself reluctantly into its snowy grip. As I stood there looking downwards, all my earlier fears returned. The slope dropped away with startling abruptness and our deep upward tracks looked hazardous in the extreme. Ten thousand feet below us was the avalanche-strewn Kangshung glacier, coldly and impersonally waiting to receive a toppling cornice or a careless climber. I hastily shrugged these morbid thoughts out of my mind, and started packing the loose snow into a little ledge so that I could safely belay Tenzing across the rock pitch. My stance was far from perfect, but I put the rope over my shoulders and waved to Tenzing to cross. He moved slowly on to the traverse and laboriously began to work his way over. With a sudden shock I realised how tired he was – how tired we both were! It seemed a long time before he stepped across to join me.

With a tense feeling in the pit of my stomach I started down the slope, packing the loose snow with my boot into a step that would take my weight. Each time I changed my weight into a new step, I had a moment of fear to see if it would hold. We were going very slowly, but we couldn't afford to hurry. I glanced behind. Grimly silent, Tenzing was climbing down the steps with great care. He was obviously tired, but was still strong and safe. I went on packing steps and lowering myself into them. Time lost its meaning and the great slope turned into an eternal and endless nightmare. It was with an astonished feeling of relief that I suddenly realised we were nearly at the bottom. I started traversing carefully over to the right, plunging now with renewed vigour through the deep snow, and then, with an enormous feeling of thankfulness, I stepped on to the ridge again and sank the shaft of my ice-axe deeply into the firm snow. I took in the rope as Tenzing moved up beside me. We looked at each other and we didn't need to speak – our faces clearly showed our unrestrained relief.

Almost casually I started down the ridge – it seemed so easy now after what we'd just come down – but a sudden fierce gust of wind brought me sharply to my senses and I started concentrating again. I knew our oxygen must be nearly exhausted and that we had to reach the dump left by Evans and Bourdillon before it ran out. I pushed on as hard as I could. The wind had wiped out a lot of our tracks in the snow, but it didn't take long to remake them. And then we reached the oxygen dump and another nagging worry lifted from my mind. I checked the sets on our backs. We still had

a few litres of oxygen left and couldn't afford to waste it. We
continued on down carrying the life-saving reserve bottles
in our hands. The ridge broadened and I realised we'd reached
the snow shoulder above Camp IX. I plunged down the steep
slope off the ridge, sidled around a rock bluff, and then saw
our tent only a hundred feet away. I moved eagerly towards
it, but suddenly felt very tired and weak. My load felt like a
ton and my boots were as heavy as lead. I realised that my
oxygen bottle had run out. I climbed slowly on to our tent
platform, took off my oxygen set and slumped down in the
snow. Tenzing wearily sat down beside me. It was good to
be back.

Our tent was flapping furiously in the wind and already
many of the guy-lines had come undone. Tenzing crawled
inside it and started getting the cooker going for a hot drink.
I removed the empty bottles from our oxygen sets and
connected up our last meagre reserves. I reduced the rate of
flow to two litres a minute and tested both the sets out.
Frequent gusts of wind were whipping across the ridge,
pelting me with stinging particles of snow, but I was too tired
to worry very much. Far below on the South Col I could see
the tents flapping and thought I saw some figures moving.
It was nice to know there was someone there to help us, but
it looked a long way down. Tenzing handed out a large mug
of warm, sweet lemon-flavoured water, and I drank it with
relish. We rolled up our sleeping-bags, our air-mattresses,
and our personal gear and tied them on to our oxygen sets.
We needed them for sleeping in the lower camps. We heaved
our loads on to our backs and turned on our oxygen, and
then, with no feelings of regret, I took one last glance at our
forlorn little camp that had served us so well and started off
down again.

There was no tracks visible on the slopes below us, but I
knew that once we had worked across on to the ridge we

could stick to it until we reached the remains of the highest Swiss camp. I forced a deep trail across the slope, very conscious of the weakness in my limbs and the extra weight on my back. The ridge itself dropped away in an unhealthy looking sweep of snow-covered rocks. I knew Evans and Bourdillon had had some unpleasant slips on this part of the ridge, and I was determined that we shouldn't do the same – we mightn't be so lucky! We made our way slowly down, moving very carefully but steadily. It wasn't particularly diffi-cult, just rather unpleasant, and we knew we couldn't afford to slip. Our first objective was the remnant of the Swiss tent about 700 or 800 feet below us. For a long time it never seemed to get any closer, but all of a sudden it grew much larger and there we were, right beside it.

Now we had to branch off to the right to the head of the great snow couloir leading down to the South Col. We crossed slowly over easy snow and rock slopes to the little rock ledge which gave access to the couloir, and then we looked down our last problem – the long steep slopes beneath us. With a sudden start I realised there wasn't a step showing – for some reason I had expected George Lowe's steps still to be intact. My heart sank! I was deadly tired and had no desire for another bout of step cutting. I tried the snow with the hope that it would be soft enough to kick steps down it, but it was as hard as a board. It was far too steep to attempt to crampon it in our weak condition. I had no alternative but to start cutting again. I had only chipped down about ten feet into the couloir when I heard a high-pitched roar from the bluffs above us, and next moment I was hit by a terrific gust of wind and almost torn from my steps. As I braced myself against the slope with the pick of my ice-axe dug into the hard snow as a belay, I was peppered with a barrage of small ice particles dislodged from the battlements above. After a few moments the wind disappeared as quickly as it had come.

I went on cutting step after step and Tenzing moved into the couloir behind me. A few moments later we were once again clinging to the slope, being buffeted unmercifully by a powerful gust. It seemed as though the couloir was acting as a wind-tunnel and intensifying the wind to dangerous proportions. I continued hacking a path downwards, but when I'd done over 200 feet I'd just about had enough. Tenzing – tired though he was – offered to take a turn and cut down for nearly another hundred feet. Then he moved ten feet out to the right and started kicking steps down a softer layer of snow. Thankfully I moved down behind him and we lost height quickly. I noticed that a small figure had appeared on the icy slopes above the South Col, and somehow I knew it was George Lowe. We stopped and had a rest at the crevasse at the foot of the couloir and then moved on again. We knew we were safe now, and with the disappearance of our tension the last of our energy went too. But, stiff legged and weary, we thumped on down automatically.

George's tall, strong figure was now much closer, and the thought struck me that there wasn't anyone I'd rather tell the news to first. George and I had been through a lot together in the mountains. We'd had a lot of success together and we'd had our tough moments; no one had done more than George to make this final success possible. Already I could see his cheerful grin, and next moment his strong vigorous voice was shouting out a greeting. To my tired mind he looked an absolute tower of strength. In rough New Zealand slang I shouted out the good news, and next moment we were all talking at once and slapping each other on the back. I could feel a warm glow of contentment creeping over me, and for the moment at least quite forgot that I was at 26,000 feet with a fifty-mile-an-hour wind whistling around my ears.

George took his pack off his back and produced a thermos flask of hot soup, which was rapidly consumed. He also had a spare bottle of oxygen with him, but we didn't use it. Tenzing and I took off our rope, and then continued on down the ice-slopes towards the Col. My oxygen ran out just as we reached it – we'd had just enough but no more. As we climbed slowly up the few feet to the tents, we were met by Wilfrid Noyce and Pasang Phutar. These two men had come up to act as a support party, and it was good to see them. Gregory and the other Sherpas had gone down into the Western Cwm. The wind was whistling over the Col, so we took off our packs and crawled wearily into the tents. A few moments later I was revelling in the warmth and comfort of my sleeping-bag and feeling a wonderful sense of security and companionship.

George was in the Meade tent with me, and he had a cooker going and was melting some ice for drinks. We called to Noyce to come in out of the wind, but he told us of an arrangement he'd made with John Hunt. In the event of our success he was to put two sleeping-bags in the form of a T (meaning Top) on a snow slope on the edge of the South Col where it was hoped it would be seen with binoculars from Camp IV. It was so cold and windy outside that George and I didn't hesitate to try to dissuade Wilf from doing it. 'They'll find out soon enough tomorrow' was our attitude. But realising how anxious the main party down in the Western Cwm would be to know the news, Wilf refused to be deterred by our weak-kneed suggestions. He collected two sleeping-bags and a puzzled Pasang Phutar, and crossed over the hard ice of the Col to a suitable snow slope above the Cwm. The wind was far too strong to enable them to hold the sleeping-bags in position, so Wilf lay down on one bag himself and per-suaded Pasang Phutar to lie on the other. For ten long minutes they lay there in the bitter South Col wind before Wilf felt they'd done their duty and agreed to struggle back to the tents. It was unfortunate that during this ten minutes either nobody at Camp IV was looking or one of the frequent clouds had come in between, with the result that the message didn't get through.

Noyce crawled into the tent with us. He didn't have an air-mattress so had to lie in his sleeping-bag on the cold floor. We made quite a satisfactory meal out of our rations and drank large quantities of fluid — I seemed quite unable to quench my continuous thirst. It was now pitch dark outside, and in the familiar South Col environment of our swaying, flapping tent we settled down for the night. But sleep seemed far away from my overtired body and excited brain. George didn't seem much better so we talked and dozed far into the night, tossing and turning as the freezing cold from outside crept into our tent. Soon George and I were spending all our time telling each other how cold we were. Wilf Noyce must have been a great deal colder than either of us, but an uncom-plaining 'I'm all right, thanks' was all we ever got out of him. Despite the cold, I finally drifted off into an uneasy sleep.

The morning was the same as every other morning on the South Col. I opened my eyes to a scene of complete chaos. Remnants of food, black and dirty stoves, battered tins of fuel, and repulsive looking mugs with the residue of our last drink frozen solid in the bottom. All strewn around and between our three recumbent bodies as we curled up into a ball to try to retain a little warmth. I looked at George. With his bedrag-gled beard, scaly windblown countenance, burnt lips, and bloodshot eyes, he fitted perfectly into this depressing scene. 'I suppose that's how I look,' I thought, 'or worse! It's about time we got out of here!' I cursed the maddening wind that was pummelling the thrashing canvas against my head like a pneumatic drill and then started talking to George again. Wilf Noyce didn't move. He'd slept with his head outside the door due to the lack of room, and we suspected we were going to have to thaw him back into life.

Reluctantly we emerged from our bags and overcame the lethargy of altitude long enough to light a cooker. As the warmth from it crept around the tent, life became a little brighter. Soon we were crouching around the stove like a bunch of hagged old witches slowly munching away at some food. I still felt completely dehydrated and kept drinking the water as quickly as we could melt it. We slowly prepared to leave. There were two full bottles of oxygen left, and though none of us really needed it, we decided that Tenzing and I should use it on the way down. We were each carrying our own sleeping and personal gear, and it made a formidable load. We crawled out of our tents for the last time, and clumsily strapped our crampons on to our boots, heaved our loads on to our backs, tied ourselves together on the rope, and started painfully up the slopes above the camp. We had only 200 feet to climb, but it seemed like a thousand, and we'd had more than enough when we struggled up to the top.

We looked back at the South Col – three tiny tents flapping furiously in a grim expanse of bare ice and black rocks. They looked awfully lonely down there, but we weren't sorry to leave them. We turned away and started down towards the great traverse. The steps made by the parties of the previous day were still intact, and this made travelling relatively easy. But there was no pleasure in it – I was too conscious of the weakness of my limbs and the weight on my back and the great drops underneath. All I wanted was to get back to safe ground again and have a long rest. It seemed a lifetime before we reached the end of the traverse and started cautiously descending the steep ice of the upper Lhotse face. To our tired minds it seemed even steeper and more difficult than usual, and we climbed down it with extreme care. We crossed slowly over the last exposed ice-slope to the edge of the great crevasse above Camp VII. For some unknown reason I had the impression that Camp VII was going to be deserted, but as we appeared in sight we heard a hearty yell, and there were Charles Wylie and half a dozen Sherpas standing amongst the tents. It was like a breath of fresh air to see them. We carefully crossed the unstable snow bridge over the crevasse and next moment we were the centre of an excited, chattering group. Mugs of hot lemon drink were thrust into our hands and our loads taken off our backs. It was good to be back amongst friends.

We rested for half an hour while the Sherpas dismantled the tents. Then George and Tenzing and I roped together and started off down. We were going a little better now at this lower altitude, and made quite good time down the familiar steps and fixed ropes to the site of Camp VI. Another brief rest and we moved on again. The great glistening ice bulge below the camp demanded care, but holding on to the 400-foot long fixed rope, we cramponed our way cautiously but confidently to the bottom. The track led on and we followed it numbly – too tired to remember much of its steep descents and exposed traverses. We reached the last fixed rope, and thankfully guided our way down it and collapsed on the snowy ledge at the foot of the face. The track from now on was easy – merely a matter of putting one foot in front of the other, but we found even this was hard work.

We reached Camp V, and some smiling Sherpas took our packs off our shoulders. But we didn't waste any time. We started off on the last long stretch down the Western Cwm. As we approached Camp IV we saw a few figures drifting slowly out of the tents towards us, obviously undecided as to whether we'd been successful or not. We didn't give any sign, but wearily stumped down the track. When we were fifty yards away, George couldn't restrain himself any longer and waved his ice-axe exuberantly towards the summit. The approaching figures stopped dead, as though unable to grasp the import of this signal, and then they suddenly rushed up the track towards us. Mike Westmacott reached us first, and then John Hunt, his tired face lighting up with unbelieving joy. Soon we were embracing them all, and shaking hands and thumping them all on the back. It was a touching and unforgettable moment.

But I'd had many great moments in the last few weeks, and I couldn't help feeling a touch of sadness at the thought that it was all over. I could remember so clearly Charles Evans and Tom Bourdillon, weary to death, dragging themselves down to the South Col; and John Hunt's lined and indomitable face as he handed me his tiny cross while the wind battered our tent; and the feeling of terrible loneliness as George Lowe and Gregory left us high on our little ledge; and then, at the last, Tenzing's smile of triumph on the summit.

And now our adventure was finished!

An Explanation of Some of the Terms Used in this Book

arête	a narrow ridge.
belay, to	to secure the climber's rope to a firm projection while he moves over difficulties.
belay	the projection itself – it may be a rock, an embedded ice-axe or even ice.
chang	a beer brewed from rice.
chimney	a narrow vertical gully in rock or ice just large enough to get the body into.
col	depression in a mountain range. The lowest depression between two peaks. Similar to a pass but not necessarily able to be crossed. South col is the lowest depression south of the summit of Everest. Everest has a north col but no east or west col.
cornice	overhanging mass of snow or ice along a ridge, shaped like the curling crest of a wave and generally formed by the prevailing wind. Very dangerous to climb along.
couloir	gully or furrow in a mountainside, usually filled with snow or ice.
crampon	metal frame with spikes (usually ten, $1^{1}/_{2}$ in. long) fitting the sole of the boot and secured over the boot by straps, for use on hard snow or ice.
crampon, to	to move wearing such spikes.
crevasse	a fissure in a glacier, often of great depth.
cwm	an enclosed valley on the flank of a hill. A

Welsh word similar in meaning to a corrie or a cirque.

icefall   a frozen cascade of ice, often on a gigantic scale, created when a glacier passes over a change of angle or direction in the slope of the ground beneath.

karabiner   snap-link or mousqueton – a large metal spring-loaded clip which can be fixed to the rope or piton.

monsoon   a wind in South Asia which blows from the S.W. in summer (the wet monsoon), and from the N.E. in winter (the dry monsoon). This causes two main seasons on Everest – snow and cloud from June until October; wind and cold from November until May. The 'Spring' attempt is timed for the climb to be made during a lull in the change of seasons at the end of May and beginning of June. The 'Autumn' attempt is aimed for the lull in October-November.

moraine   accumulation of stones and other débris chiselled off and brought down by glaciers. Where two glaciers meet a medial moraine is formed. Base Camp on Everest was on a medial moraine.

pitch   a stretch of difficult ice or rock between ledges or belays.

piton   metal spike with a ring or a hole in the head which can be hammered into rock or ice and which is used in conjunction with a karabiner to secure the rope passing between two climbers. Used mostly on Everest in ice walls to fix ropes to cling to while climbing.

piton, to	to hammer in the metal spikes and attach ropes to them.
rakshi	a spirit distilled in Nepal from rice.
rope	links members of a party for mutual safety and is usually one hundred feet in length. A party may be referred to as 'a rope'.
sangar	low wall serving as a windbreak.
scree	slope of small loose stones.
sérac	tower or pinnacle of ice, usually perched and liable to fall.
Sherpa	hillman of Tibetan stock from Eastern Nepal.
Sherpani	Sherpa woman.
sirdar	chief or leading Sherpa.
snow-bridge	a layer of snow bridging a crevasse.
spur	a rib of rock running down from a main ridge or arête.
step	a vertical or steep rise on a glacier or mountain slope.
traverse, to	to cross a mountain slope horizontally or diagonally.
traverse	such a crossing.
tsampa	flour of roasted and ground barley: staple food of Sherpas.
yeti	the local word used to describe an unidentified creature believed to dwell in the Himalayan mountains and which has been nicknamed the 'Abominable Snowman'.

A Note on the Author

Born 1919 in Tuakau, Auckland, New Zealand, Sir Edmund Hillary climbed into immortality on May 29, 1953 together with his Sherpa companion Tenzing Norgay, becoming the first to reach the highest point on earth, the summit of Mount Everest – 8,850 metres above sea level. Hillary has conquered eleven summits in the Himalayas, all above 6,000 metres.

Among other adventures and expeditions, in the late fifties Hillary was invited to partipate in the first mechanized expedition to the South Pole, and in 1975, he travelled by jet boat from the mouth of the Ganges to the head waters of the river high in the Himalayas.

During recent years, he has continued his global fund-raising work for organisations such as UNICEF and the World Wildlife Fund.